Scott Simon Fehr

Introduction to Group Therapy
A Practical Guide

Second Edition

Pre-publication
REVIEWS,
COMMENTARIES,
EVALUATIONS . . .

"Introduction to Group Therapy: A Prac-*tical Guide, Second Edition,* provides motivating, intelligent coverage of a new-century view of group therapy. With years of experience in conducting groups and training group therapists, the author focuses on what works in a range of settings for therapists of various theoretical orientations and levels of experience. He considers the theoretical underpinnings, characteristic interventions, relevant research, strengths and weaknesses, negative group experiences, and demands of the group setting, giving particular attention to variables that are unique to group treatment.

This book brings together the key ideas in group psychotherapy in the last cen-tury. Using case studies, the author demonstrates vividly how the therapist can choose, adapt, and implement the model most suited to heighten group experience and achieve group goals. This book gives an essential overview that will enable practitioners and theorists to gain a deeper understanding of their own work and its significance within the development of this field."

Marco A. Wildt, MD
Former Staff Member,
Psychiatry Department,
Montreal General Hospital;
Consultant Group Therapist,
Hospital for Infectious Diseases,
Brazil

More pre-publication
REVIEWS, COMMENTARIES, EVALUATIONS . . .

"This second edition of *Introduction to Group Therapy* is an extraordinarily balanced handbook for group psychotherapists. Dr. Fehr is like a great dancer on a rope. With one hand he feeds the beginning therapists with crucial information and with the other hand he provides the advanced therapist with necessary, updated refreshments. He has fully realized his intention to write a book that pays as much attention to theory as to clinical/practical issues. His two chapters about a case viewed by seventeen different experienced clinicians is very illuminating and instructive. He also sheds light on the importance and possibilities of modern technology in this case on the use of the Internet and the group psychotherapy discussion list. I recommend this book wholeheartedly."

Maria van Noort, PsyD
Editor, *Handbook of Group Psychotherapy;* Chair, Committee for International Relations, The Netherlands

"Dr. Scott Simon Fehr has positioned himself as a leading authority in the field of group psychotherapy with his latest offering, a second edition of *Introduction to Group Psychotherapy: A Practical Guide.*

In this concise and informative addition to the original text, Dr. Fehr has achieved extensive refinement in the emancipation of an overall didactic view and coherent theoretical framework of group psychotherapy for the student and professional alike. He offers a continued, needed practical application to this most important and extensively developing field. This is a definitive source for anyone interested in the field of psychology and those specifically interested in the exciting paradigm of group psychotherapy as it represents a model for human healing, understanding, and interaction."

Joseph J. Toto, PsyD
Specialty in Child and Family Psychotherapy, Private Practice, Warren, NJ

"It was with pleasant anticipation that I awaited the second edition of Dr. Scott Simon Fehr's very successful text, *Introduction to Group Therapy: A Practical Guide.* I was wondering how Dr. Fehr was going to improve on the first edition, but in fact he did. This second edition is expanded and includes seventeen contributions from senior clinicians, all analyzing the same case from different paradigms. This book is highly readable. I laughed out loud at Fehr's first-person account of his initial foray into running a group, and am impressed with the amount of erudite and practical information that is covered by an obviously very knowledgeable group psychotherapy clinician. This is the book I recommend to all residents in psychiatry who wish to include group psychotherapy in their work and experienced psychiatrists who desired a resource that is both timely and timeless."

Vincent F. Colón, MD
Morristown Memorial Hospital, Morristown, NJ

More pre-publication
REVIEWS, COMMENTARIES, EVALUATIONS . . .

"This book follows a very successful first edition of Fehr's book. It presents the subject in more detail based on the author's growing experience with group therapy, on updated bibliographical references, and on comments from scholars and students about his first edition. The foremost merit of this book is in the meticulously presented details of the actual group therapy process as supported by well-explained theories. The clarity of the author's style provides the beginner, or a student embarking on group therapy, with a secure basis from which to start to provide group therapy or group art psychotherapy.

Beyond its usefulness for beginners for whom it would serve as a basic textbook, this edition is eminently suited as a model of teaching the subject for academicians developing a curriculum for their students and to teachers of group therapy. Fehr has achieved a healthy balance between practical instructions and theoretical presentation in this elegant and clearly written book."

Irene Jakab, MD, PhD
Professor of Psychiatry Emerita,
University of Pittsburgh;
Lecturer on Psychiatry,
Harvard Medical School

"Dr. Fehr teaches group therapy in a methodical, yet personal manner. He takes the reader through a course in group therapy and shows the value of learning leadership skills from a variety of theoretical approaches. He is adamant that the key to being a good group leader is for the therapist to have experience in a group, especially as a member. I certainly support this idea.

I was pleased to see the way he handled the details of organizing a group based on the physical setting, the group contract, and both verbal and nonverbal techniques of group therapy. His presentation of problem patients and the use of a case presentation viewed by a variety of clinicians from different theoretical positions were excellent additions to this text. I recommend this book to other clinicians, new and experienced, who wish to gain a fresh perspective on the many issues involved in group psychotherapy."

Barbara W. Turner, PhD, CGP, FAGPA
Private practice,
Atlanta, GA

"Dr. Scott Fehr, an accomplished and experienced group therapist and teacher, has produced a fine, improved-upon, and expanded second edition to his already excellent *Introduction to Group Therapy: A Practical Guide*. It is an easy and enjoyable read and highly informative. It will be of great value and benefit to both students of group therapy and those already practicing group therapy. I recommend this second edition fully and with enthusiasm to those motivated to expand their knowledge of group therapy and their expertise as therapists."

Herbert L. Rothman, MD
Geriatric Psychiatrist,
Mt. Sinai Hospital,
Miami Beach, FL

The Haworth Press®
New York • London • Oxford

Introduction
to Group Therapy
A Practical Guide

Second Edition

Introduction to Group Therapy
A Practical Guide

Second Edition

Scott Simon Fehr

The Haworth Press®
New York • London • Oxford

The Haworth Press, Inc., 10 Alice Street, Binghamton, NY 13904-1580.

Cover design by Jennifer M. Gaska.

Library of Congress Cataloging-in-Publication Data

Fehr, Scott Simon.
    Introduction to group therapy : a practical guide / Scott Simon Fehr.—2nd ed.
        p. cm.—(Advances in psychology and mental health)
    Includes bibliographical references and index.
    ISBN 0-7890-1763-6 (alk. paper)—ISBN 0-7890-1764-4 (pbk. : alk. paper)
    1. Group counseling. 2. Group psychotherapy. I. Title. II. Series.

BF637.C6 F366 2003
158'.35—dc21

                                                                                    2002068752

This guide is foremost dedicated to Ellen Fehr, MS, a very fine therapist in her own right, who manages to maintain a sense of humor after living with me for thirty-one years; to my graduate students at Nova Southeastern University who permitted me to enter their lives for a brief period of time and taught me how to teach group therapy; and last, but not least, to my clients, who with their patience and guidance taught me—over the past twenty-five years in over 4,800 groups—how to become a group leader.

Thank you.

ABOUT THE AUTHOR

Scott Simon Fehr, PsyD, has had a private psychology practice with his wife, Ellen, since 1979. He was accepted as a student in the first PsyD class in the state of Florida. Dr. Fehr is a Faculty Member with the Master's Mental Health Counselor Program and APA Doctorate Clinical Psychology Program in the Center for Psychological Studies at Nova Southeastern University in Fort Lauderdale, Florida, where he teaches Group Theory and Processes and Advanced Group Theory and Processes, and supervises both Doctoral Directed Research Studies and Doctoral Practicums. He has also supervised licensed eligible post-master's and post-doctorate interns for the past twenty-two years. Dr. Fehr, a member of the American Group Psychotherapy Association (of which he is the Past President of the Florida Affiliate) and a member of the International Association of Group Psychotherapy, also taught a twelve-credit APA continuing education course on group therapy for licensed professionals over the Internet. His second book, *Group Therapy in Independent Practice,* is published by The Haworth Press, Inc. He has been a reviewer for numerous psychology books and journals, has been published in the *Journal of Independent Private Practice,* and was a Guest Editor of the *Journal of Psychotherapy in Independent Practice* (both from The Haworth Press, Inc.). Dr. Fehr is an international lecturer and has led over 4,800 psychotherapy groups. He is an avid collector of eighteenth- and nineteenth-century antiques and a perpetual student of astrophysics. Dr. Fehr believes that a number of theories in astrophysics correlate to human behavior and that if the observer can perceive the microcosm as a finite form of the macrocosm, the observer too may come to believe we cannot truly separate ourselves from the immutable laws of the universe.

CONTENTS

Foreword

I love flowers. I love to plant them and, in due time, watch the flowers bloom. A parallel to this in my life is reflected in the growth and development of graduate students. The author of this book is one of those students.

I met Scott Simon Fehr many years ago when he had long, dark hair, which has since turned gray. I hated the appearance of long hair on a man, but he was a candidate for doctoral admission, which prompted my initial interaction with him. Notwithstanding his long hair, he impressed me as a highly intelligent, eager young man with a mission in life. I experienced him to be a down-to-earth individual who was destined to become a social leader. Without hesitation, he received my positive vote for his admission to the inaugural class. I was the dean.

From the beginning, Scott's classmates—both men and women—accepted him as a leader. Today, Dr. Fehr is a faculty member at the Center for Psychological Studies at Nova Southeastern University and privately conducts a highly successful practice in group therapy.

I asked Dr. Fehr why he chose to write a book on group therapy. He responded that it was time to bring closure to a promise he had made over thirty years ago to his group therapy mentor, Elizabeth, who is deceased. She requested that he pass on what she taught him and what he had learned on his own. When I inquired as to what he desired to achieve in writing this book, he indicated several goals: (1) to stimulate the creation of more group therapists; (2) to help students and colleagues feel less intimidated and anxious when beginning group leadership; (3) to promote group therapy at the grassroots level—with students—where it has the greatest opportunity for being implemented; (4) to indicate that group psychotherapy is a first-rate modality and is not second to any other modality, as many professionals and laypeople believe; and (5) to write a book that he would have liked to have read when he was learning about group therapy. He said that many books were scholarly but not helpful when actually running group.

In the preface, Dr. Fehr has noted that, "Many of the fine books in today's market tend to have a preponderance of theory at the expense of experiential material or experiential material at the expense of theory." This book combines not only theory and practice but also practical suggestions in areas that are rarely covered in academic settings in a thorough and well-organized manner.

Although this second edition is intended primarily for colleagues who are new to group psychotherapy, it is my belief that seasoned professionals as well will profit by what it has to offer.

> *Robert D. Weitz, PhD, ABPP, ABPH*
> *Professor Emeritus and Board Member*
> *Nova Southeastern University*

Preface

Dear colleagues and future colleagues in group therapy,

Welcome to this introductory book, the second edition of the original book. The many changes in this particular edition have been spawned from the fine ideas and suggestions generated by reviewers, colleagues, and students around the world. They kindly related what areas they would like to see expanded and what areas were not included in the first edition. Their input truly helped to make this a more inclusive and better book.

Group therapy is one of the most naturalistic and therapeutic laboratories for interpersonal learning and relationships. It truly is an elegant representation in microcosm of the family, society, and civilization. Very few humans live in total isolation by choice; rather, they interact continuously with members of society. A vast majority of individuals seeking psychotherapy report that these interactions create feelings of social discomfort, personal alienation, a sense of aloneness, and diminished feelings of intimacy with others because of previously unsatisfactory and often repetitively painful emotional experiences. By its very nature, group therapy provides a corrective environment and a twofold opportunity: an adventure of self-exploration, and the possibility of a profound understanding of oneself in relation to humanity and humanity's relationship to oneself.

The book you are about to read does not include and cover every aspect of group psychotherapy or every population for which group psychotherapy is a viable modality. Rather, it has been organized to help you get a feel for the extraordinary effect of group therapy in helping to relieve human suffering.

Many of the fine books in today's market tend to have a preponderance of theory at the expense of experiential material or experiential material at the expense of theory. Although theory can be very interesting and academically stimulating, it often leaves novice group therapy clinicians somewhat bewildered when beginning the actual practice of running a group. On the other hand, a book that is mostly made up of experiential suggestions is extremely helpful but may create a sense of bewilderment after the inexperienced practitioner has run a group, because the question often arises, "What just happened here?"

This book has been created in the hope of combining both the elements of theory and experience in a reader-friendly manner. It covers such diverse topics as the historical beginnings of group therapy, theories, modalities, practical issues of how to set up an office for an effective group environment, surviving your training sites, problematic clients, contemporary issues in group therapy taken from the Internet, developing a group therapy practice, review questions, and so on.

It is my hope that readers who find group therapy a stimulating complement to individual psychotherapy will continue to learn and to seek further resources among the many excellent books available on this powerful therapeutic modality.

Good luck in your careers.

Acknowledgments

I am a person who truly believes in acknowledging those people who are and have been a positive influence in my work as it specifically relates to my specialty, group psychotherapy. No one works alone when writing a book on group. It would be antithetical to the premise underlying group psychotherapy not to acknowledge all those who have been involved. A book such as this is the culmination of the input of many individuals through the written word and, most enjoyably, verbal communication. I would like to gratefully thank those individuals who have been part of a group that has helped tremendously in bringing the first and second editions of this book to fruition.

Thanks go to the staff at The Haworth Press who have gently led a new, and now a little bit more experienced author, through three book publishing processes. I have become less traumatized when I receive the corrected galleys, and they are always much better after their efforts.

Thanks to Dr. Frank DePiano, senior editor for Advances in Psychology and Mental Health at The Haworth Press, past dean of The Center for Psychological Studies at Nova Southeastern University, and Renaissance Harley-Davidson man who has encouraged me through the trials, tribulations, stress, and joy of the book publishing experience. Thanks to my colleagues both in private practice and at Nova Southeastern University who reinforced and pushed me at those times when I needed a push.

I also thank my colleagues who were in the first and now those in the second edition. They are all listed together in thankfulness—Sharan Schwartzberg, Mary Alicia Barnes, Thomas Treadwell, Rocky Garrison, Joshua Gross, Samuel Miles, Avraham Cohen, Ronald Levant, Bennet E. Roth, Randolph C. Moredock, Mark Schorr, George Saiger, Frances Bonds-White, Larry Kreisberg, Ellen Horovitz, Danielle Fraenkel, Earl Hopper, Michael P. Frank, Steven Van Wagoner, and

xviii   INTRODUCTION TO GROUP THERAPY

William Weitz—for taking the time to write their marvelous analyses in Chapters 10 and 11.

To my colleagues Gary Sandelier, Karen Arkin, Daniel Schoenwald, Scott Rosiere, Edgar Ross, Joan Kreisberg, Francis Berman, Ava Berman, and the group from the AIME community: Nancy, Charlie, Sue, Marty, George, Barry, Ramona, Leslie, Harvey, Veronica, Michael, Phil, Jesse, Julie, and Virginia for their invaluable help on the Problematic Client section in Chapter 12.

Thanks go to David Cantor who generously provided "Group Therapy from A to Z" and his input on the negative aspects of group, and to Lori Gutman, who forthwith is referred to as the "Glossary Lady," as she patiently read through the glossary and supposedly learned a lot.

In addition, I wish to thank Donald Corriveau of the University of Massachusetts at Dartmouth and WebEd Unlimited, who created the springboard for the first edition by offering me the opportunity to teach a course on group therapy over the Internet; Thomas Scott of Scottcom Networks, Inc., and Ray Cafolla of Florida Atlantic University, whose computer skills were invaluable; Richard Higgins for his effort on Appendix A; my assistant Sheila Sazant, who was a sensitive and kind taskmaster during her many corrections of this book; and my dog Freud, who sat with me during the entire process of writing this book and the other two books. He never once complained, and he validated the statement, "Acquiring a dog may be the only opportunity a human ever has to choose a relative" (author unknown).

Most of all, I want to thank my analyst, Elizabeth, one of the finest human beings I have ever had the privilege of meeting and whose influence, thirty-four years later, continues to guide my life and work. You turned a farm boy into a psychologist and showed me a world I never knew existed. I am saddened that you could not have seen the publication of these books. You are deeply missed.

Chapter 1

The History of Group Therapy, Part I: Genesis, 1895-1943

THE CIRCLE

The circle is the earth upon which we walk. It is the sun from which the elements of life began on this planet. It is the solar system, the planets, and the stars.

In the beginning, a historical overview of group psychotherapy would probably be somewhat remiss without a preliminary discussion of the concept of the circle, round, or sphere, as it physically represents the process of group psychotherapy. It is a most curious global phenomenon that clans, tribes, societies, and civilizations, no matter how primitive or advanced, have continuously used the circle as a symbol in their cultures.

The circle or sphere is an entity that is self-contained; it has no beginning or end, and represents, theoretically, a perfect state in which the opposites are in mutual harmony before a contradiction begins to occur. It is the only symbol in which all points have parity and equivalency. It is the uroboros, a symbol from ancient Babylon, embodying the world, represented by a snake holding its own tail in its mouth, forming a circle. This symbol can be found in the ceremonial artwork of the Navajo Indians in America and in the different tribes and castes in Africa, India, and Mexico. It is used in the alchemical writings of wizards, magicians, and in the wheel of reincarnation. The circle is observed in the Book of Revelation and it appears consistently in the form of a mandala for meditation and unification with a supreme being. By focusing upon the mandala, one travels in search for harmony with the universe.

The circle often represents the womb or the origins from which life springs forth. It is the yin and yang of Chinese philosophy and the

1

gold ring of being united in marriage. Children all over the world, no matter how primitive, humble, or affluent, begin their primary drawings by trying to duplicate a circle, and then, as they mature, they move beyond this symbolism to more detailed representations of their internal and external experiences. The circle is the earth upon which we walk. It is the sun from which the elements of life began on this planet. It is the solar system, the planets, and the stars.

The circle can be a bit fanciful, as seen in the more picturesque concept of a group as depicted in the mythical story of King Arthur and the Knights of the Round Table. Although Merlin, King Arthur's famous magician, was often present to provide dream interpretation, it is not certain that these men were discussing unconscious processes. Perhaps they were fulfilling the requirements of a form of both the circle and group therapy. They sat in the round, each knight having parity to discuss the events of the day not only among themselves but with a leader. Quite probably their meetings were not only goal or task oriented but also included their interpersonal relationships with possible dream interpretation.

But what does all this mean and how does it relate to group psychotherapy? The circle has a historical and perhaps intrinsic attraction for *Homo sapiens.* In times of great importance, the circle, or being a physical part of a circle, offers a degree of emotional comfort, familiarity, strength, and protection. Thus it would seem that group psychotherapy, by the nature of the physical round or circle in which individuals sit, consciously or unconsciously enhances an environment for people seeking to return to a meditative and protected state in which affiliation provides a sense of belonging, acceptance of individual differences, equality, and the possibility of being healed.

The actual origin of the history of group psychotherapy remains a shrouded mystery. It can be assumed from our knowledge of cultural anthropology that group therapy has been informally in existence since the beginning of hominid time, whenever three or more individuals came together and looked to their companions and leader to discuss their problems.

Indaba, a Zulu term meaning "gathering together in a meeting with a chief or leader," may have covered such diverse topics as where to hunt and gather or issues facing the individual, clan, or society. These *indabas* not only had goal-directed behaviors but appeared to offer a degree of healing for both the individual and the tribe.

Unfortunately, time and space does not allow the acknowledgment of every pioneer and student of group psychotherapy who has contributed to the formal, ongoing development of this tremendously important modality for psychotherapy. Referencing and detailing every contribution would call for a book of its own. The individuals to be discussed repeatedly appear in the literature and are always acknowledged when a historical investigation is begun. It is not my intention to slight any other individual who added knowledge to this field.

In the formal sense, group psychotherapy is a fledgling in the field of psychology and psychotherapy, as the majority of monographs appear after World War II. Also, empirical findings concerning the efficacy of group psychotherapy greatly lag behind its actual practice. During World War II, group psychotherapy's development became known because there was a shortage of mental health providers available to administer necessary psychological interventions for many cases of war neuroses. As with many discoveries in science, group was thrust into prominence because of need.

The following sections describe the contributions of a number of practitioners to the early history of group therapy.

LeBON

Groups have never thirsted after truth. They demand illusions and cannot do without them. They constantly give what is unreal precedence over what is real; they are almost as strongly influenced by what is untrue as by what is true. (LeBon, 1920)

Gustav LeBon's topic of study was the group mind. His research focused exclusively on large groups of people. He felt that in a group an individual behaved in quite a different fashion than in isolation. Behaviors that were not expected emerged quite readily. He referred to these large groups as a heterogeneous entity, which comprised different individuals transformed into a homogeneous entity of like minds and behaviors. LeBon postulated that in a group an individual exhibited certain characteristics which previously did not manifest themselves. He explained this transformation by suggesting that three events catalyzed the change. (1) Because of the numerical size of the group, an individual developed feelings of invincibility and relinquished personal accountability in favor of the group assuming responsibility. (2) The herd or school mentality developed, in which an individual readily gave up his or her own interest to the interest of the group. LeBon labeled this as contagion. (3) The individual, almost as if hypnotized, obeyed all suggestions without conscious thought of the consequences of the group's behaviors. It appeared that the individual was no longer conscious of his or her acts and any suggestion by the leader was readily seized and undertaken. The concept of individual will no longer existed and the people relinquished their personal identities. LeBon felt that whenever people entered a group they reduced their socialized development. In isolation they may have been civilized individuals, but in a group or crowd they could quite possibly turn into barbarians who act upon instinct alone.

PRATT

In a common disease, they have a bond. (Pratt, 1907)

Joseph Pratt may be considered not only the originator of the concept of group therapy, but also the founder of a procedure related to the essence of "recovery" as a group dynamic with a homogeneous population. He focused on patients diagnosed with consumption, more commonly known as tuberculosis.

To students of classical literature and opera, this disease and its impact on European society during the nineteenth century is well described in Alexandre Dumas's book *Camille,* written in 1848, which became the source for Guiseppe Verdi's 1853 opera *La Traviata.* Pratt's patient population was not only consumptive but was also economically distressed. He felt that poverty increased the patients' problems. He chose to help these patients through an educational model in which all who agreed to be part of his study had to adhere to strict rules of behavior. These rules consisted of a change in lifestyle, as Pratt was very concerned with hygiene, food, and fresh air as a possible foundation for the cure of this insidious disease. He limited his groups to between fifteen and twenty-five members. According to Pratt's prescription, they would meet once a week and record the number of hours of daily outdoor activity and weight gain. Patients who distinguished themselves in their efforts and gains were reinforced by the intrinsic nature of their accomplishment and became a model of hope for the other individuals in the group. An unforeseen benefit also occurred: inclusion in the group had an emotionally positive effect on the patients.

Pratt's early work can be seen as quite contemporary. Today in the field of medicine, many groups are medically homogeneous and provide care for the members involved.

FREUD

> The common ego ideal of the individual member becomes the leader who takes over all the critical faculties of the group. (Freud, 1960)

Sigmund Freud, the father of psychoanalysis and one of the immortal minds of civilization, contributed to our knowledge of group therapy. Although group psychotherapy was not an area of investigation for Freud, he did work on conceptualizing what occurs to and within individuals when they are in a group. His book *Group Psychology and the Analysis of the Ego* is primarily the study of large groups. It is quite possible that his interest in this area developed from the escalating nationalism in Europe at the time of its writing. Because of his Jewish heritage, Freud, similar to so many other intelligentsia of his faith and time, was sensitive to the increasing anti-Semitism. Freud recognized and credited LeBon's work in relation to the individual and group, but he felt that the group mind could be more clearly understood through the principles of psychoanalysis. He suggested that individuals in a group relinquished themselves in favor of the group leader's goals and ideals, as the group members' attachment to the leader was a function of desexualized libido. Although the individual members of a group were linked to the leader through this desexualized libido, the leader carried no emotional attachment to any of the group members unless they could serve the leader's needs. Freud felt that this narcissism on the part of the group leader was functionally necessary. The leader represented for the members an individual who achieved mastery, independence, and self-confidence and became the ego ideal and the embodiment of all those characteristics that they themselves could not attain. Freud, similar to LeBon, felt that in a group an individual's inhibitions melted away and all the destructive instincts which remained below the surface were allowed free expression, and gratification as personal responsibility was no longer in operation. In some respects, the group functioned as a single entity that lacked a superego to inhibit the expression of primitive id behaviors.

BURROWS

> The problem in getting along is an industrial problem. (Burrows, 1928)

Trigant Burrows' concept of mental disorder was related to the individual's interaction with society. He believed that a profound conflict existed between how individuals felt about themselves and the assumed social personality they created in order to feel comfortable within their communities. Burrows perceived that individuals existed in a state of "I-ness" but felt this was not a viable entity for analysis. True analysis of the individual was more effective in relation to the group in which the individual belonged. If the group or society could be changed, the individual "I-ness" could also be positively affected. Burrows did not believe in the concept of isolation as it related to the individual. He considered all interaction to have both a manifest and latent content that needed to be further explored. He felt that group analysis was a corrective environment. In order to understand themselves, individuals could ultimately express what they really thought and felt without fear and inhibition of social restrictions. In effect, Burrows was speaking about a dependency problem. The individual depended upon the perceptions of others as the motivation for creating and maintaining the image personality that the person had come to realize as "I." Unfortunately, this image was often at odds with the real personality, causing conflict. In group analysis individuals came to realize that they were not alone in their thoughts and feelings and were privy to these manifestations in others.

Burrows' observations are quite timely and easily observed in clients today. Many people who come to psychotherapy or counseling repetitively speak about their need to be seen in a particular way by their society, community, and group. Because of this need, they have become estranged from their real selves and have sacrificed internal harmony in order to be seen in such a way that their needs may be gratified.

WENDER

The impetus to get well derives greater motivation through this
method in comparison to individual treatment only. (Wender,
1936)

Louis Wender introduced an eclectic form of therapy into group.
Although trained in psychoanalysis, he felt that strict psychoanalysis
did not lend itself well to the group arena. His patient population included individuals hospitalized for various psychiatric disturbances.
Wender observed that the act of hospitalization caused greater disturbances in the already conflicted individual, but because of the nature
of the hospital setting, a closed system, he saw a family structure begin to emerge among the patients in this environment. He felt that individuals were drawn to others similar to themselves and that group
membership created a potential for personal growth and change. If
this were the case, a group format would prove to be an effective tool
in helping this hospitalized population.

Wender appears to be one of the first individuals to promote what
we today might call a "group agreement," although Pratt (1907) might
be considered to have developed the first "group contract." Patients
included in Wender's group had to adhere to certain rules of conduct
such as confidentiality. No new members would be admitted into a
group that was already in session. Contrary to strict psychoanalysis,
Wender's groups began their sessions with a lecture format in which
the group therapist discussed analytic concepts with the patients as a
springboard for dialogue. These discussions, which appeared on the
surface to cause little anxiety, had the effect of promoting identification among the group members through their personal disclosures.
He felt that the nature of the group format helped individuals to re-
create early family experiences with their concomitant transferences
on the group members. In this case, the therapist and group members
would respond differently than the original family did. Disclosures
would not be judged and the patient would have a different experience of these disclosures, which effectively created and motivated the
development of a new functionally and qualitatively different internalized, healthier ego ideal.

Interestingly, Merton Gill (1982) also postulated this type of experience for the patient in individual psychotherapy. Wender's observations and beliefs in the effectiveness of the environment, the closed

system of the hospital, and the group generating a structure that re-creates the family is far-reaching and quite contemporary although presented over sixty years ago.

MORENO

In psychodrama, he is the dramatist of himself. (Moreno, 1940)

Jacob Moreno, MD, was a most interesting man who became quite influential in the practice of group psychotherapy. Initially, he formulated his theories from an original observation of Aristotle who perceived that when an audience watched a performance of a play the spectators often felt an identification with the scenario of the actors. As a result of this identification, the spectators had an emotional release or catharsis during the theatrical performance. Moreno concluded that if this passive catharsis could occur, perhaps an active catharsis might be attained if the spectator became the actor in the drama of his or her own life. This proved to be well validated and the foundations of psychodrama were laid.

Moreno worked to formalize his theory by introducing a different perception of the concept of spontaneity. Although he did not speak primarily of physics, his view of spontaneity was in some sense similar to the Newtonian theorem that "for every action there is an equal and opposite reaction." In this particular case, spontaneity indicated a degree of energy necessary to deal effectively with changes in one's life. If this spontaneity did not equal the amount of change that was occurring, the individual could begin to experience a sense of disequilibrium. Moreno felt that the disequilibrium experienced by one individual would begin to spread out toward other people in his or her life, very much as concentric circles move outward when a stone is thrown into a pond of still water. To correct this disequilibrium, it was necessary to devise a technique that would effectively bring about a catharsis for the individual. This technique was to focus on the drama of one's life.

Moreno felt that the Freudian approach to psychotherapy focused solely on the individual, thus limiting itself to the past, and did not take into consideration the great importance of the present and the future. Scoffing at psychoanalysis, he thought that psychoanalysts chose to try to go back into the womb and beyond as their sole focus in searching for the elusive trauma. He referred to this as the *recherche du temps perdu,* or "searching for the lost time" (Moreno, 1966). His use of role reversal, in which the individual assumed the personage of a significant other, and role-playing, a technique to practice behaviors in an anxiety-laden situation, are very effective. The former increases awareness and the latter desensitizes the individual to future stress-related situations.

BION

> The problem is the neurosis of the group and must become the focus of treatment. (Bion and Rickman, 1943)

Wilfred Bion's interest in groups was similar to that of his predecessors and colleagues as his focus was on the group as a whole, or what may be referred to as the mass group process, rather than the individual in the group. MacKenzie (1992) indicates that Bion's continuous focus on the group as a whole and not acknowledging the individual members runs opposite to the research on group supportive functions of individual members.

According to Stock and Thelen (1958), although Bion's contribution to the actual running of group therapy was limited because other areas in psychology became more of an interest, his group work generated considerable research. This research and interest continues to grow and Bion-oriented therapy groups are developing around the world, although less so in the United States than in other countries. Perhaps Bion's initial focus on groups was due to the era in which he conducted his investigations. At the time of his initial monograph of 1943, Bion was an officer in the British military and many of his perceptions appear to have a discipline-oriented feeling. There was a similarity between the treatment of his patients and the training of soldiers. He worked from the assumption that a group needed a common enemy, a goal, and a leader who was experienced and introspective while providing a safe environment in which the followers could express both their hostility and their praise. He suggested that in a treatment group of patients, neurosis was perceived as the enemy. Because of his orientation, he devised a program that would motivate patients to take on the enemy within a rehabilitative environment. Bion's interest was focused on the concept of community. Its effort in healing itself was inadvertently therapeutic to the members of the community. To achieve this aim, he chose to develop a program that was both structured and unstructured at the same time. He watched as the men in his rehabilitative experiment focused outside themselves and looked toward the integrity of the community as their common goal.

His later focus was toward analyzing the way groups actually function. He examined which factors prevent a group from working productively. He began with the premise that a work group was one in which all effort was directed toward accomplishing a task to reach a desired goal. The group was rational and effective. This work group culture, as he chose to describe it, could be adversely affected when strong emotion was introduced into the group environment. He found that feelings of helplessness, hostility, fear, optimism, and so on could begin to divert the group from its effective task at hand. Bion suggested that there was a feeling in the group as if all the members were privy to a common belief which negatively affected the change of direction in the group process. He chose to label this impediment as a basic assumption culture. He delineated three assumptions and felt that their common bond related to group leadership. This leadership was sought to meet the needs of the group and was similar to Rioch's (1970) statement that "groups got the leaders they deserve," but in this case the group got the leaders it wanted (p. 355). Bion's three assumptions were:

1. *The dependency assumption.* The group feels at a loss. It is helpless to find direction and is seeking guidance from someone outside the group. In this case, it is the group leader. The group does not know where to go, so all eyes will focus on the leader to take over and eliminate the conflict. The expectancy of the members is that the leader will produce some magical direction in which the group can proceed.
2. *The fight-or-flight assumption.* Something has occurred in the group that has disturbed its equilibrium. It could be the introduction of a new member or a new idea that either angers or frightens the members. For example, if a group becomes frightened because a new member is threatening, it would not be uncommon for the group members to displace their hostility on one another rather than effectively deal with the issue of the new

member. In the flight scenario, Vinogradov and Yalom (1989) used the example of a group that had a change in leadership. One of the coleaders left the group without adequate processing and the next time the group met, the members discussed issues of personal loss, such as the death of a loved one with concomitant feelings. The issue of the loss of the coleader was not approached at all, but was masked and avoided. A flight response can be seen when a group member or the group leader brings up a topic that generates anxiety. Either a member changes the topic or the group will not respond to the subject matter, as if it had not been introduced.

3. *The pairing assumption.* A leader is always sought when a group forms. In this assumption, the group is optimistic and has hope, and its integrity becomes a major focus. To that end, the group members pair up to support and strengthen the continuity of the group. It is likened to the people of a country eagerly awaiting the birth of a royal child who takes over and rules the country in peace and prosperity. It can also be an idea that is presented which gives positive and cohesive direction to the group. In groups that have bonded and worked well together, this assumption manifests itself when the process of termination is occurring. Members begin brainstorming about how they can keep the group in contact and integrated after the group itself has ended.

Bion suggested the existence of antitherapeutic factors that inhibit a group in accomplishing its goal. Although not directly stated, a group may have an unconscious set of rules of behavior to which each member diligently adheres. For example, if a group norm is, "No confrontation will be allowed," the group will remain on a very superficial, polite level. No matter what one does as a leader, the group will cling to this unconscious rule. The leader may provide a number of group-as-a-whole interpretations of what is occurring, but the group will not budge.

Although Bion's observations are interesting, Yalom (1975) and Malan (1976) feel that solely providing whole-group interpretations is basically ineffectual. Their belief is that such intervention does little to motivate individual members for self-exploration and examination and that Bion's perceptions of the mass group process are more effectively utilized by the leader who wishes to understand what is occurring at any one time.

The following questions are provided for review and reinforcement of the material in this chapter.

REVIEW

Part A

The circle not only has an intrinsic value for humanity but also is the physical representation of the practice of group psychotherapy. From your personal experience, can you think of other examples in which the circle is used to bring people together or to connect them?

Part B

Please answer true (T) or false (F) to the following questions.

1. (T) (F) Parity is not a feature of a circle.
2. (T) (F) Moving away from a circle to individuality offers individuals a greater opportunity for security and healing.
3. (T) (F) Children of different cultures use different symbols in their primary drawings.
4. (T) (F) The history of group psychotherapy is well documented. Psychotherapists promoted its use before individual psychotherapy.
5. (T) (F) *Indaba* is a Babylonian term meaning a gathering together in a meeting with a chief or leader.
6. (T) (F) The greatest amount of material concerning group psychotherapy was written before World War II because the focus of most psychological researchers was related to nationalism.

LeBon

7. (T) (F) Gustav LeBon felt that an individual acted very differently in a group than in isolation.

8. (T) (F) According to LeBon, in a group, the individual's concept of will no longer exists and people relinquish their personal identities.
9. (T) (F) He felt that whenever an individual enters a group or crowd he or she could quite possibly turn into a barbarian who acted upon instinct alone.

Pratt

10. (T) (F) Pratt's work is noted as the origin of group therapy.
11. (T) (F) His patient population consisted of individuals suffering from neurotic conflicts.
12. (T) (F) An unforeseen effect was the positive feelings patients felt belonging to his group.

Freud

13. (T) (F) Freud's initial work was focused solely on groups.
14. (T) (F) He found that when working with groups he was able to observe his patients' behaviors more clearly.
15. (T) (F) He felt that when an individual entered a group, he or she relinquished personal will in favor of the group leader's goals and ideals.
16. (T) (F) Freud believed that group members were linked to the group leader by a desexualized libido.
17. (T) (F) According to Freud, the group leader became the ego ideal and embodied all the characteristics the group members could not attain.

Burrows

18. (T) (F) Burrows felt that a mental disorder was contingent upon an individual's interaction with society.
19. (T) (F) He believed that there was a profound disturbance in how the individual felt about himself or herself.
20. (T) (F) All interactions did not have a latent content and manifest content.

21. (T) (F) Group offered the individual an arena for the first time to explore and express what he or she really thought and felt without societal inhibitions.

Wender

22. (T) (F) Wender felt that psychoanalysis lent itself well to group psychotherapy.
23. (T) (F) In his groups, Wender began each session with a lecture format.
24. (T) (F) He felt that by the nature of the group format, a patient had the opportunity to re-create his or her family of origin.
25. (T) (F) In a group, the patient could develop a healthier ego ideal.

Moreno

26. (T) (F) Moreno's concept of catharsis was developed from Plato's perception of watching an audience during a play.
27. (T) (F) Spontaneity meant having a response of equality in relation to dealing effectively with changes in one's life.
28. (T) (F) Disequilibrium in an individual did not affect other people.
29. (T) (F) Role reversal and role-playing were not considered important techniques in psychodrama.

Bion

30. (T) (F) The main focus of interest for Bion was the individual in a group.
31. (T) (F) His initial monograph indicated a disciplined and structured approach to motivating behavioral change.
32. (T) (F) The community and its ability to heal itself inadvertently led to its members being healed.
33. (T) (F) Groups operated on two levels: an overt, goal-directed level and an assumption level, centered around three distinct beliefs.

Chapter 2

The History of Group Therapy, Part II: 1951 and Beyond

DREIKURS

Group therapy promulgates man's search for equality. (Dreikurs, 1951)

Rudolph Dreikurs, eminent psychiatrist, and pupil and former collaborator with Alfred Adler, brought a most humanistic approach to the understanding of being human into the arena of group therapy. Historically, he extended the work of Adler in relation to education, child guidance, and group psychotherapy. His writings appear to be concerned for the individual in society, as he believed that the crux of emotional difficulty is sociological in origin and nature. His concept of group psychotherapy as the only group in existence that values the individual's shortcomings and deficits is quite a profound perception and approach. In other groups, the individual is accepted and included because of his or her accomplishments and abilities, whereas a deficit is considered a liability and the basis for exclusion. This is not the case for group psychotherapy in Dreikurs' opinion. In fact, individuals are valued for who they are and not what they have accomplished. In many cases, this acceptance is based on one's human existence and is probably an entirely new experience for many people entering a group environment. Dreikurs' insight relates to the concept that each point on a circle is equal, but in this case the parity is because one is human. He believed that every group must have a set of values, and in group psychotherapy these values are very different than in any other type of group. For example, the fact that an individual exists and participates on a continuous basis in the group confers a degree of status merely by ongoing commitment. He likens this to the relationship of members in a tribe in which the individual's value or worth is not in question. By mere physical presence in the tribe, the individual is of equal value to any other individual in the community.

Dreikurs felt that self-disclosure and being real were most necessary. They are of great value in group psychotherapy, whereas deception and emotional self-restraint are not considered positive values, as they are in other kinds of groups. In group psychotherapy they are considered behaviors of low self-esteem. Group psychotherapy, indeed, was a very different sociological phenomenon for Dreikurs. Because of his Adlerian affiliation, he perceived the role of the group leader quite differently than what was previously seen. He felt that the concept of the detached group leader who did not respond or answer questions because it would gratify the patient was in fact not creating a democratic learning environment but rather an autocratic environment, and thus reinforced the leader's sense of authority. He felt that a group leader needed to have the ability to function as an equal and to be as human as the members of the group even though he or she had more psychological knowledge. Obviously, this requires a leader to feel secure and not to hide behind a designated role in the group. Dreikurs's contribution to group psychotherapy will remain timeless as long as therapists value the equality of the human condition with its many deficiencies, while taking the risk of appearing human and imperfect in their search for their own equality.

FOULKES

> Group analysis is a powerful therapy. It is stimulating as a theory and can be prolific as a source for gathering information. (Foulkes, 1957)

Foulkes approached the use of group psychotherapy through reconciling the topographical theory of psychoanalysis (see Glossary) with its concomitant components and group as a whole with its Gestalt interpretations. He felt that psychoanalysis was an individualistic form of psychotherapy and chose to call his own work "group analysis." He felt that, in principle, groups represented a transferential arena, but unlike individual psychotherapy, where the transference was focused on the analyst, group transferences were focused on both the members and the analyst. In his perception, the theory of group analysis focused not on the individual per se, as in psychoanalysis, but on the individual in a sociologic perspective. Humans do not generally live in isolation, and personality development arises out of interrelations with the family and community. As a result, the family or community can be represented by the group-analysis paradigm, in which the focus of psychotherapy is asymmetrically balanced toward the group as a whole rather than seeking to understand in totality the individualistic world of each group member. Foulkes related that every event, whether it involved one or two people, had the effect of a group-as-a-whole encounter because each person in the group was affected. Interestingly, he used the Gestalt symbolization of foreground, figure, and background to explain these interactions by stating that the interaction itself was the foreground but occurring in the group was an existing underlying phenomenon attributed to the background. In some sense this interpretation could be correlated with the psychoanalytic concepts of manifest and latent content. The manifest content could be the dialogue and the latent content could be that which is unsaid but felt on an unconscious level.

Foulkes, in his observations, introduced a series of concepts of group interaction that leaders observe when leading groups:

1. A mirror reaction is when an individual sees himself or herself in another group member. This realization of seeing oneself in the behavior of another can be a very liberating experience. Clients who come for help often feel alone and unique in their distress. According to Foulkes, this experienced isolation is the individual's lack of effective communication of distress to the theoretical support environment—family and community. When it can be observed that the individual's feelings are not so very different from another's, an attenuation of this sense of isolation occurs.
2. Occupation is the primary reason for people to come together for a purpose as a group. In instances other than group analysis, there is a clear reason why people have gathered. In group analysis, this is not necessarily the case. In the aforementioned gathering, "occupation" refers to the coming together for a specific reason with boundaries that are not to be transgressed, but in group analysis, this would be considered a defensive screen against intimacy.
3. Translation means making the unconscious conscious. In individual psychoanalysis, this is done between the analyst and the

patient, but in group analysis it occurs between the member and the group. Foulkes felt that it was the process of communication, not the communication itself, that was of greatest importance in group analysis. As clinical supervisors, we often teach students of psychology that when working with clients it is important to listen to the tone of what they say more closely than to their words. A group leader in Foulkes's paradigm tends to be active, involved, and, in keeping with Gestalt psychotherapy, as much a part of the group as the members. Similar to Bion in influence, Foulkes's applications to group are more prevalent in Europe and countries outside of the United States, such as Israel and Australia. Why this is the case could be another area of historical investigation.

CORSINI AND ROSENBERG

The nature of the dynamics that leads to successful therapy is the central issue of psychotherapy. (Corsini and Rosenberg, 1955)

Corsini's contribution not only to psychology but to group therapy was multifaceted. His orientation was Adlerian and he believed from his studies with Dreikurs that group was of great value for change. Corsini and Rosenberg felt that there existed a paucity of agreement in the many psychological paradigms about what variables were necessary for psychological change and effective therapy due to the use of different terminologies. In fact, these semantic differences often caused restrictions, limiting the orderly development of psychology. In brief, what they set out to do was to gather information from 300 writers about what is necessary for successful group therapy. Their methodology had an Adlerian essence, as it approached the work of these writers with complete acceptance of their perceptions. After the data were compiled, ten mechanisms were isolated and specified. Of the ten, nine were labeled and the tenth was left as miscellaneous for dynamics that did not dovetail as well with the other categories. The nine other categories were altruism, universalization, intellectualization, reality testing, transference, interaction, spectator therapy, ventilation (the release of emotions), and acceptance.

Irvin Yalom's book *The Theory and Practice of Group Psychotherapy* (1975) presents a similar dynamic for psychological change and effective group therapy. Corsini and Rosenberg's efforts in the taxonomy of the underlying psychological factors inherent in successful group therapy have certainly illuminated and clarified the classifications that reconciled the many diverse perceptions of differing psychological modalities.

SLAVSON

Do group dynamics arise in therapy groups? (Slavson, 1957)

S. R. Slavson is considered to be the father of group therapy in America and the founder of the *International Journal of Group Psychotherapy.* His contribution to the literature on group therapy is legendary and the partial summary presented as follows is from one of his many provocative monographs (Slavson, 1957). This particular monograph has been included in the historical section of this book because of its search for empirical data, the profound questions it addresses, and its timeliness.

Slavson questioned and promoted the perceptions of the therapist to discriminate between perceiving the group as a unitary entity or specifically focusing upon the individual. The validations of these discriminations would in all probability determine whether group therapy will develop as a science and as a therapeutic tool due to eventual empirical findings. He also questioned the efficacy of group in relation to the patients' perceptions of their positive adjustment, i.e., did the patients improve merely because they adjusted to the group environment; did the group actually affect them positively due to the relationships that had been established; or did improvements develop and personalities change because during the group experience there was a release of anxiety which ultimately led to insight, thus creating the emergence of new positive self images?

Slavson defined the generic term *group* as a voluntary meeting of three or more individuals in a face-to-face relation under the auspices of leadership. These individuals are goal directed and the experience may or may not necessarily provide growth. In a therapy group the therapist does not take on the role of leadership per se but is an integral and indispensable part of the process. Rather, this person theoretically becomes a recipient of libidinal and transferential feelings with the possibility of being an object of dependency for the group members. Positive, negative, and ambivalent feelings are then elicited from the group members to the object of the therapist due to the role he or she has undertaken. Unlike other groups, therapy groups specifically address issues that have inhibited group members from enjoying life and human relationships. According to Slavson (1957), the individual in group therapy is specifically there for his or her own particular goals and the goal of the group as a whole is not of interest or aim. There may be a commonality in purpose of the group members, e.g., growth and change, but not necessarily a commonality in mirror issues. Slavson felt that the typical group dynamics of a generic group, e.g., social, political, educational, business, would be absent in a therapy group because the therapy group is not goal directed as its primary function. According to Slavson, the synergy that is present in other groups is not a factor in a therapy group and would, in effect, be counterproductive to the therapeutic process. He believed that the cement or bond that holds a therapy group together is anxiety. The attenuation of this anxiety becomes a goal of the individual members. As it lessens, the individual is in the process of change. Unlike other theorists, Slavson felt that cohesion should be avoided in a therapy group; for cohesion to develop, the group members would have to relinquish their individual egos and superegos for the service of the group as a whole. This concept has been repeated by other theorists. In contradiction to this, a therapy group encourages its members to retain their individuality in order for growth to occur. Slavson distinguished group therapy as a very different and special type of group that provides a distinct environment where the individual is foremost, in comparison to other groups where the group is foremost to the individual.

BERNE

The superego, ego, and id are psychic agencies. The Parent, Adult, and Child are not synonymous with these agencies but rather they are unto themselves complete ego states. (Berne, 1958)

Eric Berne is included in this list of contributors to group therapy because his transactional analysis moved away from psychoanalysis as an individual therapy overlaid upon group therapy toward a modality that stands on its own in relation to group dynamics. His transmutation from structural analysis into transactional analysis represented another new paradigm for inclusion in the group psychotherapy arena. His underlying analysis of the individual in a group environment was similar to Harry Stack Sullivan's interpersonal theory of psychiatry in which an individual cannot be seen and understood in isolation but only in relation to others. He perceived that three particular ego states are active in each individual no matter the nature of the interpersonal transaction. He chose to label these ego states parent, adult, and child.

The adult ego state is one in which the individual is inclined to deal effectively and is oriented in current reality. The individual objectively processes information in interpersonal relationships. The parent ego state is a form of modeling in which the individual introjects from either parent a particular behavioral style in his or her interactions with others, often containing either the positive, nurturing manifestation or the critical, negative manifestation of the parent. This ego state contains the many "shoulds and oughts" as presented by the parents in the structure for living. On the other hand, the child ego state is one in which the individual's emotional expression and spontaneous acts are seen. The child ego state has two components: (1) the natural child—the child that is open to exploration and fun but without the acculturation of society; and (2) the adapted child—the child who has learned through interpersonal interactions to accommodate the expectations of others.

In this we can see Sullivan's definition of self as a reflection of the approbations of important people in one's early life. Berne's supposition was that conflict arose in an interpersonal relationship when one individual was relating from one ego state such as adult and the other person was relating back in a different ego state such as parent. He labeled this "crossed transaction" and felt that it was the crux of most misunderstandings in human relationships. Berne used these three states as an explanation of problem resolution for his patients in group therapy. He felt that group therapy, with its multiple interactions, was realistically more effective in clarifying interpersonal relationships than individual psychotherapy was.

ROGERS

> The most significant social invention of this century is perhaps the encounter group. (Rogers, 1967)

The encounter group phenomenon evolved in America when great sociological change and movement toward authenticity occurred. From post-World War II to the late 1950s and early 1960s, a period of conformity and conservatism took place in America. At that time, events and people tended to be seen in a dichotomy of either good or bad or black and white. As in astrophysics, with the concept of the "big bang," a sociological phenomenon was exploding among the youth of America. Crew cuts and penny loafers for men gave way to long hair and bare feet. Nudity, sexual exploration, and drug experimentation were summed up in the slogan "sex, drugs, and rock 'n' roll." It was the era of Timothy Leary and others at Harvard who encouraged students to "turn on, tune in, and drop out," to the dismay of many parents. The 1960s and 1970s was the most creative and exploratory time of the twentieth century. Because the zeitgeist, the spirit of the time, was evident, the encounter group found its place and roots in American society and American psychology.

Carl Rogers, teacher and psychologist, experimented with student-centered teaching as a viable method to enhance student learning. He believed that allowing the free expression of personal feelings from students not only increased their learning potential but created personal change. He began experimenting with groups on an intensive short-term basis, which he later termed *encounter groups*. Rogers found that in this time-limited intensive environment, which was minimally structured, individuals would attenuate their defenses and relate with feeling to others in the group.

Rogers was a pioneer in generating data from these encounter groups. Through naturalistic observation he found that a similar process of group formation and functioning was evident in the many encounter groups he had run:

1. *Milling around.* A rather lost and confused group feeling emerged because participants were not sure how to respond in this loosely structured environment.

2. *Resistance to personal expression or exploration.* A sense of ambivalence initially arose when some members began to disclose issues of a personal nature.
3. *Description of past feelings.* Group members began to discuss feelings about nongroup relationships.
4. *Expression of negative feelings.* The initial here-and-now feelings toward other group members had generally begun with negative perceptions.
5. *Expression and exploration of personally meaningful material.* The individual began to significantly reveal himself or herself.
6. *The expression of immediate interpersonal feelings in the group.* Again, here-and-now feelings were expressed to other group members, but they now took on both positive and negative feelings.
7. *The development of a healing capacity in the group.* Group members began to help one another.
8. *Self-acceptance and the beginning of change.* This appeared to be the necessary ingredient.
9. *The cracking of facades.* As the group moved along, members' defensive styles were no longer tolerated and were addressed.
10. *The individual receives feedback.* A group participant learned how others perceived him or her; if members provided this feedback in a caring way, it could be very constructive for the individual member.
11. *Confrontation.* An in-your-face leveling with another individual. This could be both positive and negative.
12. *The helping relationships outside the group session.* Group members spent time with one another outside of the session, offering assistance.
13. *The basic encounter.* Individuals had the experience of getting much closer to one another than they had in ordinary life.
14. *The expression of positive feelings and closeness.* Warmth and closeness continued to develop out of the initial honesty of disclosing both positive and negative feelings toward one another.

15. *Behavior changes in the group.* Individuals became more sensitive to one another. Although Rogers strongly felt that the encounter group was a very positive modality for behavioral change, he saw that there were disadvantages. Some individuals did not have the ego strength to benefit from the intensity of this type of experience; in fact, it could be harmful to the integrity of their psychological well-being. Also, because of the time-limited nature of this event, there was little, if any, follow-up. Often, the feelings and changes that manifested themselves in the group members disappeared over a short period of time. Rogers felt that further investigation into the phenomenon of the encounter group was necessary and continued to believe that it was a rehumanizing of human relationships and of great importance in a society that reinforced the suppression of feelings.

YALOM AND LIEBERMAN

Pain was likely to be reaped for those who came believing in miracles. (Yalom and Lieberman, 1971)

Yalom and Lieberman's research into the casualties of encounter groups is included here out of chronological sequence because it dovetails rather nicely with Rogers' positive perception of the effectiveness of the encounter group movement. In a well-designed study, although limited to undergraduate college students at Stanford University, Yalom and Lieberman sought to determine the possible negative effects of being a participant in an encounter group. They had found that more than a few isolated cases were beginning to show up in the literature in relation to the adverse effects of the time-limited intensive experience of this particular modality. Over 9.4 percent of 170 participants in this study had developed severe enough negative reactions to be considered casualties of the experience. Interestingly, the least effective predictor of a negative effect for a participant was the group leaders themselves. The members of the group had greater predictive capabilities in relation to probable negative experiences of their fellow group members. The severity of the casualties depended upon the particular type of encounter group to which the participants were randomly assigned. The more traumatized participants were in groups in which the leader was highly charismatic, confronting, and challenging, with intrusive and aggressive behavior. The least negative effects of the encounter group experience were seen with leaders who were positively reinforcing. These leaders created a trusting, warm environment in which the individual participants could proceed at their own pace. Those individuals who invested in a magical belief that salvation was at hand by going through the encounter group were highly susceptible to having a negative experience. Perhaps client preparation and explanation of the type of group they would be entering would have helped in avoiding possible adverse effects.

RIOCH

In the real world, people got the leaders that they deserved. (Rioch, 1970)

Margaret Rioch is included in this overview because the approach she and her committee designed for understanding group dynamics is quite interesting. Working from Bion's group-as-a-whole format, Rioch chose to focus primarily on group leadership, authority, and member responsibility. Rioch formulated that analyzing a group with the observation of a modernistic empirical reductionistic rationale provided little understanding of the dynamics of group leadership. To understand group leadership, attention must shift from the individual to the group as a whole. Interestingly, there is a variable that is strongly discouraged in the design of Rioch's methodology. This variable, which is basic to the majority of psychotherapy groups, is the participants' emotionality. The emotionality and the individual are not the focus of interest; rather, the focus is the struggle of the group to either survive or destroy itself. It was proposed that how a group functions in its quest to survive will determine the type of leadership it will encourage. As far as the individual group member is concerned, in Rioch's study, it is believed that a common goal could and would unite the group for its survival. Each participant, however, had a different contribution. In this sense, the goal or the larger picture for survival, the group, outweighs the individual's narcissistic needs, and being part of the group provides a fulfilling experience for the participant. The results of this study elicited a very thoughtful perception. In the real world, "people get the leaders that they deserve" (Rioch, 1970, p. 355).

HORWITZ

An interpretation is not made without taking into consideration the individual and the group. (Horwitz, 1977)

Leonard Horwitz's concentration was on reconciling the holistic and individualistic approaches to interpretation as they related to group dynamics. He felt that working from a deductive paradigm in which only underlying group universalization themes were interpreted did not, in effect, take into account individual differences and the unique behavioral manifestations of patients in group therapy. He proposed that interpretation would be more effectively accomplished if the group leader observed the group and its members from the paradigm of inductive reasoning. In this sense, the therapist went from the particular, the individual's disclosure, to the universal, the underlying theme of the entire group. Because a common underlying principle of attention was not always evident in each session, it was very possible that the group leader would primarily focus attention on the individual participant, thus providing interpretation in the absence of a group theme. Unlike the holistic approach, which focuses solely on the group as a whole, the group-centered approach was more flexible and integratively accepting of individual differences.

ORMONT

A benefit of group therapy is providing a laboratory situation in which the individual may experiment through his worst moments before experiencing them in life. (Ormont, 1992)

Louis Ormont is included in this encapsulated historical overview for many reasons. Although his name is not as well known as those of previous researchers, he has contributed greatly to group psychotherapy through his many well-written and effective monographs. He has the distinction of having one of the largest group therapy practices in the world and over the past forty years has personally influenced over 2,500 group therapists through his classes, workshops, and training groups (Brook, 2001). His belief in and loyalty to the effectiveness of group psychotherapy is quite evident in his many written works. Group, in Ormont's opinion, is a microcosm of reality and the ideal place to solve interpersonal problems. Ormont strongly suggests that in this microcosm, the individual will re-create the behavioral patterns that are evident outside of the group arena. Because of this re-creation, the individual has the opportunity for awareness and personal change. In an interesting, individualistic, and group-as-a-whole perception, it is his belief that we are treating not only the individual but the group. By treating the group, we are using all the members as a cast of characters in an ongoing general story with individual subplots. As the individual becomes healthier, so does the group; as the group becomes healthier, so does the individual. The group moves forward almost as a living organism with its own personal identity.

According to Ormont, the surest way for a group to fail is when a therapist turns the group into individual psychotherapy sessions. An effective group is an emotional group in which interpersonal relatedness is emotionally connected. He writes, "It matters less who is speaking than who is feeling the import of what is being said" (Ormont, 1992, p. 5). For change to occur, the individual must have an emotional connection to the material being presented. The group leader must create what Ormont has called "bridges between patients" as a connection in which one individual can reach another through communication. This is highly unusual for most patients, as it requires them to reveal their inner lives, a task not easily accomplished when these types of disclosures have been negatively perceived by society.

REVIEW

Please answer true (T) or false (F) to the following questions.

Dreikurs

1. (T) (F) Dreikurs extended the work of Adler in relation to education, child guidance, and group psychotherapy.

2. (T) (F) His concept of group psychotherapy as the only group in existence that values the individual's shortcomings and deficits is quite a profound perception and approach.

3. (T) (F) He felt that the concept of detached group leaders who did not respond or answer questions because it was a gratification of the patient was in fact not creating a democratic learning environment but rather creating an autocratic environment and thus reinforcing the leader's sense of authority.

Foulkes

4. (T) (F) Foulkes approached group psychotherapy through reconciling the topographical theory of psychoanalysis with its concomitant components and group as a whole with its Gestalt interpretations.

5. (T) (F) He felt that humans live in isolation and personality develops out of this isolation.

6. (T) (F) When an individual sees himself or herself in another group member, this is called a mirror reaction.

7. (T) (F) Foulkes felt that the communication was more important in group than the process of the communication.

Corsini and Rosenberg

8. (T) (F) Corsini and Rosenberg suggested that the paucity of agreement among professionals, in relation to the different variables for change in group therapy, was due to the use of different terminology.

9. (T) (F) Their methodology was to approach the different authors writing on group therapy with very strict and rigid requirements.

10. (T) (F) Corsini and Rosenberg's research can be seen in Yalom's later work on the variables for psychological change in group therapy.

Slavson

11. (T) (F) Slavson was considered the father of group therapy around the world.

12. (T) (F) He felt that in a therapy group, there was a commonality in purpose of the group members and a commonality in mirror issues.
13. (T) (F) Slavson strongly supported cohesion in a therapy group.

Berne

14. (T) (F) Berne's transactional analysis moved away from psychoanalysis as an individual therapy overlaid upon group therapy.
15. (T) (F) His underlying analysis of the individual in a group environment was similar to Sullivan's interpersonal theory of psychiatry, in which the individual cannot be understood in isolation.
16. (T) (F) The ego state that contains many of the "shoulds and oughts" is the adult ego state.
17. (T) (F) Crossed transactions occur when two people come to understand each other.

Rogers

18. (T) (F) Zeitgeist means "the spirit of the time."
19. (T) (F) Rogers initially introduced the concept of student-centered learning, in which he found that permitting students free expression of their personal feelings increased their learning and potential for personal change.
20. (T) (F) The expression of negative feelings toward other group members generally began early in the group.
21. (T) (F) Rogers did not believe that the encounter group format would rehumanize human relationships.

Yalom and Lieberman

22. (T) (F) Yalom and Lieberman sought to determine the possible negative effects of being a participant in an encounter group.
23. (T) (F) The least effective predictor for perceiving a negative effect in an encounter group participant was the group leader.

24. (T) (F) The more traumatized participants were in groups in which the group leader was highly charismatic, confronting, and challenging, with intrusive and aggressive behaviors.

Rioch

25. (T) (F) Rioch's attention focused primarily on the group member.
26. (T) (F) One variable was strongly discouraged in the design of this study: the emotionality of the group member.
27. (T) (F) The results of this study elicited the perception that, in the real world, "people get the leaders that they deserve."

Horwitz

28. (T) (F) He felt that deductive reasoning, which interpreted only universal themes in the group, did not take into account individual differences.
29. (T) (F) Every group, according to Horwitz, had an underlying theme.
30. (T) (F) The group-centered approach had greater flexibility and integratively accepted individual differences.

Ormont

31. (T) (F) The group, for Ormont, represented a microcosm of reality and an ideal place to solve interpersonal problems.
32. (T) (F) By treating the group, we are using all the members as a cast of characters in an ongoing, general story with individual subplots.
33. (T) (F) According to Ormont, a group is destined to succeed when the group therapist turns the group into individual psychotherapy.
34. (T) (F) For change to occur, the individual must have an emotional connection to the material being presented.

Chapter 3

Why Group Therapy?

One achieves mental health to the extent that one becomes aware of one's interpersonal relationships. (Sullivan, 1940)

As an introduction to the question "Why group therapy?" a client's introspective description of the experience in a time-limited, weekly, sixteen-week group is presented to give the reader an idea and possibly a feeling for this individual's experience of participation in a group. This particular group was designed as a "growth-oriented interpersonal experience" as it focused on the "self search." The names have been changed, the writer's name has been omitted for confidentiality, and the client has graciously given permission to print the following letter.

The reason that this letter begins this chapter is that many novice clinicians who have never run groups, and seasoned clinicians who have run groups but have never had the experience of being a group member, may benefit from knowing what it feels like to be on the other side.

* * *

As a whole, the group experience was one which was filled with learning, whether it was obvious or not at the time. Each feeling and experience was one which needed to be noticed and processed, in reference to the group members' individual lives and to the further interactions in the group as a whole. Many times it was not until the events within the group were processed that I would become aware of what exactly had occurred and the implications of those events. It really impacts upon me the necessity of being constantly aware of what may seem to be even the most minor of interactions or events, as these may be clues to some underlying issues which should be examined in my life and personality.

The first instance of this became apparent to me when the group was first getting started. The initial anxiety and tension was apparent with every one of the group members, with each of us having his or her own reasons for what that anxiety represented. It was not until, one by one, all of the members began discussing his or her own fears and anxieties as being a member in this particular group, e.g., meeting new people, fears of exposing oneself too quickly, fear of being judged by others and needing to be accepted. By not just skimming the assumed anxiety and instead delving into it, we were able to get our first glance into the personalities and perceptions of our fellow group members, which would be an important component to our later groups.

The next part of the group, which I experienced, was the building of trust and the development of the dialogue, which as we know is a vital aspect of the overall process. From the onset of the group, this seemed to be the focus and goal of everyone involved. It appeared though that no one was willing to be the first to place his or her trust in someone else enough to divulge some intimate aspect of his or her life other than superficialities, as this would make the person vulnerable to the others in the group. The issue was brought up over and over, yet it never seemed to be the moment anyone would choose to open up. There was one point where John revealed some negative feelings about Bob, yet beyond that we were at a standstill. There was a great deal of storytelling and discussion about various topics, but the group never felt like someone was really putting himself or herself on the line. This seemed like it dragged on forever, and then finally someone began revealing personal issues. This appeared to have an effect on others in the group and there then appeared to be a great deal of sharing and self-revelation. It struck me that the development of the trust was something no one could predict or schedule, but was rather a feeling, which each member had to gauge for himself or herself, and only then could the group move forward.

Once the group began to become more and more open in discussing its personal issues, it was then that I began to notice the importance of a universal theme, which brought everyone into the discussion, and to create the feeling of some shared experience. In feeling that someone else shared some common emotion or situation, a bond of understanding and closeness seemed to be formed. This universality in experience allowed me to feel some connection with others in the group that I had not felt before that time, illustrating to me how important it is to highlight the shared similarities to facilitate some underlying bonds between members. One person in particular, Jane, whom I had never been able to identify with, revealed some painful experience and a facet of herself that we shared in common. When that occurred it was like there was some more common understanding between us. This feeling of commonality which later developed into cohesiveness was, for me, the development of security with these other people who were initially strangers.

One of the components of the group process that sticks out most in my mind was the effect that having a silent group member had upon the group members' experience. Ron was extremely quiet after his initial confrontation, rarely speaking about his own issues. After many sessions of this, there finally came a point where I felt it had to be addressed and so I related my own frustration at his lack of involvement. Others then expressed the same feeling at Ron's lack of responsiveness or involvement. Each of us within the group had a different feeling about Ron's lack of involvement. Mine was that I felt angry that he chose to observe instead of participate. Others felt worried that he did not trust them, and others seemed almost sad that he did not feel comfortable enough to share and really become a part of the group. To each of us, Ron's silence meant something different and created within us feelings that were likely linked to some personal issue or thing in our past. Silence brought out from each of us what it means to be around someone who is not gratifying and who is blank for all we say and show.

This series of incidents with Ron exemplified another important experience for me in the group, that of seeing another individual similar to someone from my past and dealing with that person the same way as I dealt with the original person. Ron's silence embodied every cool, detached, and ungratifying person I had ever dealt with before, especially that of my father and a significant other. I found myself enraged by his lack of emotional response, both verbal and physical, and his unwillingness to open up and try to become more a part of the group through sharing of himself. In relating this to him, I became more and more enraged and frustrated, almost wanting to jump on him physically and force emotion out of him. Only after I was shown that my feelings for Ron were primarily due to my unresolved feelings for the others like him in my life did I stop attacking him and felt some revelation as to why this affected me so greatly, as I was reliving these difficult issues from my own life outside of the group. Upon realizing this and thinking about it for a number of days, a profound change seemed to take place. It was one of those surreal experiences where I thought to myself, "My God! Where have I been? Look at all the pain I had put myself and others in my life through expecting them to fulfill an emotional lack I had experienced in the past with my family."

This experience of seeing someone in group like someone from the past was probably one of the most surprising and thought-provoking events I witnessed with the group. It seemed like I suddenly became aware in that moment what exactly the whole group process was about as I saw it unfolding in front of me. It was also at this point that it seemed the group took a turn for a deeper level of relating. We moved beyond storytelling and surface discussions and more into developing the interactions between ourselves.

The last important component of the group experience was the termination of our experience together. Some were eager to end and go on while others of us were saddened by the end of the group and the loss of the important supports we had developed over the sixteen weeks. I just realized that I did not say goodbye to Ron; I don't remember if anyone did? I guess that just hit me as being so sad. I felt very sad about leaving the other members and I did not even thank him for his help. I really wonder if it hurt him or if that's just his way of avoiding the feelings he was having at the time? I really never realized how important it is to have some kind of closure and to be able to share with others how important they were to me and how they had touched my life.

Through this group, I was able to gain a greater understanding of myself, my own issues, and how they impact upon my life in the everyday world. One of my own greatest personal stumbling blocks, which became apparent in the group and is apparent in my life, is becoming an active part in my relationships with people as I am usually not at ease with people I don't know well in my day-to-day functioning. I have a tendency to close up and withdraw from those around me, being very passive and detached, typically due to fear of rejection or of fear of being judged. By being open in the group and facing the possible rejection from others, I was able to face some of my own fears and see that many people are accepting and supportive. It allowed me the chance to see that I need to get past these fears, as they prevent me from meeting people and establishing relationships with others.

An aspect of myself as a group member which surprised me a great deal was the fact that others saw me as one of the more outspoken and participative members. I typically shy away from this type of activity and feel like I am more withdrawn and less outspoken. I guess this illustrates for me the differences within myself, from when I do not know others to when I become more comfortable and at ease. It seems odd that I never even noticed this difference within myself, but I assume this just relates to the fact that as I get to know people better I lose that concern and excessive self-monitoring that goes along with meeting new people. Along with this outspokenness, I have been told that I need to be more direct and somewhat more assertive in my dealings with others, especially when confronting them on issues which I perceive as being critical or anxiety provoking for me. I have attempted to work on this and I know it's something I will continue to work on in the future.

Another thing about myself I also noticed within the group was my fear of other people expressing extreme sadness or hurt. This left me feeling like I did not know how to react to them, like I was completely at a loss. I wanted to show them some kind of comfort in some way, yet it felt like I had no idea how to even reach out to them or what to say that would show I cared. I'm able to deal with anger and rage without a problem, but it seems dealing with these other feelings leaves me feeling uncomfortable and unequipped to cope with it.

One instance that stands out foremost in my mind was when I discussed with the group the issues I was having with my bigoted neighbors. I was extremely anxious, fearful, and upset at the time, and because I had very few people who I could talk to in my outside life, it meant a great deal when the group was so comforting and allowed me to deal with my own feelings. At that moment, it hit me exactly how much the group meant to me and what it felt like to have people really care about me and be empathetic to what I was going through at the time. I think that incident has made me think about how much I need to have friends who are caring and sensitive people in my own life, something which has been absent for far too long.

* * *

As you can see from the sensitive description of this client's experience in group therapy, there were many beneficial experiences. These experiences increased awareness in the client's relationships with others and insight into this individual's own personality in a relatively short period of time.

Because group is a relationship-oriented modality, an individual's historical experiences with others can be clearly manifested. Toseland and Siporin (1986) suggest that group therapy can be consistently efficient and cost effective compared to individual psychotherapy. Harry Stack Sullivan (1953) suggests that the experiences an individual has with others can cause psychological disturbances. These disturbances can be ameliorated with new experiences with others in order for the individual to be well again.

Homo sapiens are relationship-oriented animals and are thus inclined to have many diverse interpersonal experiences. Interestingly, humans are capable of having relationships and experiences with people, places, and things. These experiences can be both positive and negative and can have a profound effect upon the development of individual personalities. What and who we are as human beings depends upon and positively correlates with the memories of these interpersonal experiences. In many cases, especially with individuals seeking some form of therapy, previous relationships have not provided experiences that were effectively beneficial and the memories of those relationships, both conscious and unconscious, have affected the way these individuals relate to others. Generally, their relationships are problematic, distressing, and at times unstable, thus being the motivation for clients to seek some form of psychotherapy.

It would appear that we are always in some form of a relationship from the moment of conception until death. Whether awake and conscious or asleep and dreaming, a dialogue between others and ourselves or dialogues within ourselves are continuously being manifested. Even the schizophrenic walking down the street talking to himself, or the psychotic individual who believes he is Jesus Christ or Napoleon, is in some dialogue and relationship with a significant other. The only times that a relationship or dialogue with another may not be evident is when an individual is unconscious, in a drug-induced stupor, or considered brain dead, but we do not know for sure what is truly occurring for these unfortunate individuals.

In a sense, human beings are never quite alone. Whether this is by choice or genetic predisposition, some form of a relationship always exists. Because we are by nature relationship oriented, prolonged physical aloneness is the most severe existential punishment a human being may experience, as can be seen in the example of solitary confinement.

Group therapy is a wonderful modality for helping clients come to know themselves and their relationships with others, because it is a social microcosm of the family, society, and civilization (Corey, 1995; Ormont, 1992; Rutan and Stone, 1993; Yalom, 1985). Overall, the people who voluntarily seek or have been referred by their therapists for group therapy are not from a population of highly disturbed individuals. In fact, these people are generally functioning and are highly aware that something is not quite right in their interpersonal relationships; they see group therapy as a possible arena for solving this difficulty.

The microcosmic benefit of group therapy is that in this environment, the individual begins to manifest his or her true personality with its concomitant strengths and weaknesses. It is this true personality that we, as therapists, hope to elicit in the members of the group; it affects the unsatisfactory relationships individuals have with others and with themselves.

Most people manifest two different personalities, which at times overlap and at times can contradict each other. The social personality is the one the individual uses to relate generally to the outside world. This personality is often the one that is deemed appropriate for the situation, although internally the individual may feel very different. The individual usually saves the real personality for those people with whom he or she feels safe and comfortable. The real personality often causes the disturbance in interpersonal relationships, as it contains the true historical story of the individual's life with both its negative and positive experiences with others.

Group, by its design, creates an environment in which the real personality feels safe to emerge. It is in this emergence that the therapist and the members have the opportunity of helping individuals become aware of how they are affecting their environment and how their environment is affecting them. This is not to suggest that the social personality is not addressed; in fact, it is. Initially, we must often work with the social personality before the individual is prepared to allow others and himself or herself to view the entity that has been kept hidden for myriad reasons truly known only to the individual.

Yalom (1970) created a system of classification to empirically measure the efficacy of a member's experience in group therapy. He arrived at eleven factors that were consistently experienced by members in a therapy group. These factors or therapeutic mechanisms that help group to be effective are instillation of hope, universality, imparting of information, altruism, development of socializing techniques, imitative behavior, catharsis, corrective recapitulation of primary family group, existential factors, group cohesiveness, and interpersonal learning.

It has been my experience that universality, at least in the beginning, is the most profound of these eleven factors. With universality, individuals no longer feel alone. They see themselves in others and the dreaded fear of having unusual or strange thoughts and feelings is attenuated. When I was a group member, the realization that there were other individuals who felt similar to the way I felt was a great relief. It was a marvelous motivation to seek further similarities between these people and me.

How do we create this safe environment that will elicit all the real personalities, as group therapy generally has eight to ten members? According to Franz Alexander (1946), for a client to be helped the individual must have a "corrective emotional experience" that will ultimately mend the previously dysfunctional experience. We must create certain parameters for a client for this to occur. First and foremost, the group members must feel a sense of concern from the therapist about them. Perhaps this is something they have not felt from another person in a long time. If clients are to trust the process of group, they must trust the leader and eventually they will begin to trust one another. Members must come to feel that they can discuss anything in group without fear of being punished. Clinicians and educators are continuously amazed at how many people live their lives in avoidance of punishment, whether real or imagined. If we create a punitive environment, the possibility of an individual not opening up increases. Certain clinicians feel that reliving the punitive experience helps the client, but it may backfire and cause the member to drop out of the group before reliving an emotionally painful life situation. Clinicians who are having problems with consistent dropouts may want to evaluate their personalities, as there may be a punitive component of which they are unaware.

Transference, a salient component of group, is an extraordinary phenomenon that enables the emergence of an individual's past experience and true personality. It is through the members' interactions with one another that both the members and the leader begin to see the manifestations of the difficulties that have brought these people into group therapy.

Group therapy is one of the most extraordinary of the therapeutic modalities. It is honest, true, and has tremendous therapeutic benefits for the individual members. New behaviors generated from the group therapy experience, in comparison to individual psychotherapy, are more easily generalized to the "real world" due to the fact that group is a microcosm of society and the family. The therapeutic environment of individual psychotherapy, a one-one experience, is unique in the sense that one person is giving the other person his or her full attention for an hour, which is rare in the real world. It has the potential to make major corrective gains for individuals who have dysfunctional family histories. For many members, group provides an opportunity to observe the world of others, an involvement they have previously denied themselves due to their individual interpersonal difficulties.

THE GROUP THERAPIST

All I ever wanted to be was to be myself. Why was that so difficult? (Hesse, 1919)

The personality or characteristics of the group leader are often the concern of many novice and seasoned clinicians. If you really want to be an effective group leader, you should go into group therapy as a member and have the experience of being on the "other side of the desk." This suggestion tends to cause discomfort to many therapists who generally use the analogy that they "did not have to have a heart attack to be a heart surgeon." But no one is free from interpersonal difficulties, which, if worked out, would improve that person's effectiveness as a group leader. No matter how aware we think we are of ourselves, it is important to get feedback from others. This is especially true if the feedback provides little personal gain for the other person. Often therapists expect their clients to lend themselves to certain experiences that they themselves are not willing to undertake. This causes some discomfort for me as a therapist; the translation is that I cannot benefit from that which I am practicing. It also creates a dichotomy which implies that the client is sick and the therapist is healthy, thus reinforcing a medical model overlaid on a psychological paradigm. I once heard a senior clinician respond to a question posed to her by a client in group therapy. The client innocently asked whether the therapist's children ever had any difficulties while growing up. The therapist responded, "Absolutely not; they did not grow up in a sick family as you did."

There has been and probably will continue to be a large amount of research into what makes a good therapist or good group leader. In a sense, the focus of effective group leadership is more easily and simply understood if we look toward our clients as the guide to successful therapy. This is not to suggest that the many characteristics proposed by colleagues are not of tremendous merit, such as warmth, trustworthiness, empathy, and acceptance (Corey and Corey, 1992; Trotzer, 1989; Decker, 1988; Kottler, 1992; Rogers, 1965; Yalom, 1985). Others look at group leadership in terms of whether the individual is right for the specific type of group (Cribbin, 1972; Forsyth, 1990). As an educator and supervisor of new clinicians, it has been my observation that beginning group leaders are too focused upon their own actions, such as, "Am I being too warm, too transparent, too opaque, too cold, too gratifying, too verbal, too uninvolved, too disclosing?" Because of these valid concerns, they often miss what is occurring in the group at that moment. We cannot be effective therapists with all individuals who come to seek our services. This is a reality of life, as it is true that not all people who meet us are going to like us. It really does not matter whether you are warm, cold, opaque, transparent, gratifying, nongratifying, tall, short, thin, etc. Of paramount importance is that, upon termination, your clients leave therapy feeling hopeful, more aware of themselves and others, capable of sustaining positive relationships, and better able to effectively interact with the vicissitudes and capriciousness of life. If you can accomplish this by being detached and cold or warm and accepting, then you have been an effective therapist. I also believe that each client is unique and what and who you are may be the nearly perfect fit for effective psychotherapy to be accomplished. In effect, try being yourself and not someone else or someone you think you should be.

> There is no need to be scared to death every time I open my mouth for fear that I'll say something that's not perfectly accurate and entirely beyond reproach or criticism. No need to pick my words with such care that I end up by expressing myself much less clearly than if I had just said the first thing that came into my mind. (Rogers, 1965, p. 113)

It has been my experience that clients will tell you how they feel about you and your work. At that time, you may wish to make certain changes in your method of working. The one thing that is of greatest necessity, the sine qua non of creating a safe environment, is to develop a personality that is as free as possible from judging others. Very often therapists are unaware that their personal judgments are reflected in their therapy. What the therapist may be unaware of, the client is often very much aware of, especially if it is a sensitive issue in the client's life. Obviously, this is not an easy task. If you are perceived to be judgmental by your clients, they will be inhibited from disclosing as much as is humanly possible within their personalities. If you can reduce your judgment, you will begin to see marvelous results in your work. In my opinion, one of the most effective ways to become aware of personal judgments of others and to work those judgments through is to go into some form of therapy, preferably group.

REVIEW

Part A is related to "Why group therapy?" and the client's letter. Part B is related to the group therapist.

Part A

At this time, before you venture further into this text, what do you feel are the benefits of group therapy for the client?

What is the gender of the client who wrote the letter in the beginning of this chapter? Why did you choose that specific gender?

Part B

What do you feel are effective characteristics of a group leader and what are your feelings about a group leader becoming a group member as part of his or her training?

Chapter 4

Modalities: Structural Empiricism and Application to Group Therapy

> Structure: 1. Something made up of a number of parts assembled in a particular pattern; 2. The way in which parts are combined or arranged to form a whole. (*Webster's II*, 1984)

In general, group psychotherapy is designed to be an experience of minimum structure (Donigian and Malnati, 1997; Ormont, 1992; Rogers, 1967; Rutan and Stone, 1993). A lack of structure creates a naturalistic environment in which the group members experience themselves and theoretically manifest who they are as a more realistic entity rather than having the buffer of structure which provides the facade for socially approved behaviors. Basically, the only structure provided for the members is the group contract, whereas the structure provided for the leader is the modality he or she chooses as an intervention paradigm.

Psychology, like all social sciences in contemporary society, spawns new and different modalities that wax and wane over time. Some are fads, with a degree of provocativeness and sincere intentions, but they fade as quickly as they are introduced. Others withstand the test of time, efficacy, and empirical study to be included among the modalities that have endured.

The fourteen modalities described in this chapter and in Chapter 5 have withstood the test of time, but are not necessarily accepted or embraced by all members of the profession. They have remained viable and durable. They are presented briefly as a refresher for the reader. In-depth understanding can be obtained from books, journals, etc., devoted solely to each modality. Other modalities are excluded not because of lack of efficacy, but rather to use the space for more familiar foundation theories.

ADLERIAN

The individual psychology of Alfred Adler took a very different directional turn from Freud's psychoanalysis; for instance, biological determinism and sexuality were not considered of great importance. Adler believed that growth was the foundation of psychology, not neurosis or personality abnormalities. Inherently, behavior is a function of fulfilling growth. Human beings have goals with purpose and anticipate the future while creating meaning in their lives. Adlerians emphasize the perceptions and the phenomenological world of the individual and explore the meanings that individuals attribute to their experiences. Adlerians reject Freud's notion of determinism, which says that what we are born with limits to our behavior. Rather, they feel that how we create, act in, and understand our experiences of life causes our behavior.

Adler's growth model views the patient holistically as a person who is unified with regard to life goals and social experience. He suggests that within the human experience, individuals have the potential for a natural and positive upward progression, as if the innate goal in life is to maximize one's potential. This goal is subjective, and each individual is unique with regard to his or her own perceptual reality. Adler felt that a person can influence and create experiences and events throughout life and does so in an attempt to achieve goals while perfecting the self. When individuals experience failure, they strive to correct that failure by creating a more self-satisfying experience.

When running group therapy, the Adlerian therapist takes active steps to establish and maintain a therapeutic relationship and works toward goal alignment. The leader explores and analyzes the individual dynamics and communicates a basic attitude of caring and reassurance. Members develop insight about themselves and assume the responsibility for taking positive steps to make changes. The leader uses methods such as confrontation, interpretation, and analysis of existing practices to challenge beliefs, goals, and self-disclosure. The leader demonstrates focused attention while observing the social context of the individual behavior. The members are assisted to accept and benefit from their assets. Members are encouraged to develop the courage needed to generalize what is learned in the group to the world outside. The goals of an Adlerian group modality are to create a therapeutic relationship that inspires members to examine their basic life assumptions and to achieve a more extensive understanding of their lives. A patient is helped to become aware of his or her power to change and each group member is encouraged to accept responsibility for his or her life and lifestyle and for any modifications of this lifestyle considered necessary for change.

PSYCHODRAMA

Psychodrama allows the expression of feelings in a spontaneous and dramatic way through the use of theater. Therapeutic breakthroughs can be sudden. In psychodrama, the group members act out a difficult situation in their lives in order to acquire deeper meaning and understanding. By acting out the situation, the individual has an opportunity to re-create or get in touch with feelings that were previously elicited and had an effect on the individual's life. After this enactment, the dramatization is discussed. The actors (the individuals acting out the drama) and the audience (the other group members) may achieve a catharsis during this discussion phase as a degree of contagion may occur among members if the enactment has a special meaning for other group participants.

Psychodrama, by the nature of its design, allows people to play various roles in the group environment and to receive feedback about the impact of their actions on others and the impact of others' actions on them. Psychodrama is a directive modality that has been applied with success in many mental health facilities such as hospital clinics, day care centers, crisis units, therapeutic communities, drug and alcohol programs, and countless other settings (Blatner, 1988).

Psychodrama has successfully utilized many interesting concepts, for example, dealing with the present, which allows the individual to deal with a past event as if it is occurring in the present; encounter, which occurs when individuals confront significant others during the course of a dramatization; creativity, which encourages individuals to express their sense of God's purpose; and tele or "therapeutic love," which is expressed as a flow of feelings from one to another that creates growth in the individual and strengthens the bonds and the cohesion of the group members. The encouragement of individual spontaneity is most important in this particular modality, as it becomes a way of fostering creativity through openness, newness, and a willingness to take risks while the group member experiences both conflicts and resolutions in integrating external reality with internal desires.

Another technique allows the exploration of unexpressed emotions. By doing this, the individual may practice in the present imagined events with their concomitant consequences. This is a form of rehearsal for effectively dealing with anxiety-laden fantasies of future situations. The use of reality testing becomes an important exercise as this allows the individual to test behaviors while other group members help to provide alternatives the individual may not have considered. The use of role theory becomes important as it examines the many roles an individual plays throughout life, whereas catharsis and insight, although not a goal of psychodrama, often occur as a positive indicator of growth.

Psychodrama is uniquely designed for group therapy. It uses the group to help the protagonist reach an understanding of his or her situation. The therapist is the director and helps the protagonist spontaneously act out an event to gain a deeper understanding of it. The techniques that the therapist chooses focus on the protagonist's struggle and draw upon the protagonist's and the group's creativity for understanding and resolving that struggle. To that end, group members help play auxiliary egos that assist the protagonist and help him or her better understand relationships with significant others. Those not acting as auxiliary egos serve as the audience. This audience gives support and feedback to the protagonist, which helps that person understand the effect of his or her behaviors on others and how that effect produces behavioral responses toward the protagonist that may be negative. By this awareness, the protagonist can effectively change his or her method of relating and create an environment that is of greater benefit.

EXISTENTIALISM

The existential perspective does not emphasize a particular set of techniques for therapy. Rather, it is a philosophy based on understanding an individual's subjective experiences. The therapy process involves the exploration of certain concepts that characterize belief in proactivity and teleology. The concept of self-awareness stresses the idea that one is capable of being aware of one's choices in life, although limitations do exist. One can still be aware of the ability to choose within these limitations. The concept of personal responsibility and self-determinism is most important as it correlates with not only having the ability to make choices but to be responsible for those choices and determining for oneself the direction of one's life. In other words, one's life is the result of one's choices.

The meaning of anxiety and its place in an individual's life is another important concept in existentialism. Everyone lives with anxiety. Because of the uncertain consequences of one's choices, anxiety is pervasive, as is the awareness of the reality of death. Death is stressed in existential therapy as a fact that must be accepted for an individual to enjoy life. If one lets death restrict one's choices in life, then freedom is lost.

Since our lives must eventually come to an end, life holds meaning by its very existence. This is our search for meaning. The existentialists believe that the universe is a void. Therefore, it is up to the individual to create meaning for existence. To succeed in one's search for the meaning of existence, the individual must pursue authenticity as part of the process as it involves exploring all possibilities, exercising choices, and moving forward. Contrary to this is inauthenticity, which is experienced when we fail to grow and discover our possibilities. Hence, inauthenticity leads to guilt over our lack of fulfillment and completeness in life. The existentialists stress the view that we make our own paths in life and ultimately everyone is alone in creating meaning, making choices, and being responsible for those decisions. To be genuine to others, the existentialists feel an individual must first accept that one is alone.

The existential group leader functions as a facilitator of a therapeutic alliance between himself or herself and the members of the group and serves to enhance a meaningful relationship between members. The leader's orientation is not objective but subjective, as this helps group members express their subjective feelings in order to realize their unique existence in the world. Once they become aware of their existence, the group leader confronts the members about their responsibility for this existence and about their inescapable freedom. A leader may confront group members, which further enables these individuals to note how they are denying their freedom.

The existential group leader continues to aid the members in facing the anxiety that is generated when they accept their freedom, their responsibilities, and the inevitability of death. Individuals in group are encouraged to reflect on the accomplishments in their lives and to determine their level of satisfaction and authenticity. If change in an individual is necessary, the group creates a safe arena in which it can occur. With the group's support, members are asked to challenge their value systems and decide if they are being true to themselves.

PERSON CENTERED

The person-centered perspective maintains a strong belief in the ability of an individual to achieve full potential. This approach holds a positive view of humanity. Moreover, it claims that a person has the capacity for self-actualization but only in an environment that includes three attitudes. These attitudes include genuineness, unconditional positive regard, and empathy. The therapist utilizes these attitudes in a therapeutic setting to promote one's self-actualizing tendency.

Genuineness refers to a congruence of inner experiences and outer expressions. A person who is genuine does not pretend to be someone he or she is not. Genuineness results from awareness, acceptance, and trust in oneself. Unconditional positive regard is an acceptance of an individual just the way that person is. This means that the individual's thoughts and feelings are not judged, and nothing is expected of him or her. Furthermore, it is a genuine feeling of warmth and a sense of caring. This feeling is genuine only if it is not possessive and not based on one's own dependent needs. Empathy is defined as an accurate sense of another's feelings to the point that the person feels understood. In some respects it is like two tuning forks set to register middle C. When one tuning fork is struck and begins to vibrate, the other tuning fork begins to vibrate at the same frequency. Empathy allows an individual to listen to others more clearly and to help others to hear their expressions of meaning.

A therapist in a person-centered group needs to possess these three attitudes for the therapy to be effective. The group leader functions more as a guide than a director in facilitating a client's path to self-actualization. The members are the ones who are responsible for the group's direction, which is a nondirective approach to group therapy. Moreover, the clients in the group are the center of attention and take part in experiencing the leader's style of listening, reflecting, summarizing, clarifying, and sharing.

A client's journey toward self-actualization is not disrupted by the group leader's interpretation and advice. Rather, the person-centered group process remains unstructured and enables meaningful and honest interactions between members to occur. Clients' experiences with this group allow them to become aware of the incongruities between their inner beliefs and outer behaviors. In other words, individuals become more appreciative and trusting of who they really are because of the understanding and accepting nature of the group. The person-centered group setting encourages members to express feelings they would otherwise withhold. Since there is no structure, it is up to the group members to find direction. Through this struggle they find ways of expressing themselves and in so doing learn from their struggle.

TRANSACTIONAL ANALYSIS

Transactional analysis was developed by the late Eric Berne. It is an interactional modality and structural analysis built upon the idea that an individual makes decisions based on current beliefs. Berne's transactional analysis moves away from the overlay of individual psychotherapy onto group therapy by creating a therapy that stands on its own in relation to group dynamics. His underlying analysis of the individual in a group environment focuses similarly to Harry Stack Sullivan's interpersonal theory of psychiatry, in which an individual cannot be seen and understood in isolation but rather in relationship to others. Interpersonal problems begin to emerge when an individual's beliefs are no longer logical and the results prove to be undesirable. Identifying these illogical beliefs is the fulcrum necessary for change, as a new basis can and must be established for decision making. For this to occur, the individual must become cognizant of three ego states: (1) the parent, the ego state that functions from imposed external sources, primarily the individual's parents, which incorporates the introjection of the positive nurturing or the critical negative parent; (2) the adult ego state, which works objectively and makes decisions based on current knowledge and current reality, objectively processing information in interpersonal relationships; and

(3) the child ego state, which is most related to our emotionality and spontaneity. This ego state has two components: (a) the natural child, who is open to exploration and fun without the acculturation of society; and (b) the adapted child, who learns through interpersonal interaction to accommodate himself or herself to the expectations of others.

Berne's supposition is that a conflict arises when one individual is relating from one ego state, for example, the parent, and the other person is relating from another ego state, say, the child. He refers to this type of communication as a crossed transaction. Change comes about and is aided by acceptance of the idea that one's current behaviors are influenced by the beliefs one developed as a child and the recognition of the life script that is guiding one's behavior.

In a group therapy situation, this modality challenges the members to reach various levels of awareness. Members must become aware of their current problems and available options. Of salient importance is the task of learning which ego state an individual is using during interpersonal interactions and whether this ego state is appropriate. When this is accomplished, the individual has the opportunity of effectively making changes in behaving, feeling, and thinking. However, for this to occur, individuals must become aware that they are in control of their lives and capable of making these changes. Responsibility for change rests with each individual. Group members engage one another and evaluate past behaviors while developing new ones. Challenging one's life script and perceiving how it interferes with attaining one's personal interactional goals is important for change to occur and for the development of a new lifestyle.

GENERAL SYSTEMS THEORY (GST)

In opposition to modernistic theory, which promotes reducing everything down to its smallest unit, Von Bertalanffy (1968) proposed that to know the whole one must look at the interaction and not at finite parts. His postmodernist view, in contradiction to the reductionistic model, lends itself well to understanding the dynamics of group therapy. A group is not only seen according to individual units but needs to be understood and observed in how these units interact with one another and the manifestations that these interactions create.

Donigian and Malnati (1997) propose that three elements exist in each group at all times, constituting the entity or social system. These three elements, which are in continuous interaction, are (1) the group leader, (2) the group members, and (3) the group as a whole. Each element affects every other element. With the concept of system in mind, the group therapist focuses on the interactive pattern of the subsystems or elements and how each subsystem is affecting the other subsystems. This isomorphic connection indicates that a parallel process, and in some cases a mirroring process, is in operation in all the systems. For example, this process occurs in the group therapy experience of anorexic patients who may create a status value system regarding who is the thinnest, which aligns with and reinforces the presenting problem (Lonergan, 1994).

As a modality for group, general systems theory (GST) works effectively. Obviously, the group leader must be very much aware of the multiple interactions and how they affect every individual in the group, the group itself, and the therapist. GST is effective in observing boundary difficulties of the individual members and the group as a whole. In some groups, the boundaries are too open; in others, the boundaries are too closed and do not allow growth and change. An example of a group that is too open (Lonergan, 1994) is one in which group members continuously arrive late and constantly discuss people outside of the group system. A group with a rigid boundary would tend to be one in which the members wish to keep the status quo intact. This reduces anxiety in the group and everyone remains the same without any change or growth. This tendency is seen in groups that are generally homogeneous (Lonergan, 1994), such as a group composed solely of graduate students in psychology. In this case, the leader needs to introduce certain stimuli to shake up the group and create disequilibrium. As has been previously proposed, no change or growth occurs in any area without some degree of conflict.

GESTALT

The Gestalt paradigm focuses on the unification and wholeness of a person through individual awareness of one's thoughts, feelings, senses, and fantasies. This awareness yields personality change by means of solving problems and identifying impasses. Gestalt therapy is a here-and-now experiential modality which proposes that for an individual to be in touch with himself or herself, it is necessary for the individual to be in concert with the present. The future and the past are important, but their significance is in relation to their influence on the present.

A Gestalt therapist focuses inquiry by using "how" and "what" types of questions rather than "why," because "why" questions put clients into their heads and either back in time or ahead in time, thus taking individuals out of the moment and out of their feelings while reinforcing rationalizations. It is when clients assume responsibility for what they feel and think that the greatest therapeutic value occurs as this acknowledgment increases the individual's personal awareness. Increasing personal awareness provides clients with the opportunity to perceive a greater in-depth understanding of the meaning of their lives. In other words, individuals come to realize that they are responsible for the experience they give to themselves.

Uncomfortable events in one's life can hinder awareness in the present. This impasse requires that the individual confront this "unfinished business" by facing, exploring, and expressing aversive feelings to resolve the block.

The Gestalt modality specifies that an individual may possess five different levels of neurosis and these levels must be divested of their influence before an individual can grow into psychological maturity. The first level is the facade of people not being themselves, the phony level. To progress to the next level, individuals must be honest with themselves. When this is accomplished, clients are ready to take on the second level, the phobic level. This is the fear of seeing who one really is. For individuals to accept who they truly are means allowing the images they have built up for protection in the outside world to diminish.

Personality integration for group members through self-awareness is the leader's goal. This is believed to occur through the use of a number of Gestalt techniques. The group leader encourages clients to overcome the third level, the impasse in their lives, to reach maturation. The impasse level is a time of being stuck in a dependency position in which individuals seek others to make their decisions. Resolution of this level comes about through the effective development of awareness by helping clients focus on such things as language patterns, which can diffuse a client's power or discount their feelings, and nonverbal communications, which help clients become aware of how they are responding to overt verbalizations of others such as nonverbal responses revealed in body posture. These nonverbal communications are explored in the search for underlying meaning. The group leader assists clients in gaining responsibility for their feelings, accepting the denied aspects of themselves, and reliving their dreams in the present. When individuals begin to accept responsibility, they are ready to proceed to the fourth level, the implosive level. This requires that individuals develop a degree of courage to face their personal defenses as they come close to their real selves. Release from the implosive level to level five, the explosive level, is accomplished through letting go of the false image the individual has created. This is when individuals feel a surge of the emotionality that was inhibited.

The Gestalt therapist does not interpret for group members but helps them to develop the ability to make their own interpretations. In effect, this method encourages personal responsibility for the client as it promotes independence rather than dependence on the therapist. Perhaps one of the more provocative techniques is role-playing, in which an empty chair is used to represent a significant individual in one's life. The client is encouraged to speak to this empty chair as if the person with whom the client is experiencing some conflict is actually sitting there. Initially, this can be a difficult exercise as the participant may feel self-conscious. With continuous encouragement on the part of the group leader, the client comes to disclose thoughts and feelings to this phantom individual.

RATIONAL EMOTIVE BEHAVIOR THERAPY

This paradigm posits that people are not disturbed by childhood experiences but are in conflict because of their conscious or unconscious need to disturb themselves. Disturbance results when individuals internalize unrealistic or irrational goals or values held by esteemed members of the family, society, and/or group. To compound matters, individuals evaluate themselves negatively when these goals and values are not reached or accomplished. Individuals emotionally punish themselves by repetitively evaluating their theoretically failed efforts. These efforts are called negative self-connotations. By employing irrational beliefs such as shoulds, oughts, and musts, the individual ultimately depletes self-esteem.

The goal of rational emotive behavior therapy (REBT) is to challenge the irrational beliefs of the client and to help the individual develop a rational belief system. The relationship between client and therapist is of little importance. Interestingly, this may translate into an irrational belief that the client must have a fine relationship with the therapist or the therapy cannot work effectively because the client continues to be stuck in the belief that everyone must like him or her. The main emphasis in this relationship is the therapist's ability to confront, challenge, convince, probe, and elicit new thinking and behavior patterns from the client. It is believed that this change in thinking effectively helps the individual make long-term changes and eliminates previous self-defeating behaviors. It is not to suggest that the REBT therapist is uninvolved or uncaring, but the focus is primarily on the client. The REBT therapist demonstrates unconditional acceptance and collaboration in the work, supports the client's efforts, mentors, and accepts the individual. Obviously the therapist does not accept or support the client's irrational beliefs.

REBT, like Gestalt, is often a technique-oriented paradigm. One technique used consistently is the ABC of behavior. This technique has been designed to teach the client that (1) A is the activating event, (2) B is the stimulus eliciting the belief that an individual has about the event, and (3) C is the emotional consequence of the event or how one interprets the event. The REBT group leader contends that B, the individual's belief about the event, affects his or her emotionality, or B causes C. This causal relationship determines how the individual feels. By helping clients understand this causal relationship, the group leader is helping clients to become aware of their responsibility for their own feelings. As clients come closer to understanding the ABC of behavior, the therapist introduces D to change the irrational belief by (1) challenging self-defeating behavior, (2) detecting illogical beliefs, (3) debating irrational beliefs unsupported by evidence, and (4) discriminating between irrational and rational thinking. Upon completion of this stage, clients are encouraged to approach E, the effect of disputing. At this stage, individuals are urged to look at and acquire a rational and realistic philosophy of life, accept others, realize that everyday life can be frustrating at times, and, most important, accept themselves.

The REBT employs a number of other techniques:

1. Changing of absolutes such as "shoulds," "oughts," and "musts" into affirmations that it is all right not to be perfect, and realizing that making a mistake is not the end of the world, as acceptance of oneself is of greatest importance
2. Thinking of the worst-case scenario and making a conscious change in how the individual feels, without traumatizing himself or herself
3. The use of humor as a tool of change, because most people seem to take themselves much too seriously; when they begin to laugh at themselves, change occurs
4. Creating a situation in which the individuals are ordinarily embarrassed or ashamed to help them realize that what others think of them is less important than what the clients think of themselves
5. The differential use of rewards and penalties to assist clients to commit to changes in their lives

REVIEW

Please circle the letters that you feel complete the statements.

1. In an unstructured group, basically the only structure provided for the members and the leader is
   a. group contract.
   b. fees and group contract.
   c. modality and location.
   d. group contract and modality.

2. Adlerian psychology took a different direction than Freudian psychology in that
   a. the individual was not the focus of attention.
   b. the society of the individual was not considered important.
   c. biological determinism and sexuality were not of great importance.
   d. the use of psychological terminology was not considered important.

3. Adlerians feel that
   a. human beings have destiny.
   b. human beings are influenced by their genetic makeup.
   c. meaning is created for us at birth.
   d. human beings have goals with purpose, and anticipate the future while creating meaning in their own lives.

4. According to the Adlerians, the innate goal of life is
   a. survival.
   b. to maximize one's potential.
   c. to strive for security.
   d. to make a lot of money and retire early.

5. In an Adlerian group, members
   a. are forced to look at themselves.
   b. remain in the here and now.
   c. keep themselves from getting too excited as this interferes with therapy.
   d. are assisted to accept and benefit from their assets.

6. Psychodrama is a
   a. nondirective therapy.
   b. humanistic-cognitive modality.
   c. directive modality.
   d. nonspontaneous modality.

7. The group in psychodrama is used to help the protagonist
   a. learn how to make friends.
   b. reach an understanding of his or her situation.
   c. help him or her reduce anxiety while being in a room with others.
   d. focus on structure as it is a noncreative modality.

8. Group members in psychodrama help the protagonist
   a. better understand his or her relationship with significant others.
   b. learn how to keep feelings in check.
   c. provide a rational approach to problems.
   d. develop an attitude of not caring what other people think about him or her.

9. Existentialism is a
   a. method to help others control their behaviors.
   b. modality with specific techniques.

   c. modality used primarily for people who cannot benefit from cognitive therapies.
   d. philosophy based on understanding an individual's subjective experiences.

10. The meaning of:
    a. anger and its expression is salient to this modality.
    b. time and place is of great importance to existentialism.
    c. anxiety and its place in the individual's life is an important concept.
    d. this modality is embracing the world with all its positive and negative experiences.

11. According to the existentialists, inauthenticity is experienced when
    a. the individual fails to grow and discover personal possibilities.
    b. the individual presents a facade to the world.
    c. the individual holds back self-expression.
    d. an individual has a cognitive deficit that can be measured.

12. The orientation of an existential group leader is
    a. objective.
    b. detached but warm.
    c. a blank screen for group members to project on.
    d. subjective.

13. In an existential group, the members are encouraged to reflect upon
    a. their past failures and how they can correct them.
    b. their future goals.
    c. making the unconscious conscious to avoid repeating previous mistakes.
    d. the accomplishments in their lives.

14. Person-centered therapy
    a. believes all people are free.
    b. includes the concept that one must accept one's limitations to be happy.
    c. holds a positive view of humanity.
    d. feels the concept of potential to be overused.

15. The concept of genuineness in person-centered therapy means that
    a. the individual is usually a generous person.
    b. the person tells it like it is but tries not to hurt the feelings of others.
    c. the individual has a congruence of inner experiences and outer expression.
    d. everyone really likes the individual.

16. The concept of empathy is very important to person-centered therapy. It is
    a. an illusion that creates difficulty in interpersonal relationships.
    b. similar to two tuning forks vibrating at the same time.
    c. a misunderstanding because of lack of feeling in a conversation.
    d. the name of Carl Rogers' band in the 1960s.

17. The members in a person-centered group are responsible for the direction of the group. This occurs because the therapist is
    a. directive.
    b. nondirective.
    c. transparent.
    d. opaque.

18. The lack of structure in a person-centered group
    a. hides from the members what the therapist is thinking.
    b. allows the therapist to sit and observe without having to take part in the therapeutic process.
    c. enables meaningful and honest interactions between members to occur.
    d. keeps the tone of the group much more civilized.

19. Transactional analysis moved away from
    a. the overlay of individual psychotherapy onto group therapy.
    b. the individual being seen as someone striving for perfection.
    c. having group members act out their conflicts.

25. Rigid boundaries are often perceived in groups that are
    a. heterogeneous.
    b. homogeneous.
    c. psychodynamic.
    d. unstructured.

26. One way to expand the rigid boundaries of a group might be to
    a. leave them alone, as this will change over time.
    b. introduce members that are similar to the ones already in the group.
    c. create disequilibrium.
    d. all of the above.

27. Gestalt therapy is a
    a. technique that focuses on the past to help the individual in the present.
    b. modality that has expanded the psychoanalytic paradigm.
    c. paradigm that is solely interested in the future choices of an individual.
    d. a modality that is experiential, which focuses on the here and now.

28. In relation to psychodynamic psychotherapy, Gestalt therapists
    a. interpret unconscious manifestations of behavior.
    b. reflect back the words of the client.
    c. elicit transference reactions in the group.
    d. do not interpret for group members.

29. A provocative and effective technique in Gestalt therapy is the use of the
    a. empty closet.
    b. closed drawer.
    c. empty mind.
    d. empty chair.

30. The goal of rational emotive behavior therapy (REBT) is to
    a. challenge clients' feelings about themselves.
    b. add joy to a client's life by reinforcing positive behavior.
    c. address the irrational beliefs of the client.
    d. create a detailed contract of behaviors to be changed.

d. the concept of empathy as proposed by the client-cente
therapists.

20. According to Berne, the individual must become cognizan
three ego states
a. id, ego, and superego.
b. mother, father, and brother.
c. grandparent, parent, and child.
d. parent, adult, and child.

21. Crossed transactions, according to transactional analysis, ha
pen when
a. individuals express themselves by cross-dressing.
b. both individuals relate from the same ego state.
c. one individual relates from one ego state while the other
relating from another ego state.
d. misunderstandings occur because persons lack appropria
empathy.

22. According to transactional analysis the responsibility for b
havioral change lies with
a. the individual's parents, as this positively affects the ind
vidual.
b. others in the individual's life.
c. the work of the therapist.
d. the individual.

23. Von Bertalanffy proposed a theory that was in contradiction t
reductionism. He believed that to know the whole, one mus
look at
a. the sum of its parts.
b. the individual parts.
c. the interaction and not at finite parts.
d. the whole and not at the parts.

24. Donigian and Malnati (1997) proposed that in each group
there exists three elements
a. id, ego, and superego.
b. past, present, and future.
c. the group leader, group members, and the group as a whole.
d. the individual's cognitions, experiences, and feelings.

Chapter 5

Modalities, Continued

Paradigm: A model or pattern; in research, a basic design speci-
fying concepts considered legitimate and procedures to be used
in the collection and interpretation of data. (Coleman, 1976)

BEHAVIOR THERAPY

The foundation of behavior therapy is learning theory. It is believed that the human experience, cognitions, emotions, and behaviors are learned and as such can be relearned. By using a didactic
model, new behaviors are taught and the individual is encouraged to
try them in the hope that they can be positively reinforced. The focus
of this paradigm is the overt problem presented by the client, which
can be worked on immediately. Insight is not a concern as it is an elusive, unobservable, and nonquantifiable phenomenon. If self-understanding occurs, it is because it was related to the changes that the
new behavior elicited.

Behavior therapy approaches the conflictual behavior as a single
case study in which data are compiled and in some cases operationalized.
This collection of data provides feedback for the client and the group
therapist on a consistent and continuous basis. This paradigm is based
upon scientific inquiry and adheres most stringently to this methodology as testing, empiricism, and clear goals are implicit in this modality as a baseline for therapeutic intervention. This model of psychotherapy has a modernistic, reductionistic approach as the undesired
behavior is quantified to determine a definite baseline against which
to measure change. The effectiveness of this technique is partially in
extracting the unwanted behavior from an individual's multiple behaviors and creating an intervention strategy that highlights a pattern

of interaction. Although the past and the present are of concern, they are less important than in other therapies. In this case, the past and present are considered a stimulus to motivation and the consequences of that motivation.

As previously mentioned, a precise therapeutic goal is formulated and in many cases this helps give the client something tangible to work on. For many people this works well, as the more introspective therapies are not as appealing for clients whose goal is specific problem resolution. The fact that there is a tangible paper-and-pencil entity with which they can observe and check the results of their efforts allows many clients to feel comfortable with this therapeutic paradigm when they are hoping to change a specific part of their personalities.

In group therapy, the behavioral therapist is a teacher who is both active and directive. Each client meets with the therapist before group to discuss (1) the concepts of learning theory, (2) the program that will be used in the group, and (3) explanations concerning group therapy, identifying behaviors to be worked on, and the development of cohesiveness. At this time a contract is developed between therapist and client. The focus of this contract is behaviors that the client wishes to extinguish or reinforce. Clients arrive at the first group session with defined similar behaviors that they desire to address and change. Defining similar issues for the group members greatly helps them learn from one another.

During the working stage of a behavioral group, individual members begin to develop their treatment plans and to apply various strategies to reach their goals. Modeling, behavior rehearsal, contingency contracts, reinforcement, cognitive restructuring, and problem solving are all possible contingencies in working to resolve the designated problem or increase the likelihood of a desired behavior. As a final stage, the leader addresses whether the clients have succeeded in their efforts and evaluates the manifested behaviors in all aspects of the individuals' lives. As in other psychotherapies, individual responsibility to maintain the new behavior is encouraged, as without this a client is not prepared to generalize the new behaviors to the outside environment. Upon the termination of this type of group, the therapist helps clients learn self-help cognitive skills such as self-reinforcement and problem solving, as a way of making the transition from the group to the world outside easier. For the new behaviors to continue, the client must develop confidence in using these behaviors. This occurs through effective use of the learned techniques in an environment different from the group. Many behavioral group therapists schedule follow-up interviews to determine whether the behaviors have become part of the individual's repertoire or further work needs to be addressed.

FOCAL CONFLICT PARADIGM

Inclusion in a group, whether the group is personal, professional, or therapeutic, ultimately leads to conflict. The focal conflict paradigm is a conflict-anxiety resolution modality. The solution to attenuating anxiety is to resolve the conflict positively or negatively. Whitaker and Lieberman (1964) have suggested that a conflict which has produced escalating anxiety has two possible resolutions:

1. Enabling solution, in which the anxiety is faced and the individual or group permits its expression in relation to a wish, idea, or feeling.
2. Restrictive solution, in which the anxiety is resolved by employing defensive measures that the individuals have used in the past to avoid discomfort.

Both of these solutions invariably attenuate the anxiety and reduce the conflict, but only one, the enabling solution, is growth oriented; the other, the restrictive solution, maintains the status quo of the individual and the group, which limits the therapeutic process.

Donigian and Malnati (1997) suggest that conflict is one of the elements that the group leader has in common with the members. Without conflict, the possibility of change does not follow. Whitaker and Lieberman (1964) have suggested, after empirical study, that each member of a group affects every other member. This concept is very much in keeping with the research in social psychology which states that a close relationship is one in which each person affects the other (Berscheid and Peplau, 1983). When an issue has been presented to the group, a member takes that issue and adds some input toward its resolution, as does another, and so on until that issue has been resolved one way or another to reduce the tension, anxiety, and conflict that the issue has engendered. Because each issue creates conflict, it creates this conflict not only for the individual but for the group as a whole. For this reason this paradigm has been referred to as a group focal conflict model.

Initially, an individual has a disturbing motive that is defined as a wish, desire, etc. A conflict over its resolution occurs because negative consequences can arise in its disclosure, a reactive motive such as fear of ridicule, embarrassment, punishment, etc. (Whitaker and Lieberman, 1964). The conflict generates anxiety because of its emotional and physical discomfort. Therefore, the anxiety needs to be attenuated. This attenuation is resolved in the two aforementioned resolutions of enabling and restrictive solutions.

It is the function of the group leader to become aware of what the conflict is and to address it in such a way that the enabling solution is implemented, as this leads to growth and change with the alteration of previous restrictive solutions. As each conflict is resolved, the group has the opportunity to move forward, resolving subsequent problems. If group members realize that the anxiety, although uncomfortable, can be effectively used and not avoided, a positive change in working with anxiety is accomplished and the defensiveness of the individual members attenuates.

PSYCHOANALYTIC PSYCHOTHERAPY

The psychoanalytic model has its foundations in the past. The past is an individual's development through the early stages of life, that is, the first five to six years of development. During the ensuing years, repetition compulsion is an unconscious pattern for conflict resolution. This paradigm may be considered a "post-traumatic stress syndrome" approach to understanding the development of neurosis in a client, as repression is a key concept of the event.

According to analytic theory, neurosis is the dysfunctional resolution of a traumatic experience. For this repression to be lifted, as the traumatic experience remains unconscious to the patient although greatly affecting the individual's experience of life and relation to others, the psychoanalytic therapist encourages the unconscious to become conscious. The theory of the unconscious is one of Freud's most profound contributions to psychology and psychiatry. He postulated that all human behavior is motivated by drives that remain outside of conscious awareness. During childhood, a child may have traumatic experiences with concomitant feelings that are too anxiety laden to deal with in consciousness. These experiences are relegated to the unconscious where the feelings remain out of awareness as a protection for maintaining the integrity of the personality. Unfortunately, being out of awareness does not mean that they do not influence the personality.

As an adult it is believed that, depending upon the patient's ego strength, an individual is better able to deal with the traumatic event and the accompanying feelings that have been repressed. This is truly the crux of this modality. As stated, the traumatic events dramatically influence the life and lifestyle of the individual. Because of this ever-present, unconscious conflict, the patient has little, if any, free choice. Rather, these choices are often a double-edged sword. The individual tries to keep the repressed material repressed but at the same time, through repetition compulsion, seeks to resolve the conflict. For example, we often hear from friends, "Why do I always get involved with the same kind of person?" The answer is because that is the kind of person with whom the individual has an unconscious conflict. This understanding, though on an unconscious level, theoretically is directing the individual to repeat this liaison in order to resolve the unconscious conflict through the use of surrogates. As the mind seeks homeostasis, this relationship occurs over and over again until the conflict is resolved. Unfortunately, the conflict remains unconscious and the individual is not aware of what is propelling his or her actions. It is only through the lifting of the repression and making the unconscious conscious that the individual has a chance to make decisions freely.

To help patients resolve these unconscious conflicts, the psychoanalytic group therapist focuses on the concept of transference and its manifestation between members and the leader. Transference is a most fascinating phenomenon and anyone who has ever run group or even lived and interacted with other people can see its manifestation and the effect it has on the individual doing the transferring and the individual with whom one is in transference.

In group therapy, the therapist hopes that transference will occur, as it provides the patient with a profound opportunity to resolve unconscious conflicts. To do this effectively, the therapist encourages group interaction. An atmosphere of nonjudgmental acceptance is promoted and tolerance of others is encouraged. The leader remains relatively anonymous and impartial so that projections onto him or her are as clean and free from factual information about him or her as possible. The leader, generally, guides with interspersing interpretations while leaving the group relatively unstructured as the members develop their own direction. The group becomes, if effectively developed, a family. This permits the development of transferences and the making of the unconscious conscious as members begin to relate to one another as if they were in their families of origin. Obviously, insight is of great importance, as is personal awareness. Dreams, free association, analysis of resistance, and the analysis of transference are important for understanding the interpersonal unconscious relatedness of the group members. The psychoanalytic paradigm states that the "truth will set you free." It certainly is a good place to start.

BASIC ASSUMPTION MODEL

Bion's (1961) basic assumption model is an interesting modality as it stresses that any group has great difficulty remaining on track. It is the role of the group leader to keep this deviation from occurring and to determine what the underlying reasons are for the need to move away from the issue at hand.

Bion and Rickman (1943) suggest that assumption levels are in operation in every group. These assumptions are based on three distinct unconscious beliefs and each assumption has certain salient manifestations:

1. The dependency basic assumption assumes that a leader is all-powerful, protective, and omniscient. The leader, through some extraordinary gift or power, brings forth a magnificent resolution to a problem. When group members hold this belief, they are manifesting a childlike faith in authority or parental security that "all will be well" when the leader takes charge.
2. The fight-or-flight basic assumption suggests that the group is in a struggle to either fight or flee from an enemy who may cause the dissolution of the group. The individual member becomes less important than the group as a whole as its preservation is most salient. With an enemy at hand, the members do not look at themselves but focus on an outside stimulus, whether it is a person or an idea that has occurred in the group that gener-

ates anxiety. This helps to keep the escalation of any intragroup emotion in check.

3. The pairing basic assumption proposes that the group can be delivered from its conflict by the appearance of a messiah in the form of a new idea that has been generated and created by the leader and another member. This assumption has been compared to the feeling of hope. In the future lies the answer to the conflict and it is brought about through a joining of the leader with another.

In each group, one of the three assumptions tends to be dominant, but this is not to suggest that the three assumptions could not be working at once or that each individual member at some time is not manifesting all three of them in various degrees. Some wonderful examples of these three assumptions follow:

> The dependency basic assumption helps the church, which is based on worshipping and depending upon a higher being; the fight/flight basic assumption helps the army, which is organized around fighting an enemy; the pairing basic assumption helps the aristocracy because subjects will become emotionally involved in the king and queen and the progeny they produce. (Lonergan, 1994, p. 197)

The basic assumptions of a group are not necessarily an aversive manifestation. According to Bion (1961) they can be used as a tool for resolution. To help resolve an issue, it is important that a group therapist be aware of both the conscious and unconscious factors that are working for and against the resolution of the problem and which factors can be effectively incorporated to reach the goal.

REALITY THERAPY

Reality therapy is a problem-solving modality that focuses its attention on the demands of reality in relation to one's interaction with society. Members of a reality therapy-oriented group are challenged by both the leader and the other members to evaluate their behaviors and to determine whether these behaviors need to be changed, and if so to commit themselves to that change. Excuses and blaming others for one's lot in life are not acceptable. Individuals must take responsibility for reevaluating their behaviors to determine whether what they are doing is sufficient to get what they want in their lives. By adhering to the tenet of personal responsibility, individuals eventually gain control over their lives.

Reality therapy, in contradiction to dynamic therapies, does not focus upon insight, attitudes, unconscious motivations, and the individual's past, but rather it is a directive, didactic modality that requires the client to take action to develop personal control. This personal control provides the tools to help the individual fulfill basic needs. According to reality therapy, the basic needs of each individual are (1) power, to achieve and accomplish the feeling of being in control of one's life; (2) belonging, to feel and to give love and to have an involvement with others; (3) fun, active participation in the joy of life; and (4) survival, physical well-being.

For individuals to develop self-control, they need to become aware of their total behavior. This understanding has four components: (1) doing, as individuals must be involved in activities; (2) feeling, as individuals need to allow the full possible spectrum of feelings and not limit what they can feel; (3) thinking, as in what individuals choose to think about and statements they choose to make about themselves; (4) physiology, as in being aware of physiological changes within their bodies. If individuals change what they are doing, this in turn affects thinking, feeling, and physiological responses. It is very much like the question, "Which came first—the chicken or the egg?" If we change attitude first does this change behavior, or if we change behavior first does this change attitude?

The goal of the reality therapy group leader is to encourage clients to face and deal effectively with reality. By accepting responsibility for their behaviors and gaining control of their lives, individual members can have a more satisfying experience of life. The therapist is usually quite active and directive, focusing on the potentialities of the clients, including the clients' strengths. Past behaviors that have proved to be negative are not discussed; rather, clients are questioned about their current choices. The therapist is quite involved in the clients' lives as this involvement helps to create a positive foundation for the development of trust between the individual and the therapist. This trust aids the therapeutic process, as it is necessary for growth.

HERE-AND-NOW MODALITY

Group therapists working from humanistic, psychodynamic, Gestalt, existential, etc., paradigms agree that a tremendous amount of positive growth for the individual members and the group as a whole occurs when members address the other members in the here and now. As group therapy generally is an interpersonal modality, it is more effective when interpersonal relationships are addressed and worked on with the individuals that are eliciting thoughts and emotions at the time they occur. When group members continuously relate their experiences outside of the group environment, which can be a defense mechanism, and try to turn the group into individual psychotherapy, the group is dealing with an individual's subjective experience, which may or may not be accurate because it is infused with many conscious and unconscious facets. If group members address one another in the here and now, there is a greater opportunity to observe how they truly relate in their interpersonal relationships.

Yalom (1985) suggests that it is the therapist's role to create and maintain this intragroup relatedness. This not only allows the individual members to observe their behaviors in the present but increases the opportunity for the individual to receive feedback from the other members who are part of the scenario. Note that here-and-now group experiences create a sense of bonding in the group as it develops cohesion.

For the group therapist, this approach can generate anxiety, especially if the members are exceptionally verbal and highly emotional in their interactions. It is not uncommon for a leader to divert the group from this type of interaction if the leader is uncomfortable with strong emotionality. Because of this, the leader needs to become comfortable with the range of his or her own feelings as an emotionally interactive group often includes the therapist directly in that emotionality. As anyone who has run this type of group knows, it can be a marvelous experience for both the members and the group leader.

REVIEW

Answer true (T) or false (F) to the following questions.

1. (T) (F) Behavior therapy states that cognitions, behaviors, and emotions have a genetic foundation.

2. (T) (F) The focus of behavior therapy is the covert problem presented by the client.

3. (T) (F) Clear goals are implicit in behavioral therapy as insight is not considered the focus of concern. This modality is reductionistic and the problematic behavior is quantified.

4. (T) (F) The behavioral group therapist is a teacher who is active and directive.

5. (T) (F) Whitaker and Leiberman (1964) believe that conflicts neither produce anxiety nor are they the focus of interest for the focal conflict paradigm.

6. (T) (F) Donigian and Malnati (1997) feel that the group leader and the group members have conflict in common and without conflict the possibility of change does not follow.

7. (T) (F) Finding an enabling solution is the role of the group leader, as this leads to change in the group.

8. (T) (F) Psychoanalytic psychotherapy states that traumatic experiences cause repression. This repression creates neurotic conflicts that cause continuous distress in the individual's life.

9. (T) (F) Freud postulated the theory of the unconscious. He believed that behavior is motivated by drives which remain outside of awareness. When a childhood trauma occurs, the individual represses the event into the unconscious in order to maintain the integrity of the personality.

10. (T) (F) Transference is a method of making the unconscious conscious.

11. (T) (F) The psychoanalytic group therapist is nonjudgmental and the tolerance of others is promoted.

12. (T) (F) Bion felt that the dependency basic assumption explains why group members seek a messiah to resolve their conflicts.

13. (T) (F) An example of the fight-or-flight basic assumption is the similarity of group to a church where there is a sense of hope.

14. (T) (F) Reality therapy, similar to psychoanalysis, focuses on the unconscious, insight, and transference.

15. (T) (F) In reality therapy, group members must take responsibility for themselves to gain control in their lives.

16. (T) (F) The therapist in reality therapy becomes quite involved with the clients' lives.

17. (T) (F) According to reality therapy, the basic needs of an individual are power to achieve and accomplish with the feeling of being in control of one's life.

18. (T) (F) When group members focus their disclosures on the past, they are in the here and now because they are making the disclosure in the present.

19. (T) (F) If a group member addresses another member, the member initiating the dialogue has the opportunity to observe himself or herself in the present with concomitant feedback from other members.

20. (T) (F) Here-and-now groups can elicit strong emotionality. This emotionality can at times be frightening for group leaders who have a personal difficulty with feelings.

Chapter 6

Preparation and Practicality

Nothing can replace preparation in group therapy. No matter how seasoned and experienced a group therapist may be, preparation and its concomitant ally, practicality, help buffer the anxiety and stress that most therapists experience when beginning a new group. This is especially true for the less experienced clinician, who is often anxious upon the realization that this is an environment of multiple interactions, which could escalate into heightened emotional confrontation. As a person giving a speech needs preparation to be effective, the prepared group therapist is able to deal effectively with the possibility of spontaneous events occurring, as he or she has created structure in a process that is primarily founded on a lack of structure.

THE SETTING

The presentation of our office not only tells our clients how we feel about ourselves but how we feel about them.

Many clients, upon initially coming to both individual and group therapy, are extremely tense, with varying degrees of anxiety. This anxiety is not at all uncommon. In the majority of cases it should not be perceived as an indication of pathology, but rather a very human response to entering the unknown. To attenuate these feelings, it is very important that the physical environment, the consultation or group room, is as restful and peaceful as possible, if it is your goal to help elicit feelings.

Starting from the top, whenever possible, do not use fluorescent lighting. Not only is fluorescent lighting cold and stark, creating harsh shadows, it also has a negative effect upon individuals who have any kind of eye disturbance, as fluorescent lighting blinks sixty times per second. This pulsating light has been shown to cause headaches even in individuals without any kind of physiological eye disorders. Consider using table lamps with soft pink bulbs. Humans become more intimate and willing to speak about their feelings when the lighting is subdued.

The comfort of your furnishings has an emotional effect on your clients. Clients who are physically uncomfortable may not be as readily inclined to disclose personal and intimate details. I have found when helping new clinicians rearrange their offices that wondrous things began to happen. Obviously, everyone has different taste in furnishings, and that is not a problem. Culturally, Americans like to have some degree of physical distance between themselves and others. It can be a problem if there is not enough space between the chairs that your clients are using. Even if this is only a few inches, it helps group members feel that they have their own territory. You will find that as the group begins to bond, the space between these individuals will begin to diminish. It is important that you understand what a client may experience when coming into this room to discuss very personal issues. The essential, indispensable ingredient is that stimulus from the outside world must be reduced to a minimum, if not totally. Distractions of any nature can turn a truly effective moment into a truly ineffective one.

Your office must always be clean. If you are untidy by nature, keep it out of your consultation room. If clients come to an untidy office or an unclean bathroom, they may feel that they are not worth your making preparations for their arrivals. It is insensitive to leave clients, especially women, with toilet seats that need to be wiped. It is not uncommon for a female member to come into group with the complaint that the bathroom is a mess and there is no toilet paper. I very much agree with the clients' feelings on this issue, as I myself do not want to use such a room. Many people come to us feeling unacknowledged and uncared for and we in fact re-create the same issue by not preparing for their arrivals. The lack of acknowledgment will make itself known whether we prepare or not, but preparation is professionally and humanly one of the more effective ways to proceed.

Never answer the phone or make phone calls during group or individual sessions. Not only is it rude and insensitive, it indicates that your time is more valuable than the clients'. Obviously, if an emergency occurs you must effectively deal with it. Many individuals have reported that their therapists often made and answered phone calls during sessions. They felt upset but were too passive to tell the therapist. Instead, they just did not return.

Personal articles should be kept to a minimum, such as photographs, your child's finger paintings (no matter how extraordinary), family awards, and so on. The less that is known about you, the more room is left for fantasy and projection by the client. A photograph of a therapist's wife, husband, lover, etc., can become an object for competition and multiple questions. This may be interpreted as a good thing as it stimulates dialogue, but I have found that a richer dialogue ensues when less is known about the therapist. As an aside, for my clients the group room temperature becomes a consistent factor of disagreement. Because I live in south Florida, air-conditioning is predominantly the energy source that we use. There is always someone in group who is either too cold or too warm. This can be especially true if the group has become emotionally heated—the environmental temperature is often perceived as much too warm.

Remember that our offices tell our clients how we feel about ourselves and the environment in which we choose to work and, most important, how we feel about them.

CLIENT INCLUSION/EXCLUSION

If we approach the task of group member selection using an analogy from genetics, we will find that all groups follow a DNA format in their development. This specifically means that the group members can be correlated to the genes in the DNA molecule, turning off and on in their interpersonal relationships with one another, which ultimately affects the structure or phenotype and outcome of whether a group will be successful or not. This success in the development of the group—whether it will be a healthy environment or an unhealthy environment for growth to occur—is specifically related to the group leader's skill in client selection for a particular group. Obviously in some situations, the group leader does not have a choice in whom he or she would wish to have in a group. We often see this, for example, in some inpatient facilities where transient patients are placed haphazardly into groups. The format for these placements are frequently related to whether there is space available in the group. Unfortunately, this makes a successful group outcome very difficult. Careful selection of group members is inextricably related to successful prognostication and prediction for the group's future growth to occur. According to Yalom (1985, 1995) a group's future has been sealed before the first session commences. His powerful statement truly indicates the importance of whom you choose to place into your groups: the future is sealed before it begins due to the combination of the members selected.

Unfortunately, theory and reality often clash in relation to client selection or inclusion. This is especially true when the powerful variable of economics comes into the decision-making process, as the concept of ethics seems to be the first casualty of this ubiquitous force.

As you are aware, managed care has enveloped the psychotherapeutic community and has delivered rigid guidelines regarding money spent on psychotherapy and allowable time for services to be provided. Group psychotherapy has become an attractive option because it is less costly and clients can receive longer psychotherapeutic treatment than the managed care companies allow for individual psychotherapy. This reasoning is solely economically based with little, if any, concern for whether a client is initially a good candidate for group psychotherapy. This being said, we should focus our attention on what are considered effective theoretical considerations for a client to be included in group psychotherapy.

Client selection for group therapy is not currently an exact science, nor will it probably become one, as the infallible prediction of human behavior seems unlikely. With this in mind, the best safety net or buffer against including an inappropriate client in a group is preparation. The determination for inclusion is not a simple task, as it must take into consideration a number of relevant variables. Often these variables focus on the candidate for the group, but other relevant variables include the group leader and the mental health provider who has referred a candidate for this particular modality. Friedman (1976) suggests three propositions that may influence a mental health professional considering group therapy for a particular individual:

1. *Nonlegitimate (objective) approach.* The referral to a group has little, if any, consideration for the efficacy of treatment for the candidate. The candidate is an object of training for novice clinicians.

2. *Illegitimate (subjective) approach.* The referral occurred because the therapist has negative feelings toward the candidate and either wishes the individual out of his or her practice or feels more comfortable seeing the individual with other people at the same time, thus reducing their individual time together.
3. *Legitimate approach.* The clinician feels that group therapy is the treatment of choice for a particular candidate, as it provides greater therapeutic value.

At its most simple, there are two basic ways that an individual is considered for group therapy: (1) voluntary, and (2) involuntary. Voluntary inclusion means the candidate has either suggested or agreed to the group therapy experience; involuntary inclusion means that the individual has no choice as he or she is a hospital patient, has been ordered by the court, or was forced by a parent (in the case of a teenager). The involuntary client can be, initially, most difficult for the novice and the seasoned clinician alike, as the candidate may perceive group therapy as a punishment for some wrongdoing (Donigian and Malnati, 1997).

Yalom (1985) believes that the most promising candidates are motivated by interpersonal problems of an existential nature, such as low self-worth, loneliness, or difficulties with intimacy and the inability to love, whereas Rutan and Stone (1993) feel that most patients are potential candidates for group. Rutan and Alonso (1979) go so far as to suggest that when considering group therapy for a candidate, the question to ask is, "Are there mitigating factors against considering group therapy for this patient?"

The Ethical Guidelines for Group Counselors (American Association for Counseling and Development, 1989) encourages the screening of candidates for group therapy who will not negatively affect the group process and can benefit from and are compatible with the goals of the group. Candidates should not be damaged by the group experience. Corey and Corey (1997) report that they look closely at the initial interview to determine how much effort the individual is willing to expend in making changes.

There appears to be agreement about who is not a good candidate for the therapy group. Clients who are in crisis, such as those experiencing escalating anxiety such as panic attacks or pathologic behaviors such as psychosis, according to Rutan and Stone (1993), are not considered good candidates for group therapy. They suggest that individuals with poor impulse control should not be considered for this modality, as there is the possibility of danger to the other group members. Yalom (1985) also excludes for heterogeneous outpatient intensive group therapy those who are "brain damaged, acutely paranoid, hypochondriacal, addicted to drugs or alcohol, acutely psychotic, or sociopathic" (p. 228). This is not to suggest that individuals with these diagnoses cannot be candidates for group therapy but that they are more effectively treated in homogeneous groups.

Although there are a number of reasons for inclusion in a psychotherapy group, there are also a number of reasons for exclusion, especially if the groups are designated heterogeneous and outpatient. As initially mentioned, the group leader should make adequate preparation for determining who is going to be in the group and should carefully review the reasons for those decisions. Many clinicians feel that a preliminary interview is sufficient for evaluation, and in many cases this may be all that they are allowed by either economics or the policy of the institution in which they are employed. But this is not the most effective approach for selection, as it does not allow a relationship to develop between the therapist and the client. A group that is time limited and has a particular theme, such as children of alcoholics, bereavement, etc., may lend itself more effectively to an initial interview.

If a candidate is to be placed in an ongoing group without a time limit for the purpose of personality restructuring, it is important for a relationship to be established between the therapist and the client before group becomes the modality of intervention. Individual psychotherapy will effectively create that relationship in a shorter time than will placing a candidate with eight to ten strangers. It is important for us to know our clients. It is likely that certain experiences in each person's life will not be disclosed in a group situation. If these secrets cannot be disclosed easily by the group member, it is quite possible that these issues are affecting the manner in which the group member is acting in his or her interpersonal relationships. If this is the case, the group member may have less opportunity to make as many behavioral changes as possible, as he or she will be limited by fear of judgment. This is one of the benefits of group. It provides an arena in which an individual learns to take interpersonal risks. However, by initially providing a safe environment, individual therapy for a period of time is, in the long run, a very helpful preparation for both the individual and the group. Although theoretically we encourage members to discuss "all and everything," initially, individual psychotherapy lends itself more effectively to that end, as the individual becomes more comfortable with personal disclosures. After testing the waters with the therapist, clients generally have an easier transition into group therapy and an easier time expressing what they feel, as they have now had the experience of their personal disclosures being met without judgment and have been warmly encouraged by the therapist. For many individuals, this type of acceptance of their personal disclosures can be new and often quite frightening. Obviously, each therapist chooses, when possible, which form of client selection is most comfortable and which lends itself more effectively to the types of groups the therapist is considering.

COHESION

Cohesion is the attraction of elements to come together and bond. It is a very important phenomenon in group therapy. Through this attraction of the members toward one another, the leader, and the group as a whole, motivation toward effective behavioral and personality changes of the individual participants begins to take place. No two groups are exactly alike. They may have similarities, but there are always certain features and components that make them different. This is very much like each individual in society who, although similar to others in his or her species, is uniquely different in either appearance or manifest behavior. If we correlated a psychotherapy group to the concept of genetics, we would find that the individual members would represent the genotype of an entity while the group as a whole or its manifest unique structure would represent the phenotype. How the genes, or clients in this case, interact with one another will determine how the structure of the entity or group as a whole emerges.

Although individual modalities may approach the art of psychotherapy differently, the cohesive relationships of the group continue to be one of the most important components of successful treatment, (Yalom, 1985). When a group is cohesive, the members work harder, disclose on a more intimate level, attend regularly, explore the self with greater introspection, take greater interpersonal risks, and effectively make substantial changes in their personalities. Corey (1995),

MacKenzie (1990), Rutan and Stone (1993), and Yalom (1985) suggest that cohesion, although a necessary element, is not enough for a group to move forward and for its members to change but rather is an element that needs to be present for the therapeutic process to develop. Cohesion, in a sense, is like hydrogen and oxygen. Separately they have importance, but when combined they create water, a necessary ingredient for survival. Cohesion is a necessary ingredient for group survival.

For many individuals, belonging to a group that acknowledges feelings of acceptance is rare indeed. It is very similar to Dreikurs' (1951) comparison of group therapy to a primitive tribe in which the individual's value and/or worth is simply due to membership in the group. In fact, inclusion in a psychotherapy group is perhaps the only membership that accepts an individual because of deficits rather than accomplishments. For many group members, their previous group experiences have been aversive, beginning with their families of origin, peer groups, social groups, etc.

By observing contemporary gangs and their attraction for youthful members, we can see, no matter how destructive inclusion may be to the individual, that the appeal of belonging, being accepted, and possibly understood is stronger than the dislike of feeling isolated and alone. Human beings are relationship-oriented entities. To be part of and accepted into something greater than oneself is powerful, especially if one feels this inclusion is of personal benefit. This need to belong, no matter how initially stressful, can be an excellent tool for the group leader in providing an environment that has the potential for healing. Yalom (1985) summarizes:

> Cohesiveness refers to the attraction that members have for their group and for the other members. The members of a cohesive group are accepting of one another, supportive, and inclined to form meaningful relationships in the group. Cohesiveness seems to be a significant factor in successful group therapy outcomes. In conditions of acceptance and understanding, patients will be more inclined to express and explore themselves, to become aware of and integrate hitherto unacceptable aspects of the self, and to relate more deeply to others. Highly cohesive groups are more stable groups with better attendance and fewer turnovers. . . . Cohesiveness favors self-disclosure, risk-taking, and

the constructive expression of conflict in the group-phenomena that facilitate successful therapy. (p. 69)

But how do we encourage this most wonderful element in our groups? Corey and Corey (1997) suggest that it is possible to engender cohesion and to reinforce its continuation in the following ways:

1. *Developing cohesion through group members disclosing their feelings concerning their issues on trust.* In reality, it is important for group members to feel safe before revealing intimate details of their personal lives.
2. *Clearly defined goals.* These goals need to be similar to the personal goals of the members or they will go in different directions, hardly encouraging cohesion. For example, why would a person without an addiction problem join a group of individuals choosing to reduce their dependence on an addictive substance?
3. *Encouraging participation by all group members.* Although many suggest that a silent member may be benefiting greatly from the group experience, it seems highly unlikely that cohesion can be established if all the participants are not actively involved. For example, if we try to glue two pieces of wood together, how strong will the bond be if we only place the glue on certain parts of the seam and not run it along the whole seam?
4. *Creating a here-and-now approach to group therapy.* In this approach the members relate to one another directly and take collective responsibility for the direction that the group may take. Ormont (1992) suggests that it is effective for therapists to create bridges among members by encouraging them to interact. He stresses that one of the greatest downfalls of a group is when it turns into individual psychotherapy. The greater the involvement that each member has with every other member, the greater the chance that group cohesion will develop.
5. *Effectively dealing with conflict.* Any time a group of individuals gets together, conflict is sure to ensue. This is part of the therapeutic process in a group. Group members should learn and seek to understand and resolve conflictual situations. Conflict does not bring people together but rather creates a barrier to closeness. However, when a healthy resolution is reached, the individuals in the conflict often feel closer than they did before.

6. *The level of appeal of the group for the individual members.* If members are attracted to the experience and to the other members in the group cohesiveness will be reinforced. Members will look forward to coming to group and being with one another.

7. *Honesty and openness about one's thoughts and feelings.* These are very necessary elements of cohesion. If there are covert feelings and thoughts or undisclosed agendas in the group, this leads to fragmentation and very tight boundaries in which risk taking is almost nonexistent.

As you can see, cohesion is an element that must be present for a group to run effectively, move forward, and grow. As in any relationship, the development of cohesion takes time but can be encouraged through the input of the group leader. Cohesion cannot be forced on a group of people but needs to develop through their interactions with one another. If you can encourage honesty and interaction among your group members, the chances that cohesion will develop are quite good and the members, as well as the leader, will have a marvelous experience.

THE GROUP CONTRACT

It is in the interest of all groups to have a group contract, which is basically those rules and regulations that must be adhered to for continuous inclusion in the group. Rutan and Stone (1993) use the term *group agreement* for their format for inclusion, although it is of no consequence it is called a contract, agreement, rules, or the Magna Carta of group inclusion. It is important that these rules are understood and accepted by all group members. It is also of iconic value to understand that once a group has begun, changing a group contract can cause disastrous effects within the group, especially if it creates a special dispensation for one individual member. Some requirements that have been useful are listed as follows. Depending upon your individual populations and settings, you may wish to add or remove some of the suggestions to best suit your professional needs:

1. All members must arrive on time. Generally, group announcements are made at the beginning of each group, such as "Gary S. will not be here tonight because he has a cold." A group member who is not attending a session must notify the leader beforehand and disclose the reason or reasons for his or her absence. This information is then

passed on to the group. In private practice, many clinicians have a twenty-four-hour cancellation policy or the individual is charged for the missed group. Other group therapists require that clients pay for the month in advance whether or not they attend.

2. Confidentiality is the icon for building trust and must be strongly presented and maintained. Unfortunately, we have little control over what group members say and do when they leave the group room and return to the outside world. Yalom (1990) feels that members continually discuss group issues outside of sessions and to try and curtail this activity is next to impossible. He suggests instead that we encourage group members to bring back into group all that had previously been discussed outside of the group.

To reduce some of the need to disclose to others outside of the group or to minimize rebelliousness against rules by a group member, I clarify that if a member wishes to speak about the experience there is little I can do. I explain that this need to discuss group issues outside can dissipate the experience, and it is therapeutically of greater benefit if the individual speaks about group experiences inside the group. Sometimes the individual does have the need to check the perceptions of the other members, especially when he or she feels the group is incorrect in its perceptions of him or her. For instance, a member may ask an outsider, "Sheila, my group said that they felt I was insensitive. Do you see me that way?" If this is the case, I require that the names and intimate details of other group members are never disclosed. If it comes to my attention that a member has broken the rule of confidentiality, that person is removed from the group.

3. Any and all feelings and thoughts are permissible for expression, and disclosure is encouraged. However, it is required that these disclosures remain solely verbal and are not to be physically acted upon with any other member or the leader.

4. Members socializing outside group is discouraged as it initiates the development of subgrouping and bonding at the expense of the other group members and reinforces secrets. For instance, one member might say to another, "Please don't talk about what I just told you when we are in group." Although we have very little control over what members choose to do when they are outside the group arena, we can try to encourage the concept that if members do meet for coffee before or after the group they are responsible for bringing that meeting into the group itself. I explain the concept of subgrouping

and how it works against not only maximizing the group experience but against the individual's personal therapeutic growth. The American Psychological Association group-psychotherapy forum (on the Internet, <www.group-psychotherapy.com>) addressed this issue and the majority of clinicians who responded were against any kind of outside meeting of the group members. However, there are certain realities and, to play the devil's advocate, the majority of clinicians are not going to develop social relationships with their clients. As a result, we do not have the opportunity of actually observing the group member in a real social situation and must rely solely on the members' subjective interpretation of events outside the group environment. If members do meet outside of group and are honest and willing to disclose and discuss those meetings, we have the opportunity of perceiving the members in their naturalistic behaviors. Arnold Lazarus (personal communication, 1982) related that in individual psychotherapy, he has taken patients outside of the consultation room to observe them in other situations. Obviously, the decision will remain with the group leader as to how to proceed in this area.

5. Although many of our group members are astonished by this statement, it is very important to advise that, "You cannot have a sexual relationship with anyone in group." It is not uncommon for members to develop sexual feelings and interest in other members, whether of the opposite or same sex. This is quite natural and can be very effective for dialogue, investigation, and interpretation but can be dangerous for both the group and the individuals if acted out. I have often found that the underlying attraction is of a transferential nature, which has the most profound, therapeutically beneficial effect when analyzed. If two clients choose to break this rule, they are removed from group, as a relationship has been formed that destroys the equality of the individual members.

6. In a direct-payment situation, I require each member to pay at the end of each session, and members are charged for cancellation if I am not notified twenty-four hours in advance. You may find, when implementing this rule, that some offer excuses why they feel they should not have to pay for the missed session. The client may exhibit tremendous anger toward you when you adhere to this rule, which can become an effective issue in therapy. Other colleagues require members to pay for the session before going into the group room.

As previously mentioned, the population, setting, and time structure, for example, whether the group is to be time limited or ongoing, will determine the nature of the group contract. Each individual leader will determine which rules are suitable. I suggest, when possible, that a copy of these agreements be given to each new group member and that members sign the document after a clarifying discussion. A copy is then put into the new group member's file. This helps the new group member to avoid forgetting what the contract rules of agreement are for inclusion.

REVIEW

Part A is related to the setting, Part B deals with group cohesion, and Part C relates to the group contract.

Part A

You have been given carte blanche in designing your group room. Expense or size is not an issue. For your own knowledge, how would you set up your group room?

Part B

Do you agree with Corey and Corey's (1997) suggestions for engendering the development of cohesion? If so, which techniques do you find to be the most effective? If not, why? Can you think of any other procedures that might improve the development of cohesion?

Part C

Select two different client populations that interest you. Design a group contract that is both effective and appropriate for the populations you have chosen. Also, what are your feelings about a group contract being changed after the group has begun?

Chapter 7

The Life Cycle of a Group

The life of a group is analogous to the life cycle of a human being in a compressed form. If we look at the life cycle or developmental stages from perhaps a different perspective than the usual, we can see that the stages of psychosocial development proposed by Erik Erikson (1956, 1959, 1968) compare rather interestingly and, in some prominent cases, similarly to the developmental stages of group therapy proposed by many contemporary authors.

In Eriksonian terms, a series of crises occurs that must be resolved before a human being can progress further in social development. The resolution of these crises is never quite complete. Often, progression and regression occur in future and past developmental stages. Erickson's psychosocial stages are theoretical constructs that are not effectively quantified but rather are guideposts for observation. He described abstractly the physical, psychological, and emotional developmental stages or tasks that were necessary for individuals to move forward and obtain the maximum benefits of life.

Each stage relies on the effective completion of the previous stage, as the remnant of an unresolved crisis affects behavior in the ensuing hierarchy of development. If this seems to be psychodynamic in origin, it is. Erikson's orientation was dynamic and his descriptions of development relied heavily upon his training in this modality. As a refresher, a list of Erikson's eight stages is presented as follows. See if you can find a relationship to the subsequent theorists' contributions to understanding the stages of group development. Remember that with Erikson, we are looking at the individual and with the subsequent theorists, we are looking at whole-group development, which is a unitary component of a process, course, or order of classification. The two may not be mutually exclusive, but the developmental stages of a group inherently involve a two-track phenomenon: (1) the recapitulation of an individual's developmental stages and (2) the developmental life cycle of the group itself.

To return to Erikson's (1956) developmental stages, the first five stages relate to infancy, childhood, and adolescence, and the last three relate to adulthood:

1. In *trust versus mistrust,* the main task is gradually realizing that the world is predictable and safe to explore with maximum comfort and minimal uncertainty.
2. In *autonomy versus shame,* the task is to develop feelings of control over one's behaviors while maintaining self-esteem.
3. *Initiative versus guilt* is the introduction of self-initiated behavior and the reduction of imitation with a sense of identification and responsibility for one's actions.
4. *Industry versus inferiority* is the development of a sense of self-worth through interaction with one's peers by refining skills.
5. *Identity versus identity diffusion* is the development of the sense of identity, a self that is constructed from the integration of other possible selves, e.g., male, student, son, etc.
6. *Intimacy versus isolation* requires the ability to develop close relationships with others and to make personal commitments.
7. *Generativity versus self-absorption* requires developing adult roles and responsibilities that contribute to the community and feeling worthwhile through productivity.
8. In *integrity versus despair,* the task is accepting the meaningfulness of life, the inevitability of loss, and the termination of the life cycle.

Other authors have described group developmental phases in three, four, and five stages depending upon the author's frame of reference.

Yalom (1985) delineates three stages of development. Stage one is a time of orientation, disinclination to participate, and a search for understanding and meaning of the experience; the second stage, a transitional phase, involves rebelliousness, conflict, and control; and the third stage is referred to as the working stage, as self-disclosure increases with group members developing greater cohesion and trust. Schutz (1973) perceives the three stages as inclusion, control, and affection.

Rutan and Stone (1993) view group as developing linearly in four developmental stages. The first is formation, which involves anxiety and trust issues as the group members seek to find commonalities among themselves. The reactive phase follows in which there is a search for power with oppositional behaviors manifesting as members begin to test the group norms with a rebelliousness toward the group leader. This reactive phase is a progressive development and not to be perceived as negative by the group leader. The mature phase is a time of developing cooperation in which the members begin working together and affiliation becomes evident, with less concern about outside relationships. The group begins to function more effectively without the input of the leader and much of the therapeutic process is accomplished by the members. The termination phase is the time to say good-bye. It is a time of pain, exuberance, and, in some cases, relief, eliciting a replay of previous endings in the lives of many of the members.

Bernard and MacKenzie (1994a), Corey (1995), and Corey and Corey (1997) also perceive a four-stage group developmental process. Bernard and MacKenzie (1994a) differentiate development into the engagement stage, the differentiation stage, the working group, and the termination stage. Corey (1995) and Corey and Corey (1997) describe the initial stage of orientation and exploration; the transitional stage, dealing with resistance; the working stage of cohesion and productivity; and the final stage of consolidation and termination.

Other theorists describe five stages, including Mahler (1969), who proposes that the stages of group development are formation, involvement, transition, working, and ending. Hansen, Warner, and Smith (1980) delineated their five stages as initiation of the group, conflict and confrontation, development of cohesiveness, productivity, and termination. A five-stage process was also considered an effective approach by Donigian and Malnati (1997), who expanded on the previous comprehensive literature review of Hansen, Warner, and Smith (1980) while perceiving group through the modality of general systems theory (GST). Remember that these stages are not always distinct and progressive but rather fluid. They vacillate between progression and regression depending on the experiences of the group and the duration of its existence.

According to Yalom (1985), these constructs basically offer the group leader some form of structure to help him or her avoid feeling overwhelmed when certain behavioral characteristics begin to manifest in the group's ongoing process. These developmental stages can also be

compared to the normal curve of an airplane taking off from one destina-
tion and landing at another. In relation to the normal curve, these stages
can be skewed, depending upon the amount of time in each stage, or
never realized depending upon the success of the group's active existence. For example, in a time-limited, sixteen-week program, these
stages may be more easily seen than if the group is ongoing. With ongoing groups, in which members come and go, it is possible for the
astute leader to see these developmental stages manifesting in the individual members as new members arrive and old ones terminate.

When comparing, for example, the developmental stage of termination to an airplane taking off and landing, the descent is noted to
be not only over the airport but begins long before the termination of
the flight, as does termination in group. For the same reason, if we
choose to view the developmental stages as an overlay of the normal
curve, we perceive it as being skewed. Each author who writes about
the developmental stages appears to use different terminology to describe similar events. This can be confusing but the more practice a
group leader has, the greater the clarification.

The five-stage developmental process is presented next, as it lends itself well to the novice clinician. Approaching these stages with the idea
that a therapy group is a social system in evolution helps us to perceive a
development that is familiar to group leaders who reflect upon their own
life experiences or other group experiences of the past or present.

STAGE ONE:
ADAPTATION · ORIENTATION · FORMATION ·
INITIAL ENGAGEMENT · INCLUSION

Stage one is a time of heightened anxiety for both the group members and the leader. Here we have a group of people coming together,
theoretically to discuss and disclose intimate details of their lives with
strangers. Prior to the gathering, there may be a great deal of fantasiz-
ing concerning not only the other members of the group but about oneself in the group, for instance, "What will they think of me? Will I seem
stupid or unattractive?" In the beginning, the group members often feel
a degree of disorientation, as most leaders do not encourage structuring
and would rather permit the group to structure itself. The norms, correct procedures, the permitted behaviors, and the structure should be
covered in the group contract or agreement. Generally, the group mem-

bers are detached and relate information that is deemed "safe" as they try to protect themselves from feelings of vulnerability. Often a leader makes preliminary introductions and each person discloses some basic information that one would disclose in any situation, such as name, profession, etc. The group leader may introduce the concept of anxiety and how everyone is feeling about being together, but this topic may elicit a certain defensiveness and denial in some members. This is often the stage when group members think, "What am I doing here with these people?" Members begin to analyze one another covertly. Generally the analysis focuses on individual differences rather than similarities. Most disclosures are cognitive in an almost unconscious group agreement that anything which elicits strong feelings is to be avoided. Ambivalence about the group and its development is prevalent. It is a time of advice-giving by individual members and there can be a period of dropouts as certain group members rationalize that this situation is not for them. This is a good time for the group leader to observe the defense mechanisms individual members use in interpersonal social situations and when they are unfamiliar with people.

STAGE TWO:
REACTIVE PHASE · CONTROL · DIFFERENTIATION · DISINCLINATION TO PARTICIPATE · TRANSITION · CONFLICT AND CONFRONTATION · RESISTANCE

This is the stage that often causes uneasiness for both the novice clinician and the more seasoned practitioner who knows of the storm that is about to come. It involves power and control with confrontation and conflict. Group members are beginning to feel more comfortable because they feel less vulnerable than in stage one. They are willing to take certain risks, often at the expense of the group leader. Covert self-talk is given overt expression with statements such as, "I have been thinking about this for awhile and I really think you [the group leader] don't know what you are doing." This statement could be said in a relatively normal voice or at the top of one's lungs, depending upon the degree of emotionality felt by the group member or members. It is a time of testing the limits and determining who is going to be in control of the group. It can be the "alpha dog syndrome" with intimidation as a component. It may include the beginning of subgrouping—members allying with one another against other members, against the leader, or in relation to the group as a whole. Members begin to confront and in some cases attack one another in their need to see who has the mettle to remain in the group. There appears to be an unconscious need to get on with the work at hand and to want to work only with people who are going to commit themselves to the group process.

At times this stage almost seems like dealing with adolescents going through puberty, but it is very important for the life of the group and its members. All this storm and stress is necessary, as it is truly the beginning of trust. It is a bit of trial by fire, but should not be diverted by the group leader who may feel it is not a good thing. In fact, it is a very good thing not only for the members but also for the leader. This stage helps the group leader begin to see how much control he or she needs in life. If group members are expected to submit to the leader's dominance and need for homeostasis, as spontaneity with strong emotion causes discomfort, then the leader needs to become introspective about personal issues with possible countertransference undertones that are overflowing into the group arena. This stage is definitely the precursor to the beginning of group bonding. Although uncomfortable for the therapist, the members are beginning to pull together to face a common enemy—the group leader. In comparing it to the concept of nationalism, having a common enemy creates strong cohesion in the citizens of a country. Take a deep breath. It will pass like any other storm in nature. But if it does not, it is an indication that the group is reluctant to move forward into a stage of bonding, unity, and togetherness. If this happens, the group leader would be wise to address the issue, as this stage is very important for the further development of the group.

STAGE THREE:
TOGETHERNESS · COMMITMENT ·
COHESION · BONDING · ATTRACTION ·
IDENTIFICATION · FAMILY

Stage three develops after the difficulty of stage two has been resolved. The leader becomes less active in the therapeutic process and the group begins to take more responsibility for the issues that brought the individual members into group therapy. Individual differences among the members are now beginning to be viewed as characteristics of the other members rather than idiosyncratic disturbances, as judgmental perceptions are beginning to diminish and members begin to seek similarities. Members begin to embrace self-disclosure on a more intimate level as they are feeling greater trust and less vulnerability. The facade of the social personality that manifested in stages one and two begins to change into more of the reality of who the person is and, interestingly, the recapitulation of the individual member's characteristic role in the family of origin is emerging from the opaque and defensive personality initially used for protection. Although the leader is beginning to ease back in involvement, this is a time for concentrated observation (not that there is ever a time when concentrated observation is unimportant). Care must be taken as the true personalities of the group members begin to risk being seen.

STAGE FOUR:
MATURE · WORK · RESOLUTION · PRODUCTIVITY · TASK ORIENTED · COOPERATION

Stage four is a time of cooperation. The individual group member is primarily interested in relationships with the other members. The sense of emotionality again begins to rise as individual members are seriously working on issues that have caused them personal stress and discomfort. In this period, there is less discussion of the past, present, and future with greater stability in the here and now. This is very important because the "present" is a time frame with which most people have little familiarity. It is the time when the individual is most in contact with himself or herself. Being in the moment appears to create discomfort for many people, as you can see by thinking about your own day. How much of your thinking is spent on what you have to do next in your schedule or on how well you did or did not accomplish something in the past? This focus on the moment in group therapy is the salient characteristic that helps the members create behavior change as they have a clearer opportunity to be in touch with the essence of who they are. This is a time of greater openness and a willingness to explore feedback with minimum defensiveness.

Psychodynamically, it is an opportunity to make the unconscious conscious. The group has become an entity. It has solidified, having a history with memories, like a family offering support and acceptance to its individual members.

STAGE FIVE:
TERMINATION · FAREWELL · CLOSURE · THE END

The termination of a group often causes heightened emotionality. Members may feel great sadness, as it touches upon personal loss issues in their own histories. There is a sense of accomplishment related to the understanding they have achieved about themselves and joy in having had an experience unlike any other in their lives. It also can be a relief for members who have found the closeness of the group uncomfortable. It is not uncommon for certain members to want the experience to continue and to try to devise different ways of doing this to avoid letting go. Plans for future get-togethers or the exchanging of phone numbers are discussed; others are willing to go on and put the group experience behind them. Often there is a rehashing of the experience, with individual members relating their experiences with one another and the therapist. This can be a difficult time for a therapist who has become emotionally involved with the group. Depending on the leader's history, terminations may elicit certain feelings that are counterproductive to the group's effective ending. This is not to suggest that a leader is not expected to feel anything at the end of a group that has been part of his or her experience but rather to suggest that it is important that the leader be aware that certain feelings are going to manifest at termination. Generally, if the experience has been positive for the group leader, his or her feelings may include loss, sadness, not wanting to let go, etc. If the experience has not been positive, relief at the termination may be the predominant feeling. As the leader gains experience, the intensity of emotion at termination is not as pronounced as it is for the novice clinician. It becomes more a component of one's personal and professional history.

REVIEW

1. Erikson's psychosocial stages are in actuality
   a. rigorous empirical evidence.
   b. existential tenets of development.

c. theoretical constructs.

d. humanistic understanding of how an individual develops.

2. Each of Erikson's stages relies on
   a. physical development.
   b. emotional development.
   c. cognitive development.
   d. effective completion of the previous stage.

3. Erikson's orientation was
   a. behavioral.
   b. existential.
   c. dynamic.
   d. cognitive-behavioral.

4. In intimacy versus isolation, the individual develops
   a. feelings of being worthwhile through productivity.
   b. ability to develop close relationships.
   c. a realization of the meaningfulness of life.
   d. a sense of identity.

5. According to Rutan and Stone (1993), the reactive phase of group is
   a. a time of harmony among the members.
   b. when the members are in positive transference with the leader.
   c. a time when oppositional behaviors begin manifesting toward the group leader.
   d. when the group leader begins to feel negativity toward the group members.

6. Hansen, Warner, and Smith (1980) delineated how many stages of group?
   a. one
   b. two
   c. four
   d. five

7. The developmental stages of group are
   a. fluid, progressing forward and backward.
   b. consistently moving forward.

    c. pretty much determined by the first session.
    d. nonexistent.

8. In relation to the normal curve, the developmental stages of a group could be seen
    a. as distinct and rigid.
    b. always the same.
    c. often as skewed depending upon the time in each stage.
    d. more likely in a long-term ongoing group.

9. During stage one, there often tends to be a heightened sense of
    a. intimacy.
    b. anger.
    c. silence.
    d. anxiety.

10. Before the initial group session, it is very possible that members have been
    a. trying to contact each other to say hello.
    b. figuring out what they are going to wear to the first session.
    c. wondering how other people in their lives are going to perceive them now that they are becoming a part of a group.
    d. fantasizing about the group and its members.

11. In stage one, group members generally
    a. try to get involved with one another.
    b. relate information that is deemed safe.
    c. bring up the issue of cost of the group experience.
    d. praise the leader.

12. Stage two may be considered
    a. a harmonious stage.
    b. a working stage.
    c. a spiritual phase.
    d. the stormy phase.

13. A change is often seen in stage three which manifests itself as
    a. covert self-talk becoming overt expression, with statements such as, "You stink as a group leader!"
    b. members relating how wonderful the group therapist is.

    c. members beginning to disclose warm feelings toward one another.

    d. discussing intimacy and feelings of sexuality.

14. Stage two is a time when
    a. members decide that they want to do things outside of the group together.
    b. most members remain silent.
    c. subgrouping begins.
    d. positive disclosures toward other members escalate.

15. The therapeutic process changes in stage three. A common characteristic is
    a. a greater sense of irresponsibility on the part of the group members.
    b. the group leader provides most of the input to discussion.
    c. the group leader begins to be less active.
    d. members start moving away from one another emotionally.

16. The social personality that was initially evident in stage one
    a. is exhibited as the tension rises in stage two.
    b. is reinforced by the group members as a positive manifestation for dealing with the outside world.
    c. is used only in stage two to demonstrate appropriate behavior.
    d. changes into more of the reality of who the person is.

17. In stage four, the group members begin
    a. to focus on their relationships with one another.
    b. to focus on their relationship with the leader.
    c. to talk more about issues outside of the group environment.
    d. to want to drop out of group.

18. We see in stage four
    a. an increase in discussion of the past.
    b. an increase discussion of the future.
    c. issues of interpersonal relationships outside of the group.
    d. less discussion of the past, present, and future with greater focus on the here and now.

19. Stage four appears to be a time
    a. of openness and willingness to explore feedback with minimum defensiveness.

    b. of increased defensiveness.

    c. of escalating anxiety because of the nature of the disclosures.

    d. when most decompensations begin to emerge.

20. Psychodynamically, stage four elicits
    a. an increase of the defense mechanisms.
    b. increased negative transferences to the group leader.
    c. transformation of members' aggressive drives toward sub-limation.
    d. the facilitation of making the unconscious conscious.

21. Stage five is the termination stage. A prevalent characteristic of this stage is that
    a. the storm and stress of stage two has not yet been worked through and must be before a positive termination can be effected.
    b. group members are usually late coming to group and do not pay their bills.
    c. the therapist is seen as a god.
    d. certain group members wish to continue the experience and keep in contact with the other members as a way to avoid letting go.

Chapter 8

Resistance and Self-Protection: Ego Defense Mechanisms and the Process of Adjustment

RESISTANCE

I am beginning to feel that what I often resist is that which I so much desire. (A client in group psychotherapy)

Similar to the ongoing *Star Trek* series, resistance is an ongoing interpersonal style when an individual is confronted with thoughts and feelings that generate anxiety. Unlike the Borg in *Star Trek* who proclaim, "Resistance is futile," this is definitely not the case in psychotherapy. In fact, it is just this behavioral manifestation that we seek to find in our clients.

Although there are thousands of books and monographs on the theories of resistance as it is related to both group and individual psychotherapy, it is often a misunderstood concept. Many times it is perceived and felt by the therapist as a negative response. The client is labeled as difficult, fighting the process, and stagnated or brought to a halt in his or her therapy. It can also generate a lot of countertransference issues in the clinician if (1) the therapist is overly ego invested in his or her work and the client is not gratifying the therapist's need to continuously see positive change, and (2) if the therapist is not aware of the benefit of this very important therapeutic manifestation.

Resistance is a prized signpost for the therapist. It frequently gives direction and understanding of previously undisclosed conflicts in the client that have remained unconscious or consciously too painful to disclose to another individual. Simply, what has occurred is that you are coming close to the core of the problem(s). In an analogy, you have advertently or inadvertently waded through the seaweed of symptomatology and found the underlying cause or causes for the ongoing conflict(s).

In dynamic therapy, resistance indicates that an ego defense mechanism is in operation in order to maintain and keep in place repression of highly charged, anxious, and emotionally uncomfortable material. Eaton and Peterson (1969) explain that resistance is perceived by many therapists as a resistance to getting well but in actuality it is really the resistance to change. Although conflict and unresolved issues may be terribly burdensome for the client, they are at least familiar, whereas change is a scary experience for most people. It represents the unknown. Briefly, do a quick self-analysis on yourself and determine how comfortable you are with change. Obviously, different people will be on a continuum from resistant toward to embracing change, but it will help to give you some idea how receptive clients are in their perceptions of change. Although clients may be unhappy in their personal situations, at least they have functioned in these situations; change once again represents the increase of anxiety. Doubts as to how the change is going to affect them are a very real concern for clients, whether consciously or unconsciously, and change in a psychotherapy environment often elicits emotional discomfort.

Interestingly, most clients are completely unaware, on a conscious level, that they are resisting. This simply occurs due to the fact that the behavior they are manifesting is a behavior they have been manifesting throughout most of their lives in situations that elicit anxiety. The sensitive therapist is encouraged to be keenly aware of issues in group that cause discomfort in the individual group members as a source of underlying, unresolved conflicts. According to Ormont (2001), it is the task of the therapist to create an environment in which we elicit resistance. By reinforcing that which is causing the resistance, it becomes "larger than life," which means that even the client is now becoming aware that he or she is resisting because it is so magnified. How does a group therapist create the resistance that is necessary for change? Actually, it occurs rather quickly on its own. Covering many topics that might create emotional stimulation in group members can move the resistance along rather effectively. This means that a group leader can introduce topics that he or she knows may cause discomfort or try and include all group members in a disclosure from another group member that would ordinarily generate anxiety. For example, I have found that even in our sophisticated society, sexuality seems to generate a great deal of anxiety. It usually is manifested in group with increased laughter and a few jokes as a means of attenuating the anxiety, but the anxiety is present. This is probably due to the very intimate nature of an individual's sexuality and the amazing misinformation adults have concerning this very human, emotional, and physical expression.

Reread the quote at the beginning of this chapter. The client is becoming aware that his or her resistance is a block to something he or she truly desires. Issues in American society wax and wane. Perhaps the most current salient issue is the lack of intimacy in people's lives. Families are being pulled apart; both parents work; relationships are correlated to our perception of products—in many cases they are thrown away when no longer working; latchkey children; transitional neighborhoods; faster-paced society; the acceleration of technology with the overload of information; escalating stress; and the Internet are just a few of the factors causing a diminished sense of connectedness and intimacy. Human beings seem to be moving farther and farther away from one another emotionally. George Carlin once said, "A man has walked on the moon, but how many people will walk across the street to welcome a new neighbor?"

A psychotherapy group by its nature and design creates an environment of intimacy. Because of this, we can expect not only the rise and fall of resistances in relation to intimacy within each group member but also the rise and fall of resistances in the group as a whole as it relates to this issue. In Chapter 6, it was pointed out that clients require space between their chairs or they feel that the other clients are getting too close. The same is true in their initial interpersonal interactions with one another in group. Clients require space and distance in these interpersonal interactions. The emotional closeness a client allows himself or herself to feel toward another client is determined by his or her level of anxiety as it relates to intimacy and emotional comfort. I have found that most clients believe that feelings have a gender. They inhibit themselves if they think that what they are feeling is opposite to their gender. When they do this, they diminish their possibility of becoming intimate with other members in the group and predominantly with other people in their lives. Because of this, it is very important that you explain to clients in group that feelings do not have a gender. They may be expressed differently by different people, but it is an erroneous assumption to believe that one gender has greater capacity for intimacy than the other. In many cases, women in group may initially be more verbal, but men have the same capacity to be as intimate and as capable to develop intimacy as women do. Although the misconstrued, layperson, popular book has proclaimed that men may be from Mars and women from Venus, the reality is that we are all from the planet Earth and of the same species and are more alike in our needs, desires, hopes, and fears than we are different.

If the group leader can promote intimacy, wonderful things will occur. This intimacy will help to attenuate resistances, promote interpersonal interaction, and provide an arena in which clients are comfortable disclosing the truth. Groups are very often a reflection of the group leader as children are a reflection of their parents. This is not to suggest that both psychotherapy groups and children are a mirror image of either the group leader or the parents that raised them. However, your being and your comfort and discomfort with intimacy will be manifested in the outcome of your groups whether you are an involved therapist or a detached therapist. Because of this, it is very important for the group leader to look squarely at himself or herself and address two personal questions: (1) how resistant to change am I?, and (2) how comfortable am I with intimacy toward others and others intimacy toward me? If you answer "not very" to both, your probability of creating intimacy in your groups will not be very good and the eventual lessening of resistance in your group members and the attenuation of the following ego defense mechanisms will not be forthcoming.

SELF-PROTECTION

There is nothing either good or bad, but thinking makes it so. (Shakespeare, *Hamlet*)

No matter what modality you use in your group, clients initially manifest defensive reactions of various degrees, as the group experience can be anxiety-provoking for the new members. This is especially true when the focus of the group's attention and heightened emotionality is a member, whether new or old. It is in the interest of the group leader to have some working understanding of defense mechanisms, as very often a member's defensive responses and behavioral style tell us more about the individual than the individual is either willing or able to tell us about himself or herself.

A defense mechanism is a psychological manifestation that is designed to protect the self from disorganization and hurt. These defensive manifestations are activated when the individual feels the escalation of anxiety in relation to a personal issue that is interpreted, whether consciously or unconsciously, as dangerous. The unconscious is not some mystical esoteric phenomenon but rather a process that is keeping something from awareness. Unconscious processes protect little-known conscious parts of the personality and are aspects of the personality that are denied and cannot be seen directly. However, people remain sensitive to these qualities and therefore tend to see them in others via the psychological mechanism of projection. The reason this awareness is kept out of consciousness is later seen by the group leader, as well as the members. It is interpreted and understood during the ensuing analysis as a manifestation of a particular defense mechanism.

Conflicts and frustrations that are experienced on a day-to-day basis are usually resolved on a conscious level. Those which are more deeply rooted often lead to an adjustment effort on an unconscious level. These adjustment processes or efforts, referred to as defense-oriented reaction patterns, are generally of two kinds:

1. Responses that are easily accessible to consciousness, e.g., focusing on the conflict and consciously devoting a certain amount of energy to resolution of the problem, reducing a goal to a more realistic size, laughing something off, crying, persevering, repetitive speaking, dreaming, and nightmares (Coleman, 1976). The individual is aware of these reactions, but may not be aware of why they are occurring.
2. The second kind of defense-oriented reaction patterns are those related to ego defense mechanisms or unconscious attempts at adjustment. They are used to reduce anxiety and tension, protect the integrity of the ego, and protect the self from devaluation and hurt. These defenses remain unconscious and automatically operate when the individual feels in psychological danger. This danger can come from external threats such as devaluating failures and negative criticism, or internal dangers such as unconscious desires that arouse guilt, for instance, an attraction to something that one consciously perceives as morally aversive.

The manifestations of these ego defense mechanisms are a very common human phenomenon as they are a buffer against the impact of deprivation, failure, and feelings of guilt. In some cases, the vicissitudes of these reactions can cause a gain for the individual when they manifest in certain degrees of sublimation, identification, and compensation. As previously stated, ego defense mechanisms are not necessarily pathological, as each individual in daily life uses many combinations of these psychological responses to deal with anxiety-laden life issues. It becomes a serious problem when the individual predominantly uses these defense mechanisms to deal with life and other individuals, which causes continuous self-deception and the distortion of reality.

Unlike many of my colleagues, I teach psychology while doing therapy. I believe the information that we possess as therapists should not be kept solely to us in an arcane manner but rather should be shared with the people who come to see us. By teaching the ego defense mechanisms and many other psychological concepts to my clients, I am giving them the tools to support their personal understanding and growth plus build a foundation for conflict resolution in their futures.

The following sections describe the most common defense mechanisms.

Acting Out

At its most dangerous, acting out can be lethal. For example, soldiers during war can be completely overwhelmed with anxiety and fear while waiting for a battle to begin. In their need to alleviate this extreme emotional and physiological discomfort, they have been known to leave the safety of their bunkers and run blindly toward an enemy. In a far milder manifestation, we see it as educators when students who generally arrive exactly on time for class or a few minutes late, arrive twenty minutes early on the day of an examination. Because their anxiety has reached a high level, early arrival at the dreaded event helps to alleviate some of the discomfort.

In group, we might perceive another form of acting out when a member shows hostility to the leader and the group for some real or imagined narcissistic injury. The group member arrives late for sessions, forgets to bring payment, or tries to involve another member in a sexual liaison outside of the group, thus breaking the group contract.

Coleman (1976) writes that in life we all have experiences of such severe anxiety that anything we can do to reduce it is embraced, no matter how dangerous the action. Remember, as the name says, acting out is a physical action. The individual is expressing unconscious conflicts that have an emotional component which the person is unable to clarify and express in words.

Compensation

Compensatory reactions are designed to defend the self against feelings of inferiority, whether real or imagined, and setbacks in life. There are two kinds of compensatory reactions: unconscious ones, in which the individual is not aware of what he or she is doing, and conscious ones, in which the individual consciously tries to change what is perceived as a deficiency, whether physically, emotionally, or intellectually. We frequently see appeals to the conscious compensatory reactions in advertising. They imply that if you buy this or that product, it will make you popular, sexy, and desired by all. These direct compensatory feelings are manifested when, for example, a woman thinks that if she uses a particular kind of makeup, she will be able to mask or hide something that she may think or others may have told her is not flattering. Certain men may think that if they make their bodies more muscular, they will feel more masculine. On the unconscious level, these feelings have developed from an individual's experiences with inadequacy and failure.

The indirect or unconscious compensation may be seen when an individual turns away from the area of disappointment and failure and develops strengths in other areas. For example, a young person who is neither adept nor clever in athletics may turn away from the physical and develop the intellectual. The goal of this defense is to mask pain and disappointment and develop mastery in another area. Depending upon the individual's subjective experience with disappointment and feelings of inferiority, we may observe the defense mechanism of overcompensation. If this occurs, the individual, rather than being well rounded in a number of areas, focuses entirely on one specific pursuit to the exclusion of all others. Compensation is very other-directed in the sense that the individual has compared himself or herself to an external ideal. When an individual has not accomplished anything that he or she feels is noteworthy but a friend or a family member has, the individual then lauds the accomplishment of the other person to whom he or she has some connection.

In group, we may observe compensation in a member who tries to appear very intellectual when in fact the member has doubts about his or her intellectual abilities. It can be seen in the overmasculine male who is unconsciously insecure about his masculinity.

Conversion

This defense mechanism involves the attempt to resolve emotional conflicts through sensory, motor, or somatic manifestations. This often represents a flight from emotional pain by increased physical illnesses. In this case, sympathy and attention compensates for the actual painful experience, which is no longer a focus as the physical problem becomes paramount in the individual's existence. During World War II, this mechanism operated in its most intense manifestation. Soldiers who had traumatic experiences began to develop psychogenic disorders, which originate in the mind and manifest physiologically, such as hysterical blindness, paralysis, and so on.

In group therapy we may see this in certain individuals who often miss group because of illness or arrive at group ill. If someone is not feeling well, the group members often reduce their focus on that individual, thus leaving the person to find safety in physical distress.

Denial

Denial is perhaps one of the most overworked defense mechanisms. Both atavistic and simple, it often dovetails with all the other defense mechanisms. It is the attempt to resolve anxiety-laden emotional conflicts by not allowing them to come into consciousness. The individual blocks impulses, needs, thoughts, feelings, etc., by denying their existence. By insulating the self from the impact of the conflict, the individual personality remains somewhat intact, but a degree of distortion of reality has occurred. It can manifest in a physiological response. An individual may faint in order to block a traumatic event. A person can become excessively preoccupied with work or a project to avoid focusing on difficult issues, for example, when an adolescent child causes tremendous distress in the home and the father puts in longer and longer hours at work. Although an anthropomorphized illustration is not very scientific, I believe that my dog Freud, when he was a puppy, manifested a form of denial. Upon arriving home, I would see that the rug was wet. I would look at Freud and say, "Did you do that?" He would look down at the wetness and then up at me with a look that said, "Not me, buddy," and would then look over at my other dog as if to say, "Maybe it was him!" It appeared that denial and projection were being manifested. However, this was difficult to validate because Freud did not speak, as he is a Freudian.

In group, we may see denial when one member tells another how he or she feels about the other member's behavior. The member receiving the feedback may respond, "No, you are wrong!" This behavior may be very obvious to everyone else.

Displacement

The following scenario is an example of displacement. A man has really had a bad day at work. His boss has read him the riot act and because he is afraid of being fired, he remains passive during the onslaught of abuse. Yet this perceived abuse and its concomitant feelings do not end there. The employee returns home that evening and screams at his wife, punishes his children, and makes the dog sleep in the yard. The emotion is displaced from its original object to safer objects that the individual believes are unlikely to retaliate. In this case, the employee's anger toward his employer is displaced onto his family. In displacement, difficult emotions such as anxiety or hostility cannot be discharged because of the nature of the situation. Also, displacement can take another form, which is devastating to the self. The individual develops masochistic behaviors involving self-punishment or intropunitive actions. Anger turned inward produces exaggerated recriminations and self-accusations that lead to severe depression and possible attempted suicide.

In group, displacement occurs when one group member confronts another. The member being confronted does not respond in kind, for whatever reason, and builds up anger. This anger is then displaced onto another group member who the other member knows will not assert himself or herself in return.

Dissociation

Dissociation is the isolation of mental processes from consciousness. These processes operate independently from the conscious mind, thus creating a split or breaking off from the personality. Theoretically, this becomes a personality of its own, with its own thought-affect manifestations. It is a core concept in relation to hysterical conversion. Examples are the famous multiple personality cases in the movie *The Three Faces of Eve* or in the book *Sybil*.

This is rather rare in groups, but could be addressed if a member relates experiences of somnambulism (walking in one's sleep), or periods of amnesia.

Emotional Insulation

Emotional insulation is an interesting defense mechanism as it reduces an individual's participation in situations that have been previously perceived as causing pain and hurt. We often see it if we try to "fix up" a recently divorced friend with a date. Generally, the response is "No!" but when we inquire, the individual usually says, "It is too soon," rather than, "I am afraid of getting hurt again."

It can also manifest itself when an individual has unrealistic goals that have repeatedly gone ungratified. For example, a rather homely man seeks to date only dazzling women but is continually rejected. This man decides that he will no longer attempt to meet women. It is a defense mechanism that insulates the individual against unnecessary disappointment. Most people are willing to take another chance and again participate in a relationship. When the individual is not, the insulation becomes a negative solution to the pain because it reduces the individual's healthy participation in life.

In group, we may perceive emotional insulation when a group member is consistently fearful of disclosing personal feelings. Quite possibly in the past when such an individual has tried to express feelings or beliefs, he or she has been punished in some way and has concluded that it is not safe to disclose.

Fantasy

Fantasy is a mental process that helps to overcome frustration. The frustration may be attenuated through the achievement of imaginary goals and their concomitant gratification of needs. Coleman (1976) speaks about two models of fantasy for gratification: (1) the conquering hero or heroine, and (2) the martyr, or suffering hero or heroine manifestation. In the conquering hero fantasy, the individual perceives himself or herself as capable of great feats and accomplishments. Admiration from others is the goal, as is respect, power, and the belief in one's great capability. For example, a graduate psychology student who is frustrated or feels misunderstood by a professor imagines himself as a well-known, highly respected professional whom other colleagues seek for his in-depth insights into human behavior. Hostility and anger are often the stimulus for the conquering hero fantasy as it helps to dissipate these uncomfortable emotions. To reduce these feelings, the individual creates mental scenarios that remove any person or obstacle which has generated those feelings. In this sense, fantasy helps to diminish the aggressive impulse by overcoming the factor that caused frustration. For example, while driving your car on a congested highway, someone cuts you off, frightening you. Chances are that if you are relatively well adjusted, you are not going to go chasing after the other driver and cut that person off. Instead, you may fantasize something unpleasant happening to the person who caused you to feel fear. By this method, you have reduced by some degree the anger you felt from being frightened.

In relation to the martyrdom pattern, we find individuals who, rather than acknowledging their feelings of inferiority, choose to translate them into doom and dread. According to them, fate has specifically chosen them to suffer. "Why does this always happen to me?" They may be aware of some personal, devastating handicap that is unknown to anyone else. They carry this belief silently. The thinking behind this type of defense generally is that when others perceive the strength the individual has mustered to survive the adversities of life, all will be sympathetic and impressed. With this particular defensive pattern, the individual literally never has to look at failed performances or personal mediocrity.

Perhaps one of the more interesting fantasies is the "great lover fantasy," which appears to be more common among men. It seems that many men are extremely concerned about how they are perceived as lovers. Because of this concern, they tend to build certain fantasies about their performances and abilities. In my experience, I find this less common among women, who seem to be more comfortable and secure in this area of physical expression.

In group therapy, we often see fantasy. A group member has suffered a narcissistic injury from another member and does not confront that individual but rather builds a scenario of retaliation. A group member is sexually attracted to another member: rather than disclosing those feelings, he or she begins to imagine a romantic scenario. At times, you may hear a group member say, "Why does this always happen to me?" or "I could write a book on all the bad things that have happened in my life."

Identification

Identification as a defense mechanism is different from identification in modeling and imitative behaviors. When identification is a defense mechanism, the individual wards off feelings of self-devaluation and inferiority by joining certain groups, organizations, etc., that are perceived by society as having some sort of status. This is an unconscious process, whereas identification as a modeling behavior is conscious and is easily seen, for instance, in the way people dress in order to fit in. As an unconscious behavior, the individual is trying to increase feelings of personal worth by this inclusion although he or she has not achieved anything personally. In other words, the person assumes status through the efforts of others. For example, certain sports fans are quite intense when it comes to their favorite teams, with a profoundly labile affect. If the team wins, they are elated. If the team loses, they experience an actual depression as if it were a personal failure. Obviously, this identification is fulfilling some need in these people.

In another example, in group therapy a member may speak about the company for which he or she works acquiring a new contract. The individual relates the acquisition by saying, "We just bought AT&T" rather than, "The company I work for just bought AT&T." In effect, this is good for the company, as it builds a certain degree of loyalty in its employees, but it is not always very good for the employee—who may be fired or laid off because of downsizing.

Incorporation

This ego defense mechanism is related to introjection. It appears to be more primitive in origin (Freud, 1946) and correlated to the oral phase of development. As the name indicates, incorporation means, in this sense, to take in and ingest. This ingestion is manifested as a psychic representation of another person or part of another person with whom one has an intimate relationship. The other individual is psychically ingested into the being of the person using the defense mechanism. It too is a defense against the awareness of one's aggression. White (1950) uses the example of a father who is opposed to his son pursuing a particular career even though the son shows promise and interest in that profession. The father rationalizes his strong stance against pursuit of that profession by expressing that he is the father and his only interest is concern for his child's future. If a person outside of this dyad were to come along and indicate that perhaps the father would be wiser in letting his child make his own choice, the father would be outraged. In this scenario, the parent has psychically incorporated the being of his son into himself and has blurred the boundaries between the two. It is correlated to the oral phase of development because, likewise, the nursing child blurs the distinction between himself or herself and his or her mother. By discounting the son's being and incorporating it into himself, the father has in effect annihilated his offspring, thus indicating another aspect of the myriad forms of aggression.

This is a very difficult defense mechanism to perceive in a typical group therapy session because it is related to the intimacy one person has with another. It can be most readily observed in family therapy, which really is a form of group psychotherapy, except in this case, the group goes home together. It is in the interest of the therapist to observe the boundaries of the family members in relation to one another. If those boundaries are blurred, the therapist would be wise to address that issue.

Intellectualization

In intellectualization, the emotional impact of a painful event is deflected and reduced by rationalizing away the personal significance of the experience, such as the death of a parent whom one loves. The individual may say, "He lived a full life," or "Thankfully he died without pain." Certainly these statements may be true. The rationalization and emotionally insulating verbalization affects the full impact of the loss. This defense mechanism is often used when one is fearful of being overwhelmed by emotion. For example, we may use this defense mechanism in relation to possible future loss, when we are waiting for another's decision about something in which we have invested ourselves. One may say, "If it does not work out at least I gave it a try." When experiencing a difficult time it is reassuring to say, "Things could have been worse." Speaking of activities that one will begin tomorrow or next week tends to help reduce the impact of the feelings lying below the surface, for example, "Tomorrow I am going on a diet," or "Next week, I am going to stop smoking."

In group therapy, this is perceived when a member is speaking about what another member has said to him or her. The obvious reaction is some degree of emotionality, but the member appears to be emotionally distant from the other member's disclosure or confrontation and rationalizes the behavior of the other individual.

Introjection

Introjection is the opposite of projection. The emotionality that is felt is turned back upon the self. It is similar to displacement; for example, an individual who may be experiencing overwhelming hatred reflects that escalated emotionality back on the self. Introjection has an essence of identification, but in this case the individual chooses to accept the values of others when these values are contradictory to one's own beliefs. This acceptance of contradictory values usually has at its core a need for survival or social acceptance. It can be summed up, "If you can't beat them, join them." You may remember the Patty Hearst story. When Ms. Hearst was kidnapped she eventually became a member of the kidnappers' group, embracing their ideals. You can easily see that her need to survive caused her to accept values that were theoretically contradictory to her own.

During World War II, prisoners in Nazi concentration camps began to take on the norms of their captors in order to survive the horrendous conditions under which they lived. We see this type of behavior in gangs. Very often the need to belong to something is so strong that individuals adopt behaviors which are quite foreign to their beliefs. In other cases, we see this in an act of attempted or actual suicide when an individual has introjected certain hated aspects of another's personality into his or her own being. Because the individual is greatly at odds with this other introjected personality, the aggression that he or she feels toward that person is directed back upon the self.

In group therapy a member who is rather passive may take sides with some of the more aggressive and assertive members in order to feel safe, even though he or she does not agree with what the others are saying or doing. Another example is a client who speaks about the tremendous anger he or she feels toward a particular parent, then behaves in a way that is similar to the parent.

Isolation

This defense mechanism has its basis in compartmentalization. The individual, for whatever personal reason(s), seeks to keep separate and distinct his or her activities in life. It is almost as if the individual lives in many different worlds and responds and interacts differently in each. The underlying motivation for isolation is to keep feelings of aggression hidden and contained. However, it is well known in psychoanalytic quarters that human beings are not meant to keep secrets and this aggression will be eventually manifested and expressed in other areas. We all know people who are very religious, humble, and pious on days designated by their religion as holy. Yet on other days not related to their religion, these individuals are very distant and different in character and personality. To watch these people, it would almost seem as if they have different personalities for each situation.

Observation of this particular defense mechanism may be a bit more difficult. It would be fortuitous to particularly look for a client's description of the many roles he or she has in life and how specifically the individual functions within each described role. Obviously, we must make adjustments in our personalities related to the situations that we are in, but maintaining some degree of consistency across the board of our personalities is effectively a healthier route to take. The more roles a client has in his or her life, whatever those roles may be, the more opportunity that client has to create confusion of whom he or she really is, if each role is compartmentalized as distinct and unrelated to each other role. Specifically observe when a client says, "I feel so very different here than I do when I am outside of here." Upon inquiry you will be able to determine how rigid this individual is in relation to the other roles in his or her life.

Projection

Projection is the inability of an individual to distinguish between the internal and the external. Its function is to self-deceive and it completely undermines and destroys personal insight. Assigning blame without taking personal responsibility is the key to this defense mechanism. Others are blamed for one's own feelings, needs, and cognitions. Almost everything that goes wrong in a person's life becomes the fault of another. Even the cosmos can be blamed for misfortunes in one's life. Projection is a way the individual avoids taking personal responsibility in the realm of thoughts and feelings. On a more simple level, we see it in children who blame inanimate objects for their distress, for instance, a kite does not fly and the child begins to stomp on it as if it were the kite's fault. We can also see this response to inanimate objects in adults. I once saw a neighbor trying to fix his car door. When he could not get it the way he wanted, he ripped the door off the car. It would seem that a very close correlation exists between frustration and projection. Obviously, I was pleased when this neighbor moved away.

In its pathological form, we see projection in operation when an individual delusionally believes that others are plotting against him or her. These feelings of persecution can become dangerous, sometimes provoking acts of violence. We can see projection working in individuals who have an overly strict moral development with rigid superegos. They often see in others those personality characteristics which they choose to hide from themselves.

Projection is a very common group manifestation, especially in the initial phases when members often tend to have less insight into their own interpersonal interactions. Group members often blame other members for making them feel certain ways rather than taking responsibility for their own feelings and thoughts.

Rationalization

This defense mechanism is employed to justify one's behaviors in the past, present, and future. Its value for the individual is in trying to uphold one's belief that the behavior or behaviors are correct and just. It is designed to reduce distress over unattained or unattainable goals. A person may work toward an aim and not achieve it. To soften the disappointment or rejection, the individual creates an explanation.

For example, a man is attracted to a particular woman who is not interested in him, and rationalizes to himself that she probably hates men. As educators, we often see rationalization in students who have done poorly on an examination, even though others have done well, when they say, "The professor was a bad teacher." Rationalization is a creative defense mechanism. An individual devises any number of reasons not to do something in order to do something else for greater gratification, for example, "I really need to go to the beach today, even though I have a pile of work that was due yesterday, because I deserve a rest." In its most nefarious and brutal form, we see it in Hitler's belief that the extermination of the Jews was justifiable for the well-being of Germany.

In group therapy, we see rationalization when members explain a particular inappropriate behavior, such as, "I use a belt to punish my children because they don't listen to me" or "I spent the mortgage money on a vacation because I felt I needed some reward for all the work I have been doing."

Reaction Formation

Reaction formation is a defense mechanism in which the individual manifests behaviors that are totally in opposition to what the individual is actually feeling. The purpose of this contradictory behavior is to protect the self from the knowledge that one may have dangerous desires. These desires are often in conflict with the morality (superego) of the individual. We can see this in the ritual behavior of a spinster who each night looks under her bed in fear that a man may be lurking there to take sexual advantage of her. It occurs among homophobic individuals who feel the need to harm others whose sexual orientation seems to be different but unconsciously is the same. Reaction formation and rationalization seem to work in tandem in some individuals. I have heard "gay bashers" say that their violence against gays is doing the "Lord's work." Very often the crusaders of public morals are those who are most attracted to the issue that they wish to remove from the public domain. Obviously, this removal would reduce their unconscious fear of losing control and indulging in their desire. By crusading, the individual has the opportunity to become immersed in the dreaded evil while rationalizing that he or she is helping humanity. A more creative reaction formation manifestation occurs in those people who feel pornography or other public issues are blights on civilization but join committees in which they view pornographic materials as fodder for their research.

In group therapy, we may observe reaction formation when a member speaks about another member in a particular way, but it seems that what is being disclosed may have some other feeling behind it. The other feeling may, in fact, be a complete opposite of what is being related. For example, "Bob, I really admire how you expressed yourself to John." In actuality, the client's feeling is one of aversion to the way Bob expressed himself.

Regression

Regression is a return to the past. With this defense mechanism, an individual seeks a behavioral pattern that provided some degree of gratification in the past. It has myriad manifestations, including dreams, play, mental disorders, and so on. Regression often occurs when an individual is overwhelmed with anxiety-provoking new situations and severe stress. Basically, the person seeks to return to a time when gratification was easier. It is a change to a less mature developmental stage. We can see this in children. For example, a new baby is brought into the home and the four-year-old boy who has had complete parental gratification, and in many cases complete control over the household, chooses to return to an earlier developmental stage in which he received more attention. He may again suck his thumb or soil in his pants. In its severest form, which is sometimes seen in psychiatric hospitals, patients cannot dress or feed themselves.

In group therapy we may see regression when a member is in transference with another member who reminds that person of a parental figure. The member begins to relate to this other individual in ways similar to those in which he or she related to a parent. It also manifests when the behavior of the group becomes childish because of an anxiety-causing issue. Certain group sibling rivalry behaviors have a regressive manifestation when a member feels that another member is getting more attention from the therapist. According to Rutan and Stone (1993), a group as a whole will experience a form of regression when a new member enters the group.

Repression

Repression is sometimes referred to as "selective forgetting." The individual restrains or extinguishes from consciousness thoughts, feelings, and desires that elicit emotional pain. These thoughts, feelings, and desires are not forgotten but rather remain in the unconscious. The retrieval of repressed material from the unconscious, or making the unconscious conscious, is one of the major goals of psychoanalysis. This repressed material is not available for voluntary retrieval but is seen in disguised forms and is symbolically portrayed in the client's dream life. In its positive sense, repression is an effective defense mechanism for protecting the self from shocking and traumatic experiences. As the desensitizing effect of repression begins to wear away, the individual comes to recall the provoking event, such as a car or airplane crash, sexual abuse, natural disaster, etc. It is the defense mechanism that an individual uses when a traumatic emotional experience occurs that the personality cannot integrate effectively.

Clients in psychotherapy may relate that they heard from someone else that a seemingly traumatic event had occurred, but they do not have any recollection of it. Some clients cannot remember anything from childhood. Repression can be a defense against unacceptable desires. By repressing these desires, the individual is able to reduce some of the anxiety related to the craving, urge, or passion. If the desire is repressed, it may manifest in a projection. Often repression and suppression are confused. Repression is an unconscious event, whereas suppression is a conscious effort not to think about an unacceptable feeling, thought, or impulse.

In group therapy, repression is not common unless an individual has a traumatic experience in the group itself. Often, the lifting of repression is more clearly evident in a group member's catharsis of a forgotten memory. Suppression is likely to occur regularly with certain members who do not wish to remember what has transpired during previous weeks in the group.

Sublimation

Sublimation is the conversion of socially unacceptable activities and behaviors into socially acceptable behaviors. As a psychodynamic concept, sublimation is often based on sexual or aggressive tendencies, or a combination of the two. As my analyst used to say, the orthodox Freudian analysts used to give as an example of sublimation, "butchers turning into surgeons, pyromaniacs into firemen, and crooks into police officers."

In group therapy, there may be a member who is always the do-gooder, never having an aggressive thought or feeling. Although similar to reaction formation, this defense mechanism is related to instinctual drives such as sexuality and aggression.

Turning Against the Self

This particular ego defense mechanism is essentially related to aggression and punishment. Anna Freud (1946) considered it to be one of the more primitive of the ego defense mechanisms because its origins probably are cultivated in the psyche of the developing child. This origin is categorically intertwined with the child's developing superego and ego. In this defense mechanism, aggression is turned back upon the self in the form of denial. The individual is denying feelings of aggression toward others and has used his or her own being as the object of those aggressive feelings. When it is drawn back upon the self, the person is actually evidencing a form of displacement. The ultimate underlying motivation is to punish oneself for having feelings that one is not permitted to have—the feelings of aggression. This masochistic stance can be extremely debilitating and often very painful depending upon the intensity of the punishment. Masochism rarely stands alone but balances on a fulcrum like a see-saw, with the other end being the sadistic stance. In the sadistic phase of this ego defense mechanism, the individual punishes others for their perceived aggression. Again, denial of one's own aggression is hidden, but its expression and manifestation is not. Guilt, as an example, is a form of punishment turned back upon oneself. Although it is related to superego functioning and conscience, it too can be a painful experience if the individual is overwhelmed by its intensity.

This ego defense mechanism can easily be seen in group psychotherapy because a client will talk about it. He or she will come in and talk about how he or she held himself or herself back the week before from saying certain things because of fear of retaliation, or he or she felt guilty for having felt that way. They often will go on to say that holding back their feelings caused them distress throughout the week and they belittled themselves for being cowardly. In this case, it is a good indication that growth will follow if the group therapist is aware of the struggle that these particular clients are experiencing. Unfortunately for some clients, the feelings they have of aggression are toward the group therapist. When those feelings come to light, some group therapists, rather than exploring the aggression with the client, turn it back upon the client. This generally occurs because these group therapists experience the client's disclosure as a narcissistic injury to them or because it touches upon unresolved aggression issues in their own personalities.

Undoing

The act of atonement, making amends for wrongdoing, is a defense mechanism that appears to have its roots in childhood. A child feels that after apologizing and making some kind of amends, whether verbally or through some form of physical or emotional punishment, he or she is theoretically cleansed of the inappropriate act or behavior and can be accepted again. Undoing is very much related to feelings of guilt and a majority of human beings seem to have a strong need to rid themselves of this feeling. Many religions offer relief of guilt after wrongdoing has been disclosed. These wrongs are nullified by some act of restitution by the individual, who is then freed from the burden of guilt. As an unconscious mechanism, though, this restitution is performed on an unconscious level. For example, a successful entrepreneur who has exploited people to achieve success may donate large sums of money to charity. An unfaithful wife may spare no effort to make her husband physically comfortable. An individual who feels that sex is dirty and wrong may need to take a number of showers after making love or may feel the need to be punished in some kind of ritualistic masochistic behavior.

In group therapy, there may be a member who is always apologizing for some real or imagined wrongdoing. It is important to remember that this defense mechanism is always related to guilt, and guilt is an emotion that we create. It is in fact the only such emotion, which means that it can be unmade.

Defense mechanisms are used to maintain the integrity of the ego and keep the personality in a state of equilibrium. During times of overwhelming stress, these defenses are less able to cope with the pressure. The personality of the individual under these conditions then begins to decompensate. To protect against the disorganization of the personality, the individual's defense mechanism is exacerbated in the attempt to stabilize the personality. This can create a burnout, like a star going nova, which ultimately hastens its decomposition. This decompensation may occur when defense mechanisms fail, producing panic attacks or unbearable heightened anxiety. If not carefully monitored, the client could conceivably have a psychotic episode.

REVIEW

Part A

In your personal experiences in life, can you remember in what situations you felt resistance? How do those previous resistant situations manifest in your current interpersonal relationships?

Part B

You have now reviewed twenty-one defense mechanisms: (1) acting out, (2) compensation, (3) conversion, (4) denial, (5) displacement, (6) dissociation, (7) emotional insulation, (8) fantasy, (9) identification, (10) incorporation, (11) intellectualization, (12) introjection, (13) isolation, (14) projection, (15) rationalization, (16) reaction formation, (17) regression, (18) repression, (19) sublimation, (20) turning against the self, and (21) undoing, some of which may manifest in some way in group therapy. Do you see yourself in any of them? You may wish to contemplate how some may be manifested in your daily interactions with others and their interactions with you.

Chapter 9

Transference and Countertransference

TRANSFERENCE

> If you always do what you always did, then you will always get what you always got. Is that what you really want? (Unknown)

The moment a client makes the decision to go into psychotherapy, he or she has entered into a transferential relationship with the yet unknown psychotherapist. This is because the client has created the belief that this particular individual, the therapist, is imbued with both magical powers and unlimited knowledge. These Olympian attributes of the therapist will make everything better and the pain which the client is experiencing will magically go away. It is very similar to a young child's belief that when in pain, whether physical or emotional, the parent or parents will make that pain go away and comfort, safety, and security will be restored. The concept of transference is as intrinsic to psychoanalysis as the concept of wet is to water. Kahn (1991) describes it poetically when he states:

> The design of transference may be thought of as musical. The composers of the eighteenth and nineteenth centuries used a form they called the sonata. (The opening movements of Mozart's and Beethoven's symphonies are examples.) In the sonata all the themes that are going to appear are stated at the beginning. From there on, everything that occurs in the form is a variation, development, or replay of those themes. . . . One might think of one's first relationships as the themes of one's interpersonal life and all subsequent relationships as the development and recapitulation of those themes. (p. 27)

Unfortunately, the rejection of traditional psychoanalysis, as reported by *Time* (Gray, 1993), has been prevalent. It is similar to "throwing the baby out with the bath water." This aversion to psycho-analysis is a result of many analytic writers creating convoluted explanations that turn people off to the true value of psychodynamic discoveries.

As an educator, I see the negative reactions of graduate students when I begin my lectures on psychoanalytic concepts and their relationship to group therapy. In some cases, convincing students that psychoanalysis and psychodynamic psychotherapy are alive and thriving is like convincing people that dinosaurs still roam the earth.

Transference is not an esoteric, mystical phenomenon. It is really a simple, quite understandable, and logical manifestation in interpersonal relations. Its basic premise is the logical assumption that when entering into each new relationship, we bring the history of our previous relationships (Debbane and DeCarufel, 1993).

Before beginning a discussion of transference and its relationship to group, a general overview of its discovery may be of historical interest to the practicing clinician (whose paradigm interests have been in other psychological modalities), and students new to analytic terminology and thought. The extraordinary phenomenon of transference was another one of Sigmund Freud's profound contributions to the field of psychology and psychiatry. While observing the work of his friend and colleague Josef Breuer, Freud observed a peculiar relationship developing between the doctor and his patient, Bertha. It appeared that Bertha felt that her relationship with the doctor had gone beyond a typical doctor-patient relationship. It is reported that Bertha, supposedly a virgin, was convinced that she was carrying Breuer's child. This proclamation did not please Breuer, and he chose to terminate his professional relationship with Fraulein Bertha and turn over the case to his friend Freud (Kahn, 1991).

The realization that patients begin to develop anachronistic and unrealistic relationships with their doctors had a profound effect on Freud's further research. He suggested that individuals tend to repeat their previous relationships in the present, especially if those relationships were problematic, making transference a form of repetition compulsion. Thus, it was proposed that patients begin to relate to the therapist similarly to the way in which they related to the people who were most important in their past (Freud, 1912).

Transference is a reaction of the client to the therapist as a "virtual reincarnation" of a significant figure from the past. It was later seen that transference manifests in other ways. The client might play out a desired relationship with the therapist that he or she may have wanted with a significant other from the past (Kahn, 1991). For example, if a client's mother was a cold, detached woman, ungiving in her love or acknowledgment, it is very possible that this client would respond similarly to older women with similar personality characteristics. Because this is an unconscious manifestation, the individual is unaware that these behaviors are being elicited due to the fact that the relationship is touching upon early unresolved conflicts. This would become especially apparent if the therapist were an older woman. This is not to suggest that this transferential reaction would occur only if the patient were in the presence of an older female therapist. In fact, this mother transference toward the therapist could just as easily manifest if the therapist were male and had certain characteristics of the cold, detached mother.

Debbane and DeCarufel (1993) suggest that transference is an oppositional event to remembering. These authors relate that there are basically two types of memory: (1) habit memory and (2) recollective memory. With recollective memory, an individual can easily remember an incident from the past and re-create that image in the mind's eye. With habit memory, a behavior is acquired, developed, and maintained through repetition, although it is not a representation of the past but rather an acting out of the past. This particular memory remains unconscious but is acted out. For example, when I was a child learning how to pick up a glass without spilling its contents, I developed fine motor skills through repetition. Today I can reach for and pick up a glass, most of the time, without spilling its contents, but I cannot remember consciously or visualize the history of how I acquired that skill. Through observation of small children and studying the literature on motor-skill development, I can assume that my fine motor developmental accomplishments generally followed similar routes of most children.

Transference may be similar to a habit memory in the sense that it is acquired through the repetitive interactions of the individual with objects and significant others, but because of the painful emotional experiences of these interactions, the individual does not consciously remember the events but rather acts them out. Reik (1972) wrote that what we cannot remember, we are compelled to repeat. These events can be both real and imaginary. If, for example, the event is tinged with aggression or sexuality toward a significant other and these feelings are not viewed as appropriate, they can be repressed.

Returning to Fraulein Bertha and her belief that she was pregnant with Dr. Breuer's child, this is a fine example of a sexual feeling toward her father that was repressed and then acted out or displaced on Breuer. Every new relationship calls up the history of every older relationship, but this is not actively understood by the individual nor is it in conscious awareness. In this sense, each relationship has the potential of reawakening and reenacting previous important relationships. The relationships that have the most profound energy are those which have been conflictual and unresolved.

Returning to the client with the cold, detached mother, he may carry within himself unresolved issues that may be stimulated in the presence of any individual who has some characteristics, real or imaginary, of the individual to whom the unresolved conflicts are transferred. Kahn (1991) speaks about transference in everyday life as a typical manifestation of being human. As an example of Kahn's belief, I once had a student, a woman in her forties, who from the moment she entered my class until about eight weeks into the course remained quite sullen and unresponsive, although her behavior with the other students in the hall was quite animated and responsive. I decided to leave it alone and observe what unfolded in her personality during the semester. One particular day, I was giving a lecture on transference. I looked up to see her hand enthusiastically waving in the back of the room, her preferred seating in my class. Surprisingly, she began by saying that she owed me an apology. Upon my inquiry, she related that the day she arrived at my class and saw me, she instantly decided that I was a man who could not be trusted and she was not about to lower her guard in my presence. In a flash it came to her. From this lecture and the particular way that I turned to write something on the board, she realized that my personal appearance reminded her of her husband's ex-partner, who ten years previously had emptied the company's bank account and disappeared with all the money. This act of dishonesty had a devastating effect on my student and her husband.

As can be seen by this example, I did little, if anything, to provoke this student's feelings toward me. Having a similar physical appearance was enough to provoke a transferential response from this student. Before she remembered, she related to me in a manner that had nothing to do with reality, who I really am, and the parameters of our relationship. If she had not come to this realization, it is very possible that she would have remained sullen during the entire semester and quite possibly looked for ways to punish me for the misdeeds of another man.

Transference can also be seen in the dream life of a client. I had a twenty-six-year-old man in group therapy. He was generally quiet and appeared reluctant to offend anyone during his membership in group. He said that his relationship with his father was always stressful, which elicited anxiety in him whenever he was in his father's presence. He felt disliked by his dad, who continually criticized his every effort, no matter what he accomplished. He felt that nothing was ever good enough to elicit any recognition from this emotionally distant parent. One night in group, he related a dream he had had the previous evening. Rutan and Stone (1993) report that dreams are very fine tools to use in group, as they allow other group members to project on the latent meaning of the dream, thus providing greater information about the group member doing the projection. In this particular dream, the young man disclosed that he was in a very large airport terminal. He was walking with his head down, the way he usually walked, when slowly he began to lift his head. When his head was up, he saw that the terminal was full of men with his father's face. Upon seeing this, he collapsed in the dream and immediately woke up.

By associating with the dream, this client began to realize that he had, up to that point, perceived all men older than himself similarly to the way he perceived his father. He related that throughout his young life he "turned himself inside out" to get recognition from teachers, coaches, employers, and any older male figure whom he perceived as significant. It was amazing to see this very heavy burden begin to melt away over the course of a few weeks. In fact, he related that he no longer walked with his head down but found that he was now occasionally tripping, which he had not done before when his eyes were continuously focused on the ground.

In both cases we have a most extraordinary process that occurs in each of our lives. Because of transference, a person begins to re-experience the range of feelings about a significant other from the past and transfers those feelings onto a significant person in the present. Initially, Freud (1912) perceived transference as an ego defense mechanism. He saw this phenomenon as a form of displacement, as it was taking from one situation and displacing it onto another. Sullivan (1953) perceived transference as a parataxic distortion and both names are often interchangeably used when describing this phenomenon. He defined parataxic distortion as an inaccuracy in perception and judgment as it relates to interpersonal relationships. He felt that individuals distort reality in their relationships due to their needs set by earlier historical experiences. In other words, individuals bring into their relationships needs from the past and expect them to be answered in the present although it is unrealistic to expect that to happen.

For this phenomenon to occur, we must look at repression. Repressed material (if you remember from Chapter 7) includes thoughts, feelings, and desires that elicit emotional pain which are restrained or extinguished from consciousness. This material is not available for voluntary retrieval from the unconscious but often appears in a disguised form in certain behavioral acts, such as transference. Repression can be used as a defense against unacceptable desires (remember Bertha).

Freud went on to say that this transferential phenomenon, the repeating of previous relational experiences, becomes a compulsion over which the individual has little control as it remains on an unconscious level and is conflictual. Because it is conflictual, the unconscious seeks a way to resolve the conflict in order to return to a state of homeostasis. Thus, the unconscious motivates the individual to seek specific surrogates with similarities to the original person with whom one has the conflict to resolve this disequilibrium.

In some cases, transference can carry a self-fulfilling prophecy. It is not uncommon for a client to try to manipulate the relationship with a therapist to re-create the earlier conflictual situation with the new "virtual surrogate." For example, if the client had a cold, rejecting father but the therapist is warm and accepting, it would not be unusual for a client to try to create a situation in which the therapist would begin to feel negatively toward the client and begin to withdraw or be less warm.

Ormont (1992) writes, "many therapists who work with patients individually believe, as Freud posited, that the resolution of the transference is virtually synonymous with cure. We group therapists share this notion to some degree" (p. 185).

COUNTERTRANSFERENCE

Know Thyself

Freud (1910) was the initial observer of what transpires between the therapist and the patient. He wrote that a process similar to transference occurs in the therapist. He chose to call this phenomenon countertransference and initially saw it as an obstacle to effective psychotherapy. In fact, countertransference was seen as an indication of unprofessional and negative behavior by the therapist. This belief about countertransference often wreaked havoc in the clinician, who felt responsible for manifesting a negative behavioral response unbecoming a psychotherapist. This continues to be true. Clinicians and students still seem defensive, feeling that they are doing something wrong, in relation to their therapy cases when the topic of countertransference is introduced.

In the therapeutic relationship, both the therapist and the client bring forth hidden dramas that can be easily stimulated, no matter how objective the therapist tries to be or how much personal therapy a therapist may have had. Logically, since we all have personal histories, these histories will make themselves known, either consciously or unconsciously.

Freud's initial belief that countertransference was an obstacle to effective psychotherapy was later questioned by his followers who felt that this phenomenon could be of value and service to better understand the patient (Kahn, 1991). Probably a sigh of relief was heard in many consultation rooms all over the world!

The new definition of countertransference was explained as any and all feelings and thoughts that a therapist may have about his or her clients. Kahn (1991) divided these responses and thoughts into four distinct categories:

1. *Realistic responses.* These responses to the client will be the same with any therapist. Kahn uses these examples: (a) the client is warm and friendly and this evokes a warm and friendly response from the therapist; and (b) the client is hostile and threatening, thus eliciting a fear response from the therapist.
2. *Responses to the transference.* These are responses from the client's transferences onto the therapist. If a client is flattering,

the therapist may feel flattered. If the client is aggressive, the therapist may feel frightened.

3. *Responses to material troubling to the therapist.* These are issues disclosed by the client that cause discomfort and anxiety in the therapist, as these particular issues are unresolved and cause conflict in the therapist's own life. A client may speak of his or her conflictual relationship with his or her father and know that this issue must be addressed and begin to assert himself or herself. This may elicit discomfort in the therapist if he or she has a similar issue.

4. *Characteristic responses of the therapist.* This is the totality of the therapist, the person he or she is in life. A therapist who is generally defensive is probably defensive when working with clients. A therapist who is generally seductive is likely to be seductive with clients.

With this in mind, therapists can begin to explore their feelings and thoughts about clients without the albatross of countertransference hanging around their necks, inhibiting the full opportunity for understanding the people sitting across from them. However, difficulty still exists as some countertransferences are effective and some are not.

The effective countertransferences are those that add clarity to the therapeutic relationship. Kahn (1991) proposes a very close correlation between countertransference and empathy. Clarity is that which promotes a deeper understanding of the nature of the relationship between the client and therapist. It evokes questions such as: (a) "What is actually happening here?" (b) "Why do I feel this way toward this client?" (c) "Why am I having these thoughts about this person?" (d) "What is being evoked inside me?" As you can see, these questions are about self-exploration and introspection.

Kahn (1991) refers to the noneffective countertransferences as being obstructive. These do not work in the service of the therapeutic situation but rather are elicited to defend the therapist. Kahn (1991) delineates five areas of obstructive countertransferences used by therapists:

1. *Issues of greater importance to the therapist than to the client.* For example, the therapist can underestimate the importance of an issue because the therapist does not want to examine it or spend excessive time on an issue that is not as stressful to the cli-

ent as it is to the therapist. If the therapist is not willing to look at a personal issue, he or she may minimize the client's disclosure or consistently focus on an issue of greater importance to the therapist than to the client. For example, a client has a fine relationship with his father but the therapist does not. The therapist continues to focus on the client's relationship with his father, looking for areas of conflict.

2. *Vicariously using clients to do things that the therapist may be incapable of doing.* In this obstructive countertransference, the therapist encourages the client to do certain things that the therapist is not ready or able to do in his or her own life. In a sense, the client is being used as a pawn. There is a degree of hypocrisy to this because the therapist is basically saying, "Do what I say and not what I do." For example, the therapist may have personal fears of dating but consistently encourages the client to go out looking for dates.

3. *The use of subtle cues to transmit what the therapist actually feels to influence the client.* Clients analyze us as much as we analyze them. The consultation room is truly not a one-way street. A therapist may say certain things to clients, but his or her body language, facial expressions, etc., may indicate just the opposite feeling. If a therapist says, "You can tell me anything," and then winces when a client speaks about a certain issue, the client realizes that not everything can be disclosed to this particular therapist. This can leave large gaps in the client's therapy. For example, the client may disclose certain sexual experiences he or she has had that create discomfort in the therapist due to the therapist's strong religious beliefs. The therapist's expression may harden or become less warm than it was before the client disclosed the sexual information.

4. *Therapist interventions that are not in the interest of the client.* This has to do with narcissistic injury. If someone hurts me, for example, I in turn may feel a need to hurt him or her back. If a client has less than positive things to say about me, I may either consciously or unconsciously await the time when I can hurt the client in return. It may not be the client's issues with the therapist per se, but the client's issue with another person. Kahn (1991) uses the example of a client who speaks about his or her father. The characteristics of the client's father and the thera-

pist's father are quite similar. If the therapist has some negative, unresolved issues with his or her own father, he or she may disclose critical and negative feelings about the client's parent.

5. *Assuming the role imagined for us by the client to fulfill the client's transference.* In this case, the therapist does not effectively fit the role that the client may wish him or her to fit. For example, if the client had a cold, rejecting mother and the therapist is neither, the client may create a scenario that will eventually evoke those kinds of feelings from the therapist. These projective counteridentification responses do little to help the therapeutic relationship. Obviously, the client has manipulated the therapist into showing a personality that he or she may not generally manifest.

TRANSFERENCE AND ITS RELATIONSHIP TO GROUP THERAPY

You Don't Look Like My Mother, Bob, and Yet . . .

The nature of group therapy, which is a microcosm of the family, society, and civilization, makes it possible for group members to have many experiences with significant others from the past in the present. In individual psychotherapy, it may be a long time before a client is able to work through these experiences and transfer those relationships onto the therapist. In group therapy, because of the multiclient environment, members have the opportunity to experience many transferences at the same time, which often develop with greater rapidity than in individual psychotherapy. The reason that these transferences develop more quickly is that other members represent who they are as people and are not presenting the demeanor of a professional therapist, who remains somewhat hidden.

Ormont (1992) writes:

> that from the very first time a member walks into a group, he distorts in his perception of the therapist and the others there—a distortion consistent with his own history. Indeed, every member misperceives in his very expectations of what the others will be like and how they will treat him, even before he meets them. (p. 163)

Stein (1981) feels that to promote the development of transferences in group, the therapist needs both to avoid any gratification of the group members and to frustrate the members' need to engage the leader in personal dialogue. By frustrating and diminishing gratification from the group therapist, the members will turn to one another for gratification, thus promoting transferential reactions.

Because group is a multiclient format, the individual brings in his or her previous history of interpersonal relationships with individuals and with groups of people. For example, if the client had negative experiences in the past with groups, he or she generally enters the group environment with a preconceived feeling that this, too, will be an aversive experience. The individual who had positive previous experiences in groups tends to believe that the new experience will also be positive.

In any case, rarely does an individual initially enter a group situation without some degree of anxiety. This is why, when beginning a group, the therapist should introduce the concept of anxiety and how each member feels about being a part of the group experience (Rutan and Stone, 1993). In doing this, the therapist will have some idea of the members' previous experiences with others in a group and how this correlates with the individuals' experiences in their families. Often, family of origin determines how an individual feels about himself or herself in relation to others, which carries over or generalizes onto other individual and group relationships.

Identifying transferences in a group is not as difficult as many students and novice therapists think it is. Whenever a client manifests any form of resistance to the therapeutic process, we may conclude that transference is in operation (Ormont, 1992). This transference, or the resistant manifestation of it, is a form of safety, as it was used in the past to protect the person from some aversive experience. Porter (1994) explains resistance:

> Human beings automatically move away from emotional pain as they do from physical pain. Operating according to this pleasure principle, from the earliest moments of life we seem to separate ourselves from, dissociate, repress, or split off experience that is painful. This protects us, but it also leads to internal fragmentation rather than internal wholeness. (p. 103)

Ormont (1992) suggests that there are a number of ways for therapists to recognize transference in groups. These four indicators are (1) pervasiveness, (2) insistence, (3) excessiveness, and (4) displacement. Pervasiveness describes a tendency to view others similarly, even though the individuals are quite different. Members display insistence when they continue to see other people according to their own perceptions and insist that these perceptions are accurate even in the face of contradictory evidence. Excessiveness is a more intense response than a situation warrants. This intensity or excessiveness is a sure indicator that something else is going on and a therapist would be wise to look for transference. Excessiveness and displacement generally dovetail because the intense response probably indicates that the reaction is a displacement from an earlier relationship.

As seen in the previous examples, transference can be viewed relatively easily if the therapist creates a group with minimum structure. By minimally structuring the group, the members have a greater opportunity to present the persons they truly are, without assuming an "appropriate role." When a person enters a structured environment, he or she will predictably behave in a manner with minimum spontaneity and authenticity, such as a student in class, an employee at work, and so on. If we do not structure the group, the members have a greater opportunity of learning more about themselves, and this lack of structure is very helpful in promoting transferences.

Transference has a powerful effect in psychotherapy. It is the profound manifestation of past relationships with significant others. It demonstrates how those relationships are played and replayed over and over again until they are resolved. Turning away from its significance denies that personal relationships and previous personal relationships are important. Can that really be true?

REVIEW

Please answer the following questions.

1. (T) (F) Kahn (1991) correlates transference to a mathematical form.

2. (T) (F) As reported in *Time* (Gray, 1993), psychoanalysis has been less popular over the past few years.

3. (T) (F) Transference is an esoteric, mystical phenomenon that can be understood only through years of training and in-depth personal analysis.

4. (T) (F) Debbane and DeCarufel (1993) believe that it is logical to assume that when entering a new relationship we bring the history of our previous relationships.

5. (T) (F) Dr. Breuer coined the term *transference* after his experience with Fraulein Bertha.

6. (T) (F) Transference is a reaction by the client to the therapist as a virtual reincarnation of a significant figure from the past.

7. (T) (F) Transferences are gender-specific. If an individual had an aversive experience with a significant female in the past, he or she will be able to work through that experience only with a therapist of the same gender.

8. (T) (F) According to Debbane and DeCarufel (1993) there are two kinds of memory. They claim that transference is a form of recollective memory and is acquired and maintained through repetition and it is not a representation of the past but rather an acting out of the past.

9. (T) (F) Reik (1972) wrote that what we cannot remember, we are compelled to repeat.

10. (T) (F) Kahn (1991) believes that transference in everyday life is a typical manifestation of being human.

11. (T) (F) Individuals who are not aware of their transferences are likely to displace onto the object of the transference negative feelings that were previously repressed.

12. (T) (F) Rutan and Stone (1993) feel that dreams, although very interesting, are of no use in group therapy.

13. (T) (F) Freud (1912) perceived transference as an ego defense mechanism. He saw this phenomenon as a form of displacement, as it was taking from one situation and displacing it onto another.

14. (T) (F) Repressed material is often easily available for voluntary retrieval if individuals are sincere about understanding their conflicts.

15. (T) (F) In some cases, transference can become a self-fulfilling prophecy. It is not uncommon for a client to try to manipulate the relationship with the therapist to recreate the initial conflict.

16. (T) (F) Ormont (1992) writes, "Many therapists who work with patients individually believe, as Freud posited, that the resolution of the transference is virtually synonymous with cure."

17. (T) (F) Freud did not feel that countertransference was an obstacle to psychotherapy.

18. (T) (F) Freud's later followers felt that countertransference was an obstacle to psychotherapy and that Freud was completely wrong in his belief.

19. (T) (F) Kahn (1991) divided countertransference into four distinct categories: (1) realistic responses, (2) responses to the transference, (3) responses to material troubling to the therapist, and (4) characteristic responses of the therapist.

20. (T) (F) Characteristic responses of the therapist generally reflect the therapist's personality. If the therapist is defensive outside of the consultation room, it is quite probable that the therapist is defensive inside the consultation room.

21. (T) (F) According to Kahn (1991), there are five areas that can elicit countertransference: (1) issues of greater importance to the therapist than the client, (2) vicariously using clients to do things the therapist is incapable of doing, (3) use of subtle cues by the therapist to influence the client, (4) interventions that are not in the interest of the client, and (5) assuming a role that a client has determined for us.

22. (T) (F) Therapist interventions that are not in the interest of the client are self-serving.

23. (T) (F) Because group therapy is a multiclient format, a group member can have many transferences at the same time, which often develop more quickly than they would in individual psychotherapy.

24. (T) (F) The reason that transferences can develop more quickly in group is that other group members basically represent who they are as people and do not present the demeanor of a professional, who remains somewhat hidden.

25. (T) (F) The individual brings to the group his or her previous history of interpersonal relationships not only with individuals but also with groups of people.

26. (T) (F) According to Stein (1981), a leader who gratifies a client's need to have exclusive dialogue with the therapist in the group setting is effectively reinforcing the client's intragroup transferences.

27. (T) (F) Resistance by a client can rule out the operation of transference.

28. (T) (F) Ormont (1992) suggests that there are four ways for a therapist to recognize transferences in groups: (1) pervasiveness, (2) insistence, (3) excessiveness, and (4) displacement.

29. (T) (F) Insistence, according to Ormont (1992), is when group members, in the face of contradictory evidence, continue to perceive others according to their own perceptions and insist that these perceptions are accurate.

30. (T) (F) Excessiveness and displacement tend to work together. Group members who have excessive responses to a particular stimulus are displacing from an earlier relationship.

Chapter 10

A Case Study

Chapters 10 and 11 are included to acquaint the reader with the application and analyses of the different modalities described in Chapters 4 and 5 to a specific case. Other paradigms have also been introduced into this case analysis to further the acquisition of knowledge. Various senior clinicians, using different paradigms, gave graciously and generously of their time and expertise in analyzing this same case. It is my hope that the reader will find these analyses interesting and educational.

THE CASE

You are treating a young woman in group psychotherapy. She has been referred to you by another client whom you treated in group psychotherapy in the past. Her presenting problem is that she is uncomfortable with other people and is having very intense moments of anxiety in social situations.

You saw her three times in individual psychotherapy before she entered group. In those three sessions she related that she is twenty-six years old, unmarried, and has recently graduated from a prestigious law school. She also discloses that she spent most of her adolescence and early adulthood studying and preparing for her career, which she knows is approved of by her parents. In fact, she relates that she feels that most of her life has been lived for their approval.

The client's parents are both professionals. Her father is a neurologist and her mother a marine biologist. She feels that she has a good relationship with her parents as she has always been the supposedly "good child," never causing them any worry or concern. The client is the youngest, with two older sisters. One is thirty years old, a doctor, and married; and the other is thirty-two years old, an accountant, and married. As reported by the client, her relationship with her sisters has been good, although she feels there was a lot of academic competition in the family.

The client has been on approximately five dates in her entire life. She is attractive, bright, and articulate with fine insight into her personality. Although she has never been in any form of therapy, her analysis of herself, although limited in certain areas, is quite good. The client feels that perhaps group will help her with her social problem and at the same time give her greater insight into her personality.

Her first three nights of group are surprising because her disclosures are not typical of someone who is used to experiencing uncomfortable anxiety with strangers. She relates that she felt quite comfortable right from the beginning and believes it to be due to the accepting attitude of the other group members.

During her fourth night in group, the client discloses that she has felt an attraction to another woman in group. She relates that she felt it the first night and did not have the courage to even think about it, but that it has been intensifying as the group continues. This causes her distress as she has wondered over the past few years whether she was gay, but has been able to put it out of her mind because she has been preoccupied with her career. Also, being gay is egodystonic to her because she is aware that this would create enormous stress, tension, and upheaval in her family, with emotionally painful parental disapproval.

GROUP ANALYTICAL-MEDICAL MODEL APPROACH

Samuel I. Miles, MD, PhD
Associate Clinical Professor, Department of Psychiatry,
UCLA School of Medicine
Vice Clinical Chief, Department of Psychiatry,
Cedars-Sinai Medical Center
Private Practice, Los Angeles, California

Before I discuss this case and my approach to it, I would like to address some issues of evaluation that, I believe, must precede group treatment. I am a psychiatrist and a psychoanalyst. As a physician, I use the medical model. This entails a process of evaluation, diagnosis, and prescription of treatment. As a psychoanalyst, I find that the process of empathic understanding followed by explanation can be therapeutic.

Diagnosis means more than just reference to the latest manual from the APA [American Psychiatric Association]. It means determination of the current problem presented by the patient in the context of that person's life history. Only after this determination is made can I reasonably decide what course of treatment to recommend for that individual.

During my early individual sessions with a new patient, I generally explore that person's life history with regard to work, social, and intimate functioning. In the process I get a sense of that person's strengths, weaknesses, and coping styles. I try to answer the question of why this person has come to me at this time from as many perspectives as possible. I consider biological, social, and psychological factors that have an impact on the individual. I consider the person from the dynamic, genetic, structural, topographical, object, and self-object perspectives.

When considering a patient for group therapy, I also consider another factor: the fit between the patient and the potential group. Unless I am starting a new group, I have some familiarity with the members of the group I am considering, and how they work together. During the evaluation sessions I will think from time to time about how the new patient might respond to people in the group, and vice versa. I usually will not accept a person with a severe personality disorder or borderline organization for group therapy, because such people are often quite provocative and may be disruptive to other people in the group. In my experience, such patients do better with individual therapy.

This patient presents problems that appear to be either a social phobia or an anxiety disorder. She has some apparent identity problems related to her sense that she has lived her life for her parents' approval. I suspect that this need for approval and the associated identity problems may play an important role in her anxiety. Group therapy appears to be an appropriate avenue to clarify, understand, and possibly resolve these issues.

On the other hand, the identity problems outlined by the patient may reflect borderline pathology, which may present a relative contraindication to group treatment. I would evaluate this possibility carefully prior to the invitation for the first group session.

In regard to her dating history, I would carefully evaluate her sexual identity in individual sessions prior to commencement of group. I would want to know why she has been on only five dates. I would ask about her sexual experiences, both heterosexual and homosexual, as well as her fantasies while masturbating. If I determined that sexual identity problems are prominent, I would recommend individual treatment, rather than group therapy, until the sexual identity issues are less problematic.

As a group therapist, my role is similar to my role as a psychoanalyst. Through my immersion in the group experience, I attempt to understand what is going on and to explain it. I intervene when I see resistance to the group functions of support and understanding, or when the cohesiveness of the group appears to be threatened. Using my knowledge of the individuals in the group, and of the group as an entity that acts as more than the sum of its individual members, I constantly try to understand what the group is doing, both consciously and unconsciously.

One of the first things I recognize as this new member joins the group is that a discrepancy exists between the young woman's description of her discomfort and her presentation in the group. She says that she feels comfortable in the group because other members are so accepting. Does she not feel accepted in other settings? Why not? If others do not ask these questions, I may, at an appropriate time. I probably would not ask too much at this time, because I do not want the new patient to feel uncomfortable. I would be thinking about these questions as I observe the group.

To some extent, the discrepancy worries me. I hope that her behavior represents strengths that the patient does not fully appreciate. However, I am concerned that it may signify a split of experience, such as a "false self" presentation. This implies narcissistic or borderline pathology with special therapeutic requirements. When this occurs, confrontation of the split represented by the emergence of the false self is a crucial component of therapy. This may not be compatible with the group's style. In severe cases, unless we are very confrontive, we may work for years on the facade presented by the patient without ever making genuine contact with the "true self." I will watch for more signs of this as the group goes on.

Her announcement during the fourth session that she feels attracted to another woman is probably a sign of resistance. A true erotic transference takes time to develop. Sexual feelings that are openly expressed so early in the course of therapy generally are covering other, more disconcerting feelings. Often, patients who had a conflicted early maternal relationship will become very uncomfortable with feelings of dependency aroused by the therapeutic situation. One way such people cope with the anxiety of the dependency is to eroticize the feelings.

Expressions of erotic feelings may also represent a sign of group difficulty. When a group is operating well, it is working on a task. When it does not work on a task for one reason or another, its functioning can be seen as regressed to one of several fixation points. The group may become focused on the activities of two of its participants, often in a sexualized manner. When this occurs the group is acting as a pairing group. (Other basic assumptions are the dependency group and the fight-or-flight group.)

I would review the recent history of the group to determine whether there is evidence for a pairing basic assumption process that is manifesting through this patient. I would look for evidence that the group is being thwarted in its tasks and is regressing. Evidence of other basic assumption phenomena in the process of the past few weeks may also indicate regression. Were there signs of excessive dependency? Did the group show signs of fight-or-flight phenomena?

If it appears that this is a pairing group, I would wonder why this patient is designated as a leader. Sometimes a group that has been operating in dependency mode will choose a new member to become part of a pairing. The unconscious fantasy may be that the union of the pair will yield a messiah who will deliver the group from its problems. I would look for evidence of this or other explanations for her assumption of this role.

I would also review the group interactions to determine whether the other woman or I was provoking the new patient's response. Was the other woman seductive? What have my interactions with the new patient been like? What have my interactions been with the other woman? How have the two women interacted? Is the new patient trying to please us (the group), or the subgroup of the other woman and me, or another subgroup through her expression of sexual interest?

Through consideration of these questions and the group's response, I would determine what intervention to make. I will intervene because I see a resistance to group or individual function. The major question for me is whether to address my intervention primarily to the individual patient or to the group as a whole. Once that decision is made, I look for an intervention which reflects the most significant affect which is relevant.

In a well-functioning appropriate group, I might explore with the client what she means when she says she "wondered whether she was gay." However, I would generally not expect to deal with this kind of question so early in treatment with a well-functioning patient. The fact that this issue is coming up at this time leads me again to consider the possibility that this patient has borderline pathology which I had missed. I would therefore be somewhat cautious, aware of the possibility that communication may be misunderstood because of splitting and projective identification. Thus, I will be prepared to intervene at times to clarify, set limits, and to interpret strong reactions when she experiences disruptions in her sense of connection.

I hope I have been able to describe adequately some of the issues I would consider in dealing with the clinical situation presented by this case. Much is left unanswered, as a group therapist must always be flexible and open to the unpredictability presented by the complexities of group interaction.

AN OCCUPATIONAL THERAPY APPROACH

Sharan L. Schwartzberg, EdD, OTR, FAOTA
Professor and Chair Mary Alicia Barnes, OTR
Level 1 Fieldwork Coordinator
Tufts University–Boston School of Occupational Therapy

An occupational therapy group may have a task focus or address a specific skill or subject matter (e.g., watercolor painting, exercise, healthy eating/cooking, social skills, stress management, leisure skills/planning, self-awareness).

In the presenting case, our observations as leaders would focus on the young woman's intra- and interpersonal functioning and her interactions with people and objects in the environment (e.g., interest, initiative, creativity). We would note her strengths and limitations (e.g., relatedness, self-regulation, level of anxiety, intra- and interpersonal boundary maintenance, verbal/nonverbal expression, judgment, insight). We would monitor her member roles (task, maintenance, and individual roles such as information giver or seeker, gatekeeper, recognition seeker) and redirect, provide, or encourage other members to provide feedback, or limit-set her verbalizations/disclosures as needed.

Because we have a client-centered occupational therapy philosophy, our approach would be to incorporate the young woman's wish to improve her comfort and to decrease her anxiety in social situations into her group contract as well as reflect this when explaining the overall purpose and goals of the group. We would hypothesize that her need for approval and the past academic competitiveness that seemed to serve as a form of sibling rivalry may display themselves in her performance in the group as seeking approval, permission, and/or praise from the leaders regarding when to begin tasks, what task to perform, how exactly to perform tasks, what the leaders want, and generally related to her and others' participation in the group (i.e., amount or type of sharing/disclosure, time/attention given to each member or other members).

We would use the example of role models of homosexual and heterosexual orientation. The use of current examples of role models in real life or fiction would set a tone of acceptance and increased safety for everyone in the group and help members apply what is learned in the group to day-to-day life.

In closing, we suggest that the leaders continue to monitor this member's possible use of defenses to avoid direct interactions (i.e., receiving feedback, confrontation), transference, and family projections in the group to other members or toward the leaders.

PROCESS-DIRECTED GROUP WORK APPROACH

Avraham Cohen, MA, RCC, CCC
Instructor, Vancouver Community College
Private Practice, Vancouver, British Columbia, Canada

This approach views human beings both as individuals and as members of a larger community. Experience can be explored in depth and breadth in various realms, including the interactive relationship between the individual, the group, and cultural, social, political, and spiritual contexts. The reflection of groups in the individual and the converse are also examined, as well as the time frames of past, present, and future. Experience is examined in the realms of emotion, cognition, sensation, movement, dreams, and imagination.

The role of the leader, or leaders, is to facilitate and also, at times, to be a conscious participant (Cohen, 1996). The leader needs to have a capacity for self-awareness, the ability to pay attention to events in the group, a capacity to be in the presence of strong emotions, a capacity for and interest in intimate relationships, a potential for being with people in creative ways, and a capacity for exercising metaskills of fluidity and flexibility (Mindell, 1995).

Given all this, how then do we understand the experience of our new group member and the group? Attention is paid to two general categories of information: primary process, information that is conscious, and secondary process, information that is not conscious. Our new member has come into an ongoing group process, which can be seen as reflective of the entry and reception process in any group, organization, or community. So, what actually happens? She reports that she feels comfortable and that the group is accepting of her. The group seems to represent the opposite polarity to her family of origin. If the group, at this point, is indeed accepting of her, then the group can work with this primary process experience by offering an opportunity to elaborate on the atmosphere of acceptance, sharing impressions and giving feedback. The facilitator can be curious about and interested in the process as it is and can be open to any emerging themes or issues.

What we have, speculatively, is an instance of a lived-out, idealized community and, for the moment, the group has emerged in its own Garden of Eden. This secondary process, the dream of the group, potentially provides material with which we can work.

As the facilitator I remember the client's original, privately expressed social fears, and at this point I am content to allow the process to unfold.

On the fourth night the young woman discloses her attraction to another woman in the group. This represents a potential rupture in the "family" culture and creates the conditions for expulsion from the garden. She has decided to say here what would be unacceptable to say to her own family. Why has she done this? We can speculate that she really feels this group to be accepting. She has consciously or unconsciously decided to go over her own edge, that is, her own limits of identity.

For the group this also represents a rupture. The initial impression of the new member is changed. The issue of diversity has emerged (Mindell, 1992). The group has an issue both collectively and individually. It is reasonable to expect and, in fact, invite a whole range of responses from the group and at the right moment suggest that we are representing and working on the process of the mainstream culture as well as our own. It will be important to acknowledge all the parts, including those that are unspoken and those represented by members who remain silent. In this approach those who do not speak are acknowledged as representing a valuable part of the group. They can be invited to speak and if they choose not to do so, then that can also be appreciated as a valid contribution. It is also important to note that the recipient of this expression of lesbian attraction will most likely have been moved to a personal edge.

As the facilitator, I want to identify and invite in all the experiences, and at the same time look for potential moments for integration. Every integration experience represents a new level that eventually has the potential to be a staging place for confronting the next edge, going over that edge, and reintegrating at the next level. It is important to have the awareness that edges, which are places of non-integration, can be valuable places in and of themselves for the group and for individuals. Going over an edge is only one of many possibilities.

Let us refocus for now. How can all this help the client and all the group members in their pursuit of growth, awareness, and resolution of personal problems? As a process-directed facilitator I am often in a stance of not-knowing. This is a special kind of not-knowing. It is conscious. I want to remain open to all possibilities that are inherent in the situation. From this position I am able to facilitate the group's process and the individual processes, including that of our newcomer. I may be aware of personal agendas that I have, and to the best of my ability I will not act on these unconsciously. One way I can deal with my own agendas is to acknowledge them to the group. It is hoped that the young lady will have an optimal opportunity to integrate any projected aspects of herself, and particularly those of the idealized family. This can help her to stand more firmly on her own feet with less concern for the opinions of others and firmer knowledge of her own purpose and direction. For the group, perhaps she represents an instance of diversity that can help them collectively and individually to recognize their own propensity to marginalize others, their experience, and parts of themselves. Through this process everyone can learn something about contact, intimacy, and the shadowy dimensions that block this.

This approach asks a lot of the facilitator and participants, and offers a great deal in return. There is intent to be "deeply democratic" as described by Mindell (1992); that is, to acknowledge all aspects of experience and bring these diverse experiences into the moment-to-moment process. This facilitates the integration of disowned aspects of the group and its members, and also provides a direct experience of being fully alive in the moment in the intentional community of the group. The group's goal is to be in a process of discovery, both personal and collective, about the nature, meaning, and ethics of being human.

REALITY THERAPY APPROACH

Lawrence Kreisberg, MS
Private Practice, Plantation, Florida

First, a brief overview of the principles of reality therapy, which were first published by William Glasser in the book *Reality Therapy* (1980). The basic premise is that each individual is solely responsible for his or her behavior. There are eight steps that encompass the work of reality therapy: (1) develop a therapeutic relationship, (2) focus on the current behavior of the client, (3) ask the client to evaluate this behavior, (4) develop plans for change, (5) get a commitment, (6) do not accept excuses, (7) refuse to use punishment, and (8) never give up on the client. Obviously, when working in a group setting it may be difficult to achieve each of these steps as one might in individual therapy. However, the general theory of clients taking responsibility, following through, setting goals, and so on is definitely an aspect of treatment that can be addressed in group therapy.

Perhaps the most important notion in reality therapy is that when people's needs, such as self-worth, belonging, and controlling their own destinies, are not being met, they experience emotional pain, disappointment, and are generally dissatisfied with their lives. This is the premise that seems to be at play in this case. It is important to note that reality therapy puts emphasis on therapists being themselves. This may eventually lead them to explore their need to please and to be hidden behind the "image of therapist," and to play the role of the mother or father. Therapists should be active, involved, and help guide clients to set specific plans of action. Reality therapists need to be confrontive yet sensitive and open to themselves about their own personal life struggles.

First, it is important that the client learn to take responsibility for the underlying hostile feelings toward her parents, who have obviously set up a great deal of competition between her and her sisters. As I believe group therapy re-creates a family, I feel that she would be comfortable in group, as the group represents an accepting, nonjudgmental, noncompetitive family environment for her underlying feelings and attractions to surface, something her family helped her to repress. It is also a place where she can set goals, make a commitment, and gain healthy support in reaching her goals.

Because reality therapy encourages a person to experience the full spectrum of feelings and encourages the client to follow through on those feelings (taking responsibility), I would encourage her to be able to eventually confront her parents on the following: her feelings of having to achieve in order to feel accepted; her sexuality (if she is indeed attracted to women); and most likely her underlying people-pleasing behavior in general. This would eventually lead her to an acceptance of herself, thus meeting her needs of belonging, acceptance, and self-worth.

As the therapist, it is important for me to be myself, to be non-judgmental of the client's feelings and attractions, and to support the client in maintaining a focus on the goals she has set. I would be confrontive with her during periods of resistance, and I would be supportive of her strength at exploring her issues. I would be open about my own struggles in psychotherapy, and relate these experiences to her when appropriate.

All of this would hopefully allow her to develop a key aspect of reality therapy: personal control and responsibility for her thoughts, feelings, and behaviors. She would then be better able to fulfill her basic needs, which in this case involves coming to terms with her sexuality, letting go of her need to be accepted through having to achieve, and becoming a "healthy adult" rather than a "good child." Of course, this would occur over a period of time, and I would supplement her group therapy with weekly individual psychotherapy.

A FAMILY ART THERAPY SYSTEMS APPROACH

Ellen G. Horovitz, PhD, ATR-BC
Director of Graduate Art Therapy, Associate Professor,
Nazareth College
Private Practice, Rochester, New York

Group therapy dynamics are not unlike that of a family, albeit an extended one. Hence, the first point of departure would be to construct a genogram for this new member within the first sessions of our individual contacts (see Figure 10.1).

This woman, whom I will hereby refer to fictitiously as Lois, would have also been advised that all group members would have their genograms posted each session within the room. The initiation into the group setting would entail visually sharing that information every group session and referring to the genogramatic constructs of each group member as relevant issues surfaced. Thus, the tempo of this group in time would begin to mirror the family constellation for each group member. This levels the playing field for the art therapist as well as the group members since familial projection almost always surfaces within a group context.

Since neither religiosity nor cultural background was stated in the presenting information, it is difficult to know exactly what Lois's belief systems and/or mythical stories were as handed down from her elders. As a result, true familial investigation will be sketchy at best.

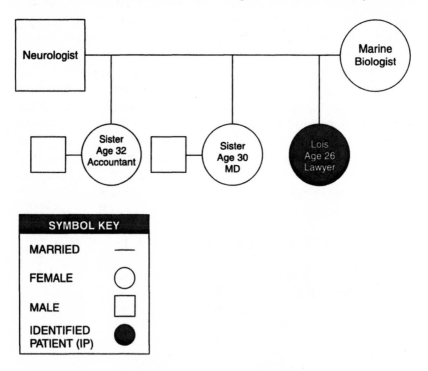

FIGURE 10.1. Lois's Genogram

What is known, however, based on Lois's intake information, is that the maxim in her family clearly underscored the importance of education. The old maxim used by real estate brokers that cries, "location, location, location" could be equivocally adopted by Lois's family system if it were supplanted with "education, education, education." Achievement, success, and academic competition seemed to reign supreme in this household. As well, if one were to adopt an Adlerian attitude, one could easily ascertain that Lois's position as the youngest child might also be replete with a continual need to measure up to the older sisters' academic and personal relationship successes. With these factors in mind, perhaps the BATA (Belief Art Therapy Assessment) would also contribute more information to the plan for treatment (Horovitz-Darby, 1994). (This assessment rules out religiosity as a predictor of pathology.) Knowing full well that culture and belief weaves our history and shapes our responses to the world around us, as the conductor of this art therapy group I would pay attention to this factor in how it tethers the group members and/or splits them asunder.

Still another unknown is how the other group members responded to Lois's proclamation that she felt an attraction to another group member. I am also assuming that this group contains only female members. Since there is no information about the response of the admired member, as the family art therapist my first stance might be to verbally flush that out and do some artwork regarding that if deemed necessary.

So assuming all of the aforementioned information, I would then pay attention to the following of Lois's struggles: cultural/familial influences; sexual identity issues; generalized anxiety of Lois (and now perhaps some of the other group members); and her need for unconditional regard.

The Group Meeting—The Family Meal

Assuming that we meet after Lois's declaration toward the other group member, after initial settling I would start the group out by simply recounting where we left off and bring up Lois's pronouncement from the previous week. Since I would be throwing this out on the proverbial art therapy table (pun intended), I might suggest that we set tonight's table around this discussion. At that point, as we begin to process the verbal reflections on Lois's admission, I would set the theme of literally setting the (art) table around this point of departure. (Since family dinners are generally a commonality for most family systems, the suggestion to "set the table" might take on a host of meanings. The idea of gathering and preparing for a meal could take place as well as the creation of an actual meal.) As well, I would open the art studio to use all materials from two- to three-dimensional media.

Next, while the members were busily deciding on the setting of the table as well as the items that were needed to create this gathering space, this sacred holding tank, I would be duly noting a variety of actions: Who took on the role of leader? What was Lois's response to the task? Did it mirror her one-down role attached to her own family system? Did she try to placate the leader or other members of the group? If she tried out the role of leader, was it fractured with insecurities, anxieties, and the competitive stance mirrored in her genogramatic issues? What did the members create to bring to the sacred dinner table? How did that dovetail with their family-of-origin issues? I am sure the reader gets the general idea by now.

The Artwork

As an art therapist, one of the most fascinating aspects is the approach to the art materials. Is it labored, free, chock-full of anxiety, developmentally regressed, anxious, tense, angry, hesitant? Some of these nonverbal cues offer insights not only into the product but also, more important, into the process of its creation. In art therapy, the focus is not only on formed art expression (although always welcomed) but also on the person's response to the plastic media. These telling clues offer insight into the maker's mental status and offer a mini-diagnostic at every session. The careful attention to detail versus a haphazard approach to the materials offers much information to the well-trained practitioner. Then, of course, there is the verbal chitchat back and forth among group members. Like a coffee klatch where group members' exchange is a free-form prattle, the discourse somehow mirrors real-life situations.

The Table Setting

Just as the making of the artwork offers telltale clues into the inner psyches of the participants, what about the seating arrangement itself? How did the structure of the group members change when the direction of creating a meal was proffered? Did the seating reflect family systems positioning? Most likely the answer to this will be mirrored in both the artistic and concurrent verbal responses. How was the table finally arranged? What did each member bring to the table setting? What offering was a member making to the sacred dining space and what did each member offer of herself to this hallowed space? What information resulted from the directive to create a table setting? Who brought the issues of the following week to the table (guised in art forms) and why? What resolve came from bringing Lois's issue to the table?

The Container

As participants created their artwork and verbalized their feelings about the directive, what was Lois's reaction to the members and the art which they brought to the table? Did the woman whom Lois admired offer up a symbolic container that married Lois to her unconditional nurturance bait? Was this perhaps the underlying attraction for Lois, or was it truly wedded to sexual attraction? Perhaps it was not either/or but both/and.

I am a great believer in symbols being myriad and replete with inner meaning for both the maker and the receiver. In art therapy sessions, even if one does not pay attention to this possibility, it clearly exists. No symbol has meaning unless digested, informed, and owned by its viewer (Horovitz, 1999). The same is true in artwork as well as the verbal associates secured to the representations. It is the responsibility of the art therapy clinician to lead participants toward this end. Often the artwork connects these symbolic offerings as easily as tributaries to lakes. The artwork is the catalyst, the glue, the never-goes-away weekly reminder to each group member as to what trail is being traveled. Artwork offers a continual reminder of what was and perhaps what will be.

ANALYSIS USING THE PSYCHODRAMATIC MODALITY APPROACH

Thomas Treadwell, EdD, TEP
Professor of Psychology,
Director of Group Psychotherapy, Psychodrama, and Sociometry
West Chester University, West Chester, Pennsylvania

The psychodramatic model is a collaborative approach—a team-work concept utilizing group members and a director to meet a protagonist's goals. It is problem focused, emphasizing the present. In brief, the psychodramatic model has three stages. Stage one, the warm-up stage, when the director uses group data to ready the group for action, identifies common group terms, and a protagonist is selected to represent the most dominant topic. Stage two is the action component, in which the protagonist's conflicts are acted out with the assistance of group members playing auxiliary roles. Stage three is the sharing and analysis stage. The analysis is usually done at the beginning of the next group meeting.

Stage One

In this case, NGM (new group member, the young woman) was selected to represent the group inadequacy. NGM was selected by the group to explore issues of inadequacy. The director has seen NGM three times in individual therapy and observed her during four group sessions, thus having some understanding of her presenting problem. The diagnoses that might be considered are social phobia and an identity disorder. However, ruling out avoidant personality features is an area the director should keep in mind.

The director first establishes that NGM is twenty-six, recently graduated from law school, and feels comfortable with her parents, although she mentions that most of her life she has been following her parents' directions at the expense of her own interests. The director clarifies that a primary reason she felt that the group was helpful was due to her fear of being uncomfortable in social settings. This fear, accompanied by her positive reaction toward this group, suggests a direction that the director and protagonist need to test.

Stage Two

The first step would be to ask the protagonist, "What area of inadequacy shall we explore this evening?" Asking the protagonist a straightforward question will usually set the agenda for the session. In this case, she wants to look at her family and why the "good child" is still with her. She also states that her parents would be very shocked to hear that she was attending group therapy.

Director has NGM develop and set a scene with the entire family—asking her to define the situation for clarification to the director and the group. Questions asked include: where are we, what is taking place, what age are you, define room and describe what is taking place in here, what time of day or evening, etc. To learn about the significant others in her life, auxiliary egos are selected from the group to play the roles of her mother, father, and two sisters. To learn about each role, the director has the protagonist role reverse with each significant other. The director interviews NGM in the role of mother, father, sister 1, and sister 2 so that each auxiliary person has information to respond to while in role. With this specific case the director should have a double for NGM. Usually, the protagonist selects all auxiliaries. The director (using data from intake, group data, etc.) sets the situation to be tested. In this case the director has NGM initiate the conversation with a significant other, that is, Dad, explaining that she is fearful of failing as an attorney.

The interaction between parents and siblings gives the director and group a view of how NGM handles herself with significant others and how significant others handle her idea of forthcoming failure. The director has to conceptualize how her thinking influences her mood and behavior based on the data gathered. The director moves from situation to situation, following the protagonist and keeping in mind the overall theme of inadequacy and NGM's question about why she never deviated from her parents' wishes.

Once the director has explored these issues, the group can move to social situations involving comfort levels. (More than likely, this theme will emerge from the scenes with significant others, although the director should complete the initial agreement with protagonist before moving on.) Have protagonist define the situation and let NGM set up the scene as illustrated previously. Using techniques of role reversal, doubling, and interview in role reversal, the director and group can gain a clearer understanding of NGM. Director and group members see her thinking pattern and behavioral response in anxiety-causing social settings. Depending on the information gained from these two situations the director may then decide to move on to the attraction issue, or perhaps the behavioral data suggest that such an issue should be delayed for another group session.

The action of the session cuts through verbal denial and helps the NGM focus on underlying issues. The use of action permits the protagonist to take control of her situation and effect positive change. It gives the protagonist a chance to see how she responds to events, thinking patterns, and behaviors in her life. She can then make concrete, conscious decisions about how to change and can practice these new behaviors in the safe, supportive environment of the group.

Stage Three

The last psychodramatic stage is sharing and analysis. The protagonist listens as group members share their life experiences related to the basic theme. Auxiliaries have the opportunity to "de-role," that is, to express cognitively and behaviorally the feelings that were attached to the roles they enacted. The "in-role" sharing is important to the protagonist and group, allowing the auxiliaries time to reintegrate and be themselves. This gives the protagonist a chance to hear what that role was like as perceived by another. Analysis is usually not incorporated at this phase, but reserved for the beginning of the next group session. The analysis or processing becomes the warm-up of the next session.

PSYCHOANALYTIC OBJECT RELATIONAL GROUP THERAPY APPROACH

Bennet E. Roth, PhD
Faculty and Fellow, Institute for Psychoanalytic
Training and Research
Faculty, Adelphi Post Doctoral Program in Group Therapy
Member, International Psychoanalytical Association
Private Practice, New York City

It must be stated from the onset that my remarks are hypothetical, for I am at some considerable distance from the patient. Contact with the patient is an invaluable source of information about what the patient wants us to know about her. There are, of course, elements of her personality that she does not want us to know and other conflicts that she herself does not know, and those that are unformed in symbolic terms. A glimmer of these can be found in our interaction with the patient in individual sessions or in the group.

She presents as a socially inhibited young woman who seeks approval from parental authority; in other words, she is highly sensitized to what others want of her and in particular what her parents want. With such a presentation she reveals to me that she has avoided the usual developmentally necessary conflicts of adolescence and the separateness and affect discharge that emerge from those conflicts. Her occupational choice seems to confirm this form of behavior; she seeks highly structured work environments in which authority is present and clear.

I have a particular interest in how people enter group therapy setups. Freud hypothesized that the two main effects of joining a group are regression and a view of the group leader as the ego ideal. The term *ego ideal* has a number of complex translations varying from superego functions to wishes for a charismatic leader. This woman entered her group without the usual anxiety associated with being in a group. Where is her anxiety? How is it expressed? Why is she not viewing the leader as "ideal"?

Wilfred Bion, an explorer of the unconscious life of groups, observed what he considered to be the universal need to pair in a group. That is, to find an ego-syntonic other that has psychic importance. I have found that there are many ways that people pair in a group, both positively and negatively. They find someone to talk to, to empathize with, to fight with, to have erotic fantasies about, and to want to expel from the group. Bion believed that pairing is an expression of some valence within each member of the pair, some aspect of the group's functioning, and some unexpressed, deeply unconscious elements that are part of the transference to the leader of the group.

Other hypotheses can be made about the patient and the group. The entire group may not have had a spokesperson (BA leader) for erotic fantasies, for wishes to be close to people other than the leader, or for unacceptable thoughts. Here, two ideas need explanation; first I will explain the BA leader. Bion assumed that the person verbalizing a conflict was a "basic assumption leader" (BA) speaking for the entire group's unconscious feeling in which the person speaking had the strongest valence for that unconscious conflict. It follows that the group has struggled to express closeness and erotic feeling and that this patient is the BA leader for the entire group's conflict as well as her own.

The patient has failed to accept the group leader as her "ideal," indicating some deeply internal conflicts with the leader of the group. In the place of idealizing the leader, she has provoked a fantasy relationship with a female member of the group. This is likely an attempt to solve her unexpressed anxiety in joining the group. It also has another very deep meaning for her behavior. She has hidden her feelings for the other members of the group by saying "how warm and accepting" the people are when she hardly knows them. In other words, she has employed a social strategy to a psychological situation by being polite and flattering and thereby attempting to control the group members' reactions to her behavior. People who continually behave this way are trying to be the therapist's "right-hand man" in the group, an interesting, symbolic, and very important role that needs to be interpreted. When a woman assumes the "right-hand man" position, she usually has sexual identity conflicts.

Transference to the leader of the group is of paramount importance, especially in the entrance phase. The leader, in reality, must contain the group's anxiety and hold reasonable rules for the group's behavior. Transference distortions of the leader will emerge as will unconscious projections of unconscious elements in the members' psychic lives. Transferences are the consistent distortions of a person. They are the result of unconscious expectancies that range from neurotic, to narcissistic, to psychotic in which the person's behavior is seen through the distorting lens of the patient's psychic past.

Within a psychoanalytic group there are vertical and horizontal transferences. The vertical is directed to the leader and the horizontal to the other members of the group. In this I am suggesting that the patient has bypassed an important aspect of her development, that is, her transference to the male (I assume) leader of the group by regressively seeking to have an erotic relationship with a female member of the group. She has at the same time assumed a "right-hand man" role in the group that is protective of herself and her identity problems. Obviously, this is the opening scene in a very complex treatment.

Although I have stated some far-reaching hypotheses regarding this patient, they are only hypotheses. Hypotheses trail after the group allowing tentative understandings of the complex interactions. That is, they will be confirmed, modified, or discarded as the treatment moves forward and as more information becomes known.

ADLER'S INDIVIDUAL PSYCHOLOGY APPROACH

Joshua M. Gross, PhD
Licensed Psychologist, Florida State University
Counseling Center
Supervisor, Predoctoral APA Internship Site
Private Practice, Tallahassee, Florida

I first note that this young woman is overdependent upon her work task in relationship to the making of friends, love, and money triptych that is central to individual psychology. The bottom line is, she is smart and comes from a smart family, probably one that emphasizes academic and professional achievement over and above personal needs and experiences. The competition with the two older same-sex siblings and the superficial good relations with the parents suggest that there are many complicated and conflicted feelings in this young professional woman. We would probably sniff this out in our first few hours of individual consultation.

The downside of a highly developed intellectual stance is the absence of the more tenuous sense of personal feeling and experience. This sounds like a very outwardly successful family and one that is a breeding ground for unconscious and unaware experiences that may be at odds with the family norms and expectations. This woman is subject to having two doctoral parents and a pair of highly achieving older siblings. The older two siblings are so close together that they are likely prone to competition between themselves. Our patient, then, has four older folks to deal with. The four- and six-year differences in age with the two older sisters sets her apart from them and she is likely prone to have been a loner in the family. Who was there for her? Did she have the space to know who she is in terms of her gender identity or her appetites and interests in general?

Obviously, she has been outwardly successful in the work realm. She has a great education, enough money to see a high-end mental health professional, friends who are in therapy. But does she know how to have fun? What are her social, recreational, spiritual, sensual, sexual, and personal feelings?

Group composition is an important theme here. I am a firm believer in heterogeneity in groups and so I believe that the issue of same-sex attraction is tolerable regarding her ability to work it out in the group. Obviously, the group tone and tenor is good enough for her to have an experience and feeling on the first night and then to mull it over for three more weeks and finally talk it out.

The issues surrounding gay versus straight are not free from politics. Some say they know from the beginning. Some seem to find out over time. Much of this range has to do with the experience of having acceptance in the family of origin that allows an expression and consciousness of one's core identity. I can see how this family would be a breeding ground for her to be unaware of her true core sexual identity. The continuing course of her overworked lifestyle would again support her lack of awareness of her underlying feelings and experiences. By focusing on work and future goals rather than dating she is able to avoid discovering feelings that fly in the face of her highly demanding and success-oriented family.

Would she view being gay as being unsuccessful? What would she guess her parents' reaction to be? Would her heterosexual older sisters be supportive? Is she really gay or is she responding to some other feelings that have been aroused by the supportive climate in the group?

The revelation of a gender-identity disturbance is frequently accompanied by a major panic and anxiety reaction. The therapist should plan accordingly. Much information is needed regarding her affective cues in the therapy situation for both individual and group work. I myself would tend to encourage her to stay in the group as long as the process was safe and productive. I do believe, however, that she would do well to undertake some individual work to sort out her real feelings and to use the group to try them out.

The group therapy setting is one of the few situations in which we can re-create our place in the family of origin once we have left the nest. In this case, it is paramount that she work through and accept her own feelings and experiences in the group. I believe that she will need the benefit of a combined individual and group psychotherapy treatment plan to achieve this goal. Much of the discovery will occur in both settings. The group will be the place where she can develop the ability to hold her feelings in the face of others. The individual work will be useful in terms of gaining support and understanding for many of the complexities and manipulations that got her into this situation in the first place.

HERE AND NOW–THERE AND THEN APPROACH

George Max Saiger, MD
Faculty, The Group Psychotherapy Training Program,
The Washington School of Psychiatry
Director, The Center for Study for Psychotherapies
for the Aging, The Washington School of Psychiatry
Fellow, American Group Psychotherapy Association
Private Practice, Rockville, Maryland

This young woman professes to be ill-at-ease in social situations and in situations that require intimacy. A good beginning question would ask why an intelligent, economically secure, and attractive twenty-six-year-old has had only five dates in her lifetime. Yet it is no big surprise that this woman felt so comfortable during her first three group sessions and that she was able to follow the rules of group so well as to disclose psychologically salient material with relative ease. It is a situation that she recognizes: she must compete with other psychologically insightful peers in this group to secure the approval and the love of the powerful leader/therapist. She takes to it like a duck to water. This is her family-of-origin situation, and she knows how to play it well.

But trouble looms: from the first night she becomes aware that she has something to disclose that truly frightens and shames her—a same-sex attraction. She has a terrible dilemma. To disclose *that* might well help her forge ahead in the good-group-member competition and win considerable favor from the therapist. Balanced against that is not only the parental disapproval that she consciously believes would follow her claim of a lesbian identity, but also a diminishing of her own sense of self-worth. It might, in some profound way, erase her competitive advantage in the group. Rather impulsively, I think, she has resolved the dilemma by going ahead with her strategy of disclosing in the group session whatever is important to her. "Truly" gay or not, she has come out.

The therapist, too, has a dilemma. The therapist wants to foster openness, but an open-and-honest approach is not coextensive with a therapeutic process. For the patient to move from disclosing to continue to be the good child to disclosing to examine her life and to change, something very profound has to happen. She has to come to feel that the group is a safe place. There is no reason to believe it has yet become that for her. The therapist needs to find a way of welcoming this disclosure as part of the group's life, while deferring close examination of it until he or she attends to the safety of the group.

Furthermore, the patient's hasty disclosure might delay its becoming safe. This is because, in my experience, people are loath to admit prejudices (including homophobia) in group. So, she is likely to be met with a chorus of disclaimers that no one in *this* group is prejudiced. That is a lie, of course; heterosexism is rife in our society, and members of therapy groups (even gay members) are not exempt. Safety will be experienced when the group is able to disclose its prejudices and, unlike her parents, to let her cause them "worry and concern" while still valuing and embracing her.

Several boundary issues in group help ensure safety: attention to confidentiality, a contract about out-of-group contact, limits about physical (as opposed to verbal) contact, and time boundaries, for example. In this situation, I would surely prefer to be working in a group in which there is no physical hugging (no matter how asexual the huggers might insist it is) and no opportunity for social contact outside the group sessions. That is to say, I would find it hard to work with enactments of any sort, which might interfere with verbal interchange.

One avenue the therapist has to further this process of making the group a safe place is to encourage an exploration of diversity within the group. This must not be limited to issues of sexual orientation. Indeed, the process will be augmented if multiple issues of diversity are addressed. Mixed-gender groups are preferable, since the difference between the male and female experience is often the one that members can most easily approach. Race, age, economic station, and religion are other issues which could also provide a focus for such exploration.

Of the modalities that have been discussed in this book, this approach is nearest to the here-and-now modality. However, as I hope is clear from the foregoing discussion, working in the here and now requires sensitivity to the there and then, to the real-life problem solving that members of minorities must face, and to knowing the properties of the systems impinging on the group. I probably borrow from other modalities as well.

Chapter 11

A Case Study, Continued

SYSTEMIC GROUP THERAPY APPROACH

Randolph C. Moredock, PhD, MFT, NCC
Counseling Center, Hazen Hall
State University of New York at Brockport

Group therapy is a mode of treatment in which several clients come together with one or two facilitators to create a safe atmosphere in which growth can take place. It should be noted that I have practiced group therapy from a systems perspective for many years and that some of the comments contained in this case review come from that experiential base.

From a systems point of view, change in a group setting occurs as clients act out family roles, project feelings about family onto other group members, and become more intimately acquainted with their family dynamics. Clients learn how these family dynamics played a part in the development of their personalities as well as how family patterns continue to affect their day-to-day functioning.

Typical tasks for group therapists include facilitating communication, ensuring emotional and physical safety, and utilizing intergroup dynamics to facilitate growth. Practitioners utilizing a systems perspective have additional tasks that include helping clients to: (1) clearly identify roles they played within their families, (2) examine family rules and dynamics that mediate their behavior (e.g., loyalty to family [Boszormenyi-Nagy and Ulrich, 1981]), and (3) develop appropriate enactments within the group that will help them test new roles and explore new parts of their identities (Minuchin, 1974).

As clients progress in the group and gain insights into their family functioning, they become able to develop a position within their family units that is more consistent with who they are as individuals separate from family influences. The notion of "formulating a position" means that clients will be able to look at their families more objectively, acknowledge their current behavior patterns within the family, and make intentional decisions about what reformulations, if any, they will undertake. However, the position will now be theirs and not be mediated primarily by family influence. This is not to say that each client will ultimately confront family members, but clients will establish the roles and responses that they choose for themselves.

Applicability of Systems Theory to the Current Case

From a systems perspective, it appears that the client has had little chance to develop her sense of self separate from her family. This is speculated because she is quoted as saying, "she feels that most of her life has been lived for their [the family's] approval." References are also made in the case material to the client "preparing for her career, which she knows is approved of by her parents." Finally, she fears intense family upheaval if she reveals her homosexual feelings. Bowen (1985) would discuss the client's identity issues from the point of view of her not being able to appropriately separate herself from her family unit. Boszormenyi-Nagy and Ulrich (1981) would talk about the woman's attachment to her family in terms of an exaggerated sense of family loyalty. In either case, the client has been greatly restricted in her growth because of conscious and perhaps unconscious family influences.

The anxiety the client reports may be caused by her fear that secrets about herself will be revealed that are dystonic to the family-mediated identity she has carefully cultivated. Since she anticipates censure from her family, she may also anticipate disapproval from others outside the family. To the extent that she has incorporated family values, the client may also be angry with herself for having homosexual feelings. In addition, she is about to embark on an adult life (in law) that she may feel is personally unsatisfying but that fulfills her family's expectations.

Her primary tasks for the group vis-à-vis her family and the rules she has adopted are (1) to develop a better sense of self both personally and apart from her family, (2) negotiate more age-appropriate roles and power relationships with her family, and (3) formulate a position with respect to her family that she will find more satisfying and that will allow her to more fully express herself within her family.

According to the case material, the client quickly began participating in the group. She attributed her rapid involvement to the accepting attitude of the group. The client's unexpected level of disclosure would be consistent with someone who has been motivated most of her life by the need for approval and who is finally receiving genuine approval. On the other hand, her behavior may also indicate a person who is socially naive and who has not been permitted to develop strong personal boundaries. The latter hypotheses are based on the client's avoidance of social situations heretofore, coupled with her tendency to give power to others.

In either case, the client suggests two contradictory aspects about her lesbian feelings to her family. The client describes her family as a unit that is powerful and capable of administering harsh punishments. Yet she also fears that they might not be able to withstand the internal conflict caused by learning information about a family member that is counter to the prevailing family ideal. Concomitantly, the client characterizes herself as someone who will be at the mercy of family reprisals but who can bring the family down by merely sharing some discordant aspect of her personality.

Because this client has operated from a one-down position most of her life, it may be extremely difficult for her to acknowledge that she has significant power within her family. The group context lends itself well to the resolution of the power dilemma because she will find peers in the group who share similar feelings. This is speculated because the issue of power is frequently a point of contention for dysfunctional families. The client will not only find those with whom she can identify in the group, she can also begin to test her ability to influence others by asserting herself in the group.

Using the group to explore new roles and interactional patterns should set the stage for the client to try new behaviors in relationships outside the group. Given the information provided, it is difficult to predict whether she will try radically different behaviors within her family. One task of the group facilitator will be to help the client clarify the reasons behind her views of her family. For example, have other family members been emotionally cut off for expressing discordant ideas, or have there been discussions about the "moral inappropriateness" of homosexual behavior? Once the client is able to develop an accurate view of her family, she can then begin to plan a course of action.

The facilitator can assist the client in this process by helping her to project as accurately as possible the potential range of family responses. Group members can be utilized to role-play the family confrontation to even better prepare for the anticipated interchange.

Even if the client decides that she does not wish to risk confrontation with her family, the exercise of formulating an accurate picture of her family will have several benefits. First, by starting to look at her family more objectively, the client can take initial steps away from a childlike position toward a more age-appropriate stance vis-à-vis her family. Second, the client can begin to differentiate family dynamics from those operating in other relationships. She may find that she can act out "forbidden" roles in extrafamilial relationships without the same fear of and concern with censure. Finally, by looking at the family more objectively, the client can begin to humanize her family. This, in turn, sets the stage for resolution of unresolved feelings, mourning of the lost family ideal, and ultimately forgiveness or some degree of rapprochement.

DANCE/MOVEMENT THERAPY— THE LIVINGDANCE APPROACH

Danielle L. Fraenkel, PhD, ADTR, NCC, LPC
Director, *Kinections*
Adjunct Faculty, Nazareth College
Rochester, New York

Dance/Movement Therapy

Dance/movement therapy assumes that an individual's movement style reflects culture, personality, and mental status. Thus, "the body, is the prime source of information, the instrument of expression and the catalyst for change" (Fraenkel, 1983, p. 32). In groups, dance/movement therapy works to expand both individual and interactive movement repertoires. Such changes can affect total functioning because the body and mind are connected. A change in one effects a change in the other. Creative processes and healing factors inherent to dance build on this reciprocal relationship.

Rhythm, synchronous and echoed movement, repetition, the symbolic use of movement, and ritual are but a few of the curative factors now used in dance/movement therapy. They are critical, for example, to movement empathy, the kinesthetic analogue of reflection, paraphrase, and verbal empathy. Movement empathy, a cornerstone of dance/movement therapy, generates and supports the therapeutic alliance, group cohesion, and factors specific to a group's developmental stage.

LivingDance

LivingDance works with natural movement that does not require training or talent. Grounded in the artistic interplay between form (technique) and content (expression), LivingDance works with the interactions among movement parameters that relate to psychological constructs and the affective, cognitive, and behavioral responses they evoke. The dance/movement therapist tends to this dynamic interplay by adopting one of four roles: teacher/director, witness/observer, choreographer, or dancer (Fraenkel, 2001). Initially, the therapist guides group members' actions, but eventually group members learn how to work more nondirectively. Whether directive or nondirective, the process draws upon the power of creativity and the innate capacity to heal. Methods include sensory awareness, creative dance, Somato-Respiratory Integration (Epstein and Altman, 1994), and improvisations related to specific psychological constructs.

Shape—A Kinesthetic Link to Identity Development

Shape, one of the movement parameters of LivingDance, is particularly relevant to this client, whom I will call FL (female lawyer). Shape refers to the kinesthetic sense of the body boundary, a somatic connection to identity development and the individual's relationship to self and others.

Theorists agree that identity is rooted in infancy. However, there are differences in perspective. Erik Erikson (1959) refers, for example, to a baby's need to master the conflict between trust versus mistrust during the first year of life. Feminists such as Wastell (1996) prefer to highlight the bonding and interdependence that characterize this period.

Dance/movement therapists take still another perspective. They recognize that the body ego is, as Sigmund Freud said, the first ego function to develop. The body ego emerges through holding, handling, and movement related to the horizontal plane. Movement in the horizontal plane relates to communication and global feelings of comfort or safety (Amighi et al., 1999)—themes that are common to Erikson's and Wastell's theories. LivingDance improvisations that focus on the horizontal plane and other movement parameters associated with "life before walking" will lay the foundation for addressing FL's social anxiety, identity conflicts, and propensity for intellectualization.

As a baby learns to walk, movement tasks associated with the vertical plane increase. Erik Erikson (1959) describes this psychosocial phase as the conflict between shame and autonomy. Wastell (1996) discusses it in relation to a toddler's boundaries and growing orientation to others. Movement in the vertical plane speaks to presentation and "holding one's ground" (Amighi et al., 1999), an overarching concept that captures the essence of both Erikson's and Wastell's perspectives. Thus, the LivingDance set of standard shape improvisations calls for "finding one's shape"—attaining the kinesthetic awareness of both the horizontal and vertical planes of the body outline. These are the planes associated with identity development in the first two years of life. Adding awareness of forward and backward movement in the sagittal plane and the front and back of the body boundary comes next.

Introductory Assessment

FL and her family have centered their lives on academic achievement. There are no references to artistic or athletic interests. Working with natural movement to which FL already has access provides, therefore, a nonthreatening, body-based approach to dealing with social anxiety. In addition, the therapist as teacher/director creates a familiar learning environment with one major difference. This academically driven young woman does not have to worry about grades.

Women who are struggling with relationships often elect, as I shall assume FL did, to attend a women's group before becoming involved in a group for men and women. To join an ongoing LivingDance group, a new client must be familiar with the movement vocabulary specific to LivingDance. This usually involves the client completing at least four individual sessions. By working individually during this introductory phase FL learned a new language. She was the center of attention, the "only child." In group, however, FL is one among many, the newest or youngest member, and, with regard to LivingDance, the least experienced. Although groups tend to trigger familial dynamics, this situation provides an unexpected parallel to her family. The youngest of three daughters in a highly educated family, she was the last to receive a professional degree.

Although assessments ordinarily examine the interactions among a constellation of movement parameters, this discussion is limited to one parameter: shape. FL enjoyed the confidence that emerged as she found her shape, but she was unable to sustain the sense of wholeness typically derived from shape exercises. Through improvisation, FL discovered that she could connect to her shape by tensing her muscles. To sustain the sense of her body boundary, she engaged in minimal movement, creating the appearance of a brittle shell, devoid of internal sensation and feeling. At these times her breath was even more shallow than usual. With the understanding that the body does not lie, it is apparent that FL is struggling with identity development, that shame and doubt are challenging her sense of self and promoting imbalances in her relationships.

Group: Using LivingDance to Work with FL's Disclosure

Before FL's disclosure, improvisations in group included three aspects of LivingDance that were new to her:

1. Alternating between holding onto one's sense of shape and "mooshing," or losing one's shape while dancing with others
2. Improvising while a designated witness observes
3. Witnessing a group member as she dances

The task of the witness is to observe nonjudgmentally, creating the unconditional regard that encourages uncensored expression. The witness attests to the dancer's experience. If she finds herself judging the dancer's level of success or comparing herself to the dancer, either negatively or positively, she considers how these thoughts and feelings relate to her life. When witnesses and dancers talk—in dyads, small groups, or the group as a whole—they learn about themselves and one another.

Since the group had already experienced advanced stage disclosures and confrontations before FL's joining (Berman and Weinberg, 1998), I expect group members to maintain the long-term norm of authenticity. Even though the group is theoretically new, it is likely that someone will relate FL's surprise disclosure to the recent focus on shape (number one aspect) and the ensuing dialogues between dancers and witnesses. Whatever the verbal exchanges, I would be sure to bring the dance back into the process. That could mean dancing shoulder to shoulder in a tight knit circle, in small groups, or alone.

With the interactive dance component of the LivingDance process still so new to FL, this would call for going back to basics: ensuring that the breath is open, muscle connections are alive, and that the sense of shape is clear. By each member being fully present in her body, each member's LivingDance will evolve in its own way. Whether the dances relate to FL's disclosure or not depends on the individual. If FL wishes to dance alone, she will do so. If she wishes to dance with others she may seek one or more women to dance with, risking rejection should others prefer dancing alone. The dances or nondances between FL and the woman she announced she was attracted to will generate feelings, as will the dances or nondances she experiences with other members of the group.

I referred earlier to the constellation of movement parameters, in addition to shape, that I would normally consider. Although I cannot do that now in depth, I will mention some of them to round out the picture. As well as attending to FL's sense of her shape and observing whether she is dancing alone, with others, avoiding contact, or being avoided by others, I will be mindful of her process and related movement phenomena. I will want to see if FL is initiating movement or picking up her cues from others. I will observe her breathing patterns, the way she carves space, rhythmic changes in muscle tension, her relationship to time and gravity, and whether her movements affect the environment or relate primarily to herself. I will attend to the roles in the group she and others assume. I may suggest movement tasks that focus on boundaries, sexual identity, relationships, and the intricate links among the oft-confused: friendship, intimacy, and sexuality. It is up to FL, however, to determine what the sensations, images, interactions, symbols, and feelings in her dances are saying.

Through dancing, witnessing, and being witnessed, FL may discover that the woman she is attracted to embodies qualities she would like to see in herself. Familial or cultural insights may emerge. FL may also begin to consider the effects of the groups becoming a safe container and group members' varying styles and roles. Operationally, that would mean that FL would be able to hold onto herself during challenging interactions, whether intimate or confronting. Additional LivingDance structures that focus on shape may help her internalize a sense of self and identity she feels free to name as her own.

FAMILY SYSTEMS APPROACH

Ronald F. Levant, EdD, ABPP
Dean and Professor, Nova Southeastern University

I will approach this case from the perspective of family systems theory (Bowen, 1978). This is a twenty-six-year-old, single, professional female, with two older, married, professional sisters, ages thirty and thirty-two, and highly educated parents (MD and PhD). She described herself as the "good child" in the family, suggesting that the older daughters may have been more trouble to their parents. She also stated that she feels that she has lived most of her life for her parents' approval. Not surprisingly, she states that there was a lot of academic competition with her sisters. In fact, she acknowledges that she spent most of her adolescence and early adulthood studying and preparing for her career.

This background suggests that this is a young person who has not yet differentiated from her family of origin perhaps due to intense family loyalty (Boszormenyi-Nagy and Spark, 1973). Because of this lack of differentiation, it can be assumed that she has not successfully negotiated the developmental stage of identity (Erikson, 1968). In this light, her lack of dating experience becomes clearer. Without a firm sense of self, how could she be ready for the stage of "intimacy" (Erikson, 1968)? Using this line of analysis, her social anxiety probably reflects her awareness at some level that, despite her tremendous academic and professional accomplishments, she is not ready for socializing or dating.

Her experience in the group is very interesting. Her ability to immerse herself in the group after only three sessions suggests again a lack of differentiation and emotional immaturity. She apparently does not know how to negotiate relationships based on a mutual process of each getting to know the other leading to an "I and Thou" relationship (Buber, 1958). Rather, in a childlike way, she senses that she will be accepted and plunges headlong into self-disclosures. There is also a narcissistic quality to her behavior in the group: She announces an attraction to another female apparently without considering what this disclosure might mean to the other woman.

It is stated that she had wondered if she was gay over the past few years. I would inquire as to why she thought this. On one hand, it may be that she has indeed felt some romantic attraction to other women, in which case I might consider a referral to a group designed to address sexual orientation. On the other hand, it may be that this was her explanation to herself of her lack of success in dating. Whatever the case may be, however, she does not seem emotionally ready for an intimate relationship, regardless of whether the relationship is heterosexual or homosexual.

She can use her experience in this group to resolve her emotional difficulties and achieve a degree of emotional maturity, which is a basic prerequisite for participating in an intimate relationship. Yalom (1985) refers to the process of interpersonal learning as one of the major curative factors in group psychotherapy. Interpersonal learning involves what others have referred to as a corrective emotional experience, which occurs when one receives significant feedback that—often dramatically—brings one's basic assumptions about self and others in interpersonal relationships into perspective. This young woman seems poised for such an experience as a result of her disclosure of attraction to the other woman in the group. Although she describes herself as "approval-seeking" (which implies that she is able to detect what people expect of her), she is likely to learn that she has difficulty seeing things from other people's perspectives and balancing her own perspective with that of others—basic requirements for mature relationships.

Further work with her would follow the family systems model, in which I would encourage her to develop a more solid sense of self by differentiation from her family of origin. This often requires frequent visits home aimed at the development of adult-to-adult relationships with her "former parents" (Williamson, 1981).

THE MODERN GROUP ANALYTIC APPROACH

Steven Van Wagoner, PhD
Adjunct Faculty,
The George Washington University Counseling Center,
Georgetown University Counseling and Psychological Services,
and University of Maryland
Private Practice, Bethesda, Maryland, and Washington, DC

The modern group approach operates on the assumption that regardless of what a client tells us about his or her life outside the group, we are most concerned with what transpires in the group. This greatly depends upon fostering an awareness in each member of developing relationships in the group. In other words, we wish to create a sense of immediacy among members (Ormont, 1992). In this context the modern group therapist seeks to help members learn about their characteristic ways of relating to others. In the case of the twenty-six-year-old law student, we could not have hoped for a more auspicious beginning than when she shared her attraction for a fellow female member, attributing the disclosure to the accepting attitude of the other members (and quite possibly to her fantasy that the therapist is also accepting and approving of the new, prized group member). In the brief background sketch provided, we know a few things about her interactions with significant others from her family (by her report), namely, that she has lived most of her life for her parents' approval (i.e., playing the good child), that she strives to cause them minimal worry, and that she competes with her siblings, ostensibly for parental approval. We must wonder if she has not already begun to reenact some of these communication dynamics in the group: currying favor with the therapist by being the good child in group and competing with other members in this endeavor. What she cannot have predicted, however, is what will happen next as others respond to her disclosure. It is in the interactions that surround and follow her disclosure that the modern group therapist is interested.

She shared that the possibility of being gay creates anxiety in her because such a disclosure would cause upheaval in her family with painful parental disapproval. We might expect that she will sense similar upheaval as the members react to her very real and immediate disclosure of attraction to another woman in group. If this occurs, we might then ask who in the room she most fears will disapprove of what she has shared. We might also ask her if she feels that she has created upheaval in the group. In this way we make immediate one of the central conflicts with which she struggles in her family. We would also want to observe the other members in the group for their various reactions to her disclosure, and help to bring these interactions into the room. The reaction of the woman to whom she has professed attraction could take many forms depending upon this woman's own conflicts and interpersonal ways of relating. She might feel dumbfounded, repulsed, aroused, flattered, or any number of feelings. Any of these reactions will evoke reactions from our client and other group members, each reflecting that person's interpersonal style and conflicts. We might also look to our client for feelings of rejection and disapproval or, in a different vein, a need to foment upheaval, thus acting out denied aggressive impulses toward a family that is perceived to stipulate approval for certain kinds of behaviors over others. In each case, she would effectively bring into her interactions in the group some of the core conflicts she has in her relationships outside the group. The permutations are endless, but a central tenet of the modern group approach is that the work of group therapy lies in the transference communications among the members, and the fact that we are working with multiple transference reactions at once—that of the person disclosing material to others, but also those of other members reacting to the disclosure. In this way, group therapy helps as many members as possible because the therapist strives to involve them in the exchange. The modern group therapy term for this is bridging, which is any technique designed to encourage emotionally laden verbal exchanges between members.

We would also want to observe members' reactions to the therapist as this exchange unfolds. For example, how does the client react to the therapist, who is most likely relatively quiet other than to bridge the exchanges between members? How do others look to the therapist as this highly risky disclosure takes place? Do others react in a competitive manner, or do they withdraw as the new member reveals so much about herself? We must be sensitive to their feelings and thoughts about the leader for introducing this person, and thus this new element, into their group. In this way we learn far more about how individuals emotionally relate to others and authority figures by witnessing it firsthand in the group. This becomes far more rich and immediate than hearing about it secondhand, as is so often the case in individual therapy, especially in the early stages.

Finally, mention should be made of the concept of resistance as it is understood and employed in the modern group approach. Modern group therapists would have begun the group with a contract that spelled out what is expected of the members in the group, typically including agreements to share thoughts and feelings about what transpires in group, to arrive on time and attend regularly, to avoid outside contact with one another, and to avoid physical contact with members in and out of the group. We expect that members will test these agreements, and as they do we help the group to observe and identify such deviations. Because we believe that the most effective group is the one that operates as a whole entity, deviations from the group as a whole must be dealt with by the group. In our case, what would happen if the new client, after sharing her attraction, is met with rejection or worse and reacts by withdrawing physically and/or emotionally? We would want to confront this resistance, ideally by asking other members how they think and feel about the withdrawal. Or perhaps several others did not participate in the exchange, and avoided the topic altogether. This would also be understood as a form of resistance, and we would hope to get reactions from those participating about the lack of involvement of others. In each of these examples, we hope to have *other members* identify and confront the resistance, not the leader. In this way we maximize the exchanges between members, empower members to take responsibility for detecting and confronting resistance, and contribute to the formation of the entire group as an agent of change. Resistance modification is at the core of modern group therapy, and thus the existence of resistance is essential to the modern group approach.

In summary, the modern group approach seeks to re-create, in the immediacy of the group interactions, the conflicts that each member characteristically brings into relationships with others. This results in an experience of others in the group similar to their experience of others in their relationships in the outside world. A reenactment of these characteristic ways of relating in the group provides the mechanism through which awareness and ultimately change can occur as the person fully experiences and understands others and their reactions in the emotionally present moment of the group. Because these moments can bring pain and discomfort, members will seek to resist this experience through various ego defenses. Modification of ego resistances, not interpretation, is the chief activity of the modern group therapist as the therapist seeks to help the group members relate their life experiences fully (including those re-created in the interactions with the group). Resolution of ego defenses facilitates this endeavor.

TRANSACTIONAL ANALYSIS APPROACH

Frances Bonds-White, EdD
Certified Teaching and Supervising Transactional Analyst
Certified Group Psychotherapist
Private Practice, Philadelphia, Pennsylvania

From a transactional analysis perspective, two things become important at the moment a person makes a personal disclosure indicating feelings or attractions to another group member. The first is protection and the second is permission. When a transactional analyst uses the terms permission and protection, we are very specific about the course of action. When a person is making emotional changes, he or she feels exceedingly vulnerable to attack from the internal parent ego state. The therapist may have to step in on the emotional level and give the client permission to explore and offer protection on an emotional level while the exploration takes place. When this exploration takes place in a group and involves feelings toward another member, the permission and protection has to be extended to the others as well.

When Patient X reveals in group that she is sexually attracted to another female member of the group, I would first "stroke" her for her courage in saying this out loud in the group after attending only three sessions. I would also ask the person to whom the attraction is directed to express how she feels about the fact that X admires her. I would ask her to speak directly to X. Being aware of the vulnerability that both of them might feel in this situation, I would invite the group to explore what it is like to be present in this moment of the group with a particular emphasis on sexual attractions they might feel for one another, both heterosexual and homosexual. As the group began to explore these attractions, I would underline any feelings of anxiety that get expressed by others, while carefully monitoring Patient X's reactions. I would also look for the expression of pleasure that can be experienced in sexual attraction, while emphasizing the group contract of no outside contact, which makes it safe to explore these feelings and desires within the group.

The goals of involving the whole group are to (1) normalize the feelings of attraction and liking for other group members, (2) protect Patient X from attack from within by getting her involved in a dialogue, and (3) listen carefully for what Patient X might be expressing for the group as a whole. By normalizing the feeling of sexual attraction as a human experience, the therapist and the group can offer both protection to the distressed child ego state of the patient and give permission to explore what sexual attraction to others is like and what prohibitions and taboos each person in the group experiences about sexuality. It will also give the opportunity to explore the distinction between sexual attraction and deep longings for nurturing and caretaking that can sometimes be mistaken for sexual attraction.

In transactional analysis, when we think of something as egodystonic we want to know to which part of the ego it is dystonic. To even think about a homosexual attraction is dystonic to X's parent ego state and to the part of her child ego state that functions in adaptation to her parent ego state. Before this group ended, I would want to check with the patient's adult ego state to see if there can be any harm in exploring the idea of being homosexual without acting on it. Since she will have the experience of the whole group exploring this topic, we have some here-and-now data for her to consider. Also, since X reports that she is in distress, I would want to find out exactly what she is experiencing emotionally. When someone reports being distressed, it is generic and I do not know specifically what he or she is feeling. When she says "distressed" does she really mean frightened, sad, or angry with herself? What thoughts is she experiencing in reaction to these emotions? Does she have any thoughts of suicide? Of quitting group to avoid the feelings of attraction? I would also check as to whether the distress is such that she needs to make an individual appointment to help stabilize herself between groups. By doing this in group, it gives both Patient X and all group members the information that an additional appointment is permissible, possible, at times desirable, and available to all.

A COGNITIVE-BEHAVIORAL APPROACH

William Weitz, PhD
Past President, Florida Psychological Association
Former Member, Board of Psychology, State of Florida
Specialty, Post-Traumatic Stress Disorder, Forensic Psychology
Clinical Director, Ruth Rales Jewish Family Services
Boca Raton, Florida

Upon initial assessment of the case, it would appear that there are many interesting aspects of a subtle nature which would affect therapeutic choices, beyond the demographic and clinical material presented. In any clinical decision making, such factors need to be considered as essential to the therapy process.

The fact that the client was referred by a former client who had been treated in group psychotherapy definitely creates positive expectations for both client and therapist. The client is coming for treatment to a specific provider because a trusted friend has conveyed a positive outcome from prior experience. The therapist has high expectations due to the personalized referral, while also experiencing some increased pressure to succeed with the client to validate the original referring party. Also, the youth, high intellect, attractiveness, and verbal skills of the client predict well for therapeutic intervention, especially when the client is positively motivated for treatment.

The practice of seeing the client individually prior to placement in a group experience also demonstrates the experience of the therapist. Even with confident, motivated, and high-skill clients, it is essential to allow some rapport to evolve between client and therapist, while also allowing an opportunity to rule out potentially disqualifying factors for group treatment. The manifestation of psychotic symptoms or additional variables that would limit the client's benefits from verbal feedback are examples of such factors. In this case, there is no evidence of disqualifying factors, yet the individual sessions are valuable and they allow some bond and reasonable expectations to develop prior to facing the group process.

The young woman has been a "model" child in many ways. She has succeeded in applying her intellectual ability, has made significant career achievements, has successfully met the high expectations of professional parents, and has maintained good relationships with her two older sisters. The fact that both sisters were equally academically and professionally successful, however, fails to allow the client to distinguish herself in these areas and, most critically, both siblings had also married. Although the client has manifested positive life development in many areas, the one limiting issue initially defined revolves around her social anxiety and her interpersonal discomfort in social situations. Although her role as the youngest child may have established her as the favorite (the baby) in the family, this potential attention and affection from parents apparently has not transferred into the evolution of high self-confidence and social risk taking. Although she was able to establish comfort in the group almost immediately, the group is conceptually a "safe" system, and the members supposedly have similar problems. Hence, it is difficult to judge the client's social anxiety and discomfort solely on the basis of her adaptation to a treatment group. It must be remembered that the client's style is to be liked and to gain external approval; hence, her initial presentation to strangers would tend to emphasize attributes that accomplish such outcomes.

Group process and feedback is an excellent modality for working with persons with high levels of social anxiety and limited social risk-taking ability, and who experience problems with intimacy. Yet it may prove a difficult place for examining sexual orientation, unless the group is specifically defined for this purpose. Thus, the issue of potential sexual attraction to another female group member and the larger question of whether she is gay present a definite roadblock for the client, especially in the group setting. One major problem for effective group process is the development of subgroups and the ensuing issues that may evolve which might not be open for honest group discussion and process. In this case, it is not clear that the issue of sexual orientation is even a major group conflict experienced by other members and thus this conflict may be seen as deflecting from the therapy agendas of others. Given the client's new awareness of the possible sexual orientation conflict, the problem remains largely an internal question that might best be handled in individual sessions with the therapist. Sexual orientation involves questions about physical acceptance, emotional style, and personal courage and choice, and individual treatment would allow the therapist to focus on these issues in a concentrated and continuous manner that would not be possible in a group format. It would thus be reasonable to maintain the client in group treatment, while adding additional individual visits to work on this selected area.

The client may experience both sexual orientation problems and the presenting problems of social avoidance and interpersonal anxiety. Having to always be the "perfect" child to gain the desired parental approval certainly may result in unspoken resentment toward powerful love objects, and the cost of devoting herself to her academic success and career goals at the expense of social development is now making itself known to the client. Through allowing the breakdown of client defense in group, the client will be better able to try out new roles and to explore the anxiety of intimate relationships in a peer format. For once, the social arena will occupy center stage and she will be able to hear group feedback and to implement behavior in a group that will help her to define the person she wishes to be. Even if she discovers that she is gay, her social skills and confidence that are also lacking can be attacked through the group process, for a goal of treatment is to assist the person to meet his or her own life needs, whether gay or straight.

A GROUP-AS-A-WHOLE APPROACH

Michael P. Frank, MA, MFT, CGP
Private Practice, Sherman Oaks, California

Bringing in a new member is a very important event in the life of an ongoing group. It is both an opening and a demand for change on the part of the new member and the group as a whole. In order for the group to be therapeutic, it must find a way to integrate the new member, and the new member must find a way to join the group. This is a challenge that we humans face in our families, our work, our social groups, and our societies. In this way, the psychotherapy group replicates life, but with a very important difference: in the psychotherapy group we openly discuss the process as it is happening. We share our thoughts and feelings. We relate the experience to our "outside" lives, present and past. We search for connection and meaning. We share the struggle. The goal is the forming of a therapeutic community in which the members are of help to one another and in the process help themselves.

Maintaining a group-as-a-whole perspective does not limit the therapist to a particular modality, but keeps the question of "how is the group responding to what is happening?" constantly in the background. This helps to both anticipate and resolve group resistances as well as mobilize the considerable therapeutic power of the group itself. The challenges to the leader who takes this approach can be daunting. It requires an extra layer of observation and understanding that is seldom taught in graduate school and can be acquired only through extensive training and experience in group psychotherapy. It requires the therapist to hold his or her own impulses to intervene one on one in check until that understanding forms in his or her mind. It demands a willingness to subjugate his or her own ego gratification and allow the group to be the therapeutic agent. In Winnicottian terms, it is an environment in which the group holds each individual and the leader holds the group.

The Group Problem

Over its life span, the group is presented with a variety of group problems that must be dealt with and resolved. (I use "problem" here not as something negative, but as a therapeutic issue that is to be solved or resolved in the course of therapy.) This case presents the group with several problems: bringing in a new member, reforming the group to incorporate the new member, dealing with the new member's "shameful secret," and helping her with both her presenting problems and those that arise in the course of her group membership. These problems must be addressed at the group level in order for the therapeutic work to be fully successful.

At least one, preferably more, session in advance, I will announce that a new member is joining the group. I give minimal information— gender, perhaps age range, first name. The purpose of this is to deal with feelings about this change so that the group does not displace them onto the new member and scapegoat her or cast her in the role of "savior." Typically, even when the group has been wanting a new member, there will be feelings of fear that she will spoil the group in some way, anger at the leader for putting the group at risk, and envy that the leader has the power to unilaterally make such a decision. Or there may be fantasies of the new member enlivening the group, or saving it from whatever difficulties it is experiencing. This, not surprisingly, can elicit considerable transference related to families of origin. At this point, the group problem is how we can tolerate these feelings without forcing the new member into an untenable role. Whatever the group does not spontaneously address, I will speculate on aloud so as to elicit or at the very least rule out what has been left unexpressed. Once these issues have been aired, the group will typically look forward to the new arrival with hopeful, curious, and empathic feelings.

At the new member's first meeting I will often start with a question, such as, "What's it like for this group to bring in a new member?" or "Well, we have a new member joining our family" or "How does this group bring in someone new?" This will often elicit remembrances of their own and others' first group meetings as well as how the group leader was experienced as helpful (or not) to the process. This immediately focuses the group on their here-and-now process and invites them to share their experience of the event. It also reinforces the norm of group self-examination as well as that the group itself is the active therapeutic agent.

The "Shameful Secret"

This patient's expressed comfort during the first three sessions is a defense. She is defending against her feelings of fear that the group will have a negative response to the disclosure of her incipient homosexuality. This is a clear example of how a member's transference to the group as a whole begins even before she attends her first meeting. She is experiencing the group as if it were her family. She is attempting to be the "good child" in the group by presenting this acceptable false self. Her disclosure of her sexual feelings in the fourth meeting is significant for three reasons: (1) she is taking the risk of disclosing her "shameful secret," (2) she is making a personal disclosure to the group member for whom she felt an attraction, and, perhaps most important in the long run, (3) she is able to talk about the difficulty she had in bringing this up in the group.

As a rule of thumb, I will always find out something new about a patient over the course of group therapy. This has held true for me regardless of whether I have had this patient in individual therapy for years or for just a short pregroup interview. Perhaps I am singularly unobservant, but I do not think so. People just respond differently and more broadly in a group than in individual therapy. The group environment allows us to observe in vivo aspects of their personality that we have only heard about secondhand, if at all. Often these observations only add additional perspective to known therapeutic issues, but sometimes they are significant in themselves, even becoming a central focus of therapy. This seems to be the case with this young woman.

Her disclosure of her homosexuality presents two therapeutic problems. The first is the resolution of her own issues that have come to light in the group. The second is the stimulation of the group's response. At this point, some therapeutic goals become evident.

First, the patient's goals include the following: mitigating her feelings of shame, guilt, and fear; resolving her transference of the awareness of her family's probable reaction to that of the group; exploring the likelihood of her projecting that transferential expectation onto the group and having the group react negatively to it; taking these awarenesses and the corrective emotional experience of the group and applying them in her "outside" life; in the long term, differentiating from her family of origin.

Second, the group goals are as follows: dealing with their own individual reactions to the disclosure; achieving a group response that is both honest and therapeutic.

Group-As-a-Whole Interventions

Here are some group-as-a-whole interventions that will likely be helpful:

- How is the group responding to _____ right now?
- We seem to be having a variety of feelings in the group. How should we deal with this?
- How is this family dealing with this information? (Addresses the transference, as well as the corrective emotional experience.)
- I notice that there are only positive feelings being expressed. I wonder what might happen if there were any negative feelings about this? (Addresses the group defense of pseudomutuality.

Invites the group to find ways to include honest expression of negative feelings in a way that is therapeutic.)

- I think the group might be angry at me for _____ . (Deflects hostile feelings from potential scapegoat in group.)
- I wonder if _____ is speaking for the group when he says that? (Invites/challenges silent group members to express thoughts and feelings.)

Why Group As a Whole?

In no other modality can the previous goals be simultaneously addressed and met. In addition, in dealing with this patient's issues, various issues of the other group members will be stimulated and brought to light. Finally, by empowering the group to be the agent of therapeutic change, we encourage the individual members to relate to others in a way that enhances their own self-esteem and provides experience in creating better relationships for themselves.

Bear in mind that this approach is not exclusive and that it can and should be integrated with the vast majority of other group modalities. Having a group-as-a-whole perspective only broadens one's awareness and effectiveness as a group psychotherapist.

A GROUP-ANALYTICAL MODEL APPROACH

Earl Hopper, PhD
Certified Group Psychotherapist, American Group
Psychotherapy Association
Psychoanalyst, Group Analyst, and Organizational Consultant
Private Practice, London, England

I am both a psychoanalyst and a group analyst, but I do not make a rigid distinction between these clinical disciplines. Formerly a sociologist, I identify with British object relations thinking associated with the Group of Independent Psychoanalysts, including Balint, Bowlby, Fairbairn, and Winnicott, to name only a few of my late teachers. Group analysis is based on psychoanalysis, sociology, and general systems theory. Although founded by S. H. Foulkes and his colleagues, group analysis draws on the work of Bion and various European and American psychoanalytical group therapists. In small but important ways group analysis is different from other forms of psychoanalytical group therapy, particularly in its emphasis on the sociality of human nature; the constraints of the social unconscious; the personification of group processes; and the attention given to parallel processes, including those within the environment of the group. As Foulkes (1975) wrote, group-analytic psychotherapy "is a form of psychotherapy *by* the group, *of* the group, including its conductor" (emphasis added) (p. 3). Of course, I have developed my own personal theoretical orientation and style of clinical work, described with respect to group analysis in Hopper (1985, 1996, 2001, 2002), and in psychoanalysis in Hopper (1991, 1995, 1997). In various ways these articles are pertinent to the task in hand.

The client/patient, who I will call Miss A, presented with a form of social phobia and a wish for "greater insight into her personality." She has been devoted to her education and nascent career as a lawyer and has complied with the norms of her middle-class family, as have her two older sisters. Her parents are not only professionals but scientists, broadly defined. However, I suspect that the therapist knows more about Miss A than is suggested by these data, and that this additional information is condensed within such phrases as "fine insight into her personality" and "her analysis of herself, although limited in certain areas, is quite good." (Nonetheless, the therapist might not know that he knows.) For example, after several sessions alone with Miss A and several sessions in the group, I would know something about: her relationship with each of her sisters and each of her parents, and the relationships between her sisters and their parents; the history and dynamics of her social phobia (its onset, the conscious meaning of "uncomfortable," "other people," and "social situations," and whether she is more anxious with men or with women or vice versa); the history of her family (the social and geographic origins of her parents); whether Miss A is living on her own, and/or in the same city as her parents and/or sisters; whether she went away to college, and, therefore, whether she returned home to start her career, etc. Such information would give me a better feel for Miss A.

Her atypical style of participation in the first few sessions of the group is indeed noteworthy, and alerts us to the complexity of an apparent social phobia. It might be assumed that Miss A feels safe because she correctly perceives that the group offers a space for the safe exploration of her thoughts and feelings, and that the members of the group respect the basic principles of abstinence, etc. However, I would be sensitive to the possibility that she has regressed precipitously, and has repeated her way of relating to her parents within her transference to the group and to me as the group's conductor (or "analyst," "therapist," or "leader"). She is behaving as a very good child/client/patient would, honoring the tenets of group analysis and making good use of the space and the other participants in it. She might even be honoring the tenets of group analysis as I described them to her during the initial interviews. Thus, I would be inclined to clarify the discrepancies between her presenting problems and her initial way of participating in the group, and to interpret this in terms of her transference of her lifelong pattern of compliance in her family, education, and fledgling career to the new group situation. I might ask her how she imagined I wanted her to be and what would please me. Ordinarily, I would be inclined to say very little and perhaps nothing at all, preferring to facilitate Miss A's entry into the group through empathic and attentive listening, but in this instance I would be the only person present who would be aware of the discrepancy between her reported impressions of herself and her style of participation and, therefore, I might well comment as described.

I suspect that Miss A's apparent ease and comfort might provoke competitive feelings among the other members of the group, especially the women. I would be inclined to focus on these processes, whether or not they were manifest, e.g., I wonder what you feel about Miss A's having taken to the group like a fish to water? In such a question I would also be hoping to elicit more information about her relationship to her marine biologist mother. I would have at the back of my mind the possibilities of various splitting processes associated with "marine," on the one hand, and "biologist," on the other, with the possibility that Miss A experienced the group as the sea/female/mother, and the conductor as the biologist/male/father parts of the mother. I would be seeking a better sense of Miss A's mother's gender identity and Miss A's perception of this. In any case, I would not want to establish an exclusive relationship with Miss A within the context of the group, and would prefer not to do the group's work for them, although in due course I would not hesitate to respond to her in a more personal way.

It is not quite clear whether Miss A and the other woman have actually initiated a pairing relationship, but assuming that they have I might invite the group to explore the possibility that Miss A and the apparent object of her interest have started a pairing relationship, and to consider what this means to the group. I would be interested to explore this relationship in connection with me and the group as a whole, and to consider the Oedipal and family patterns as well as the enactment of the pair as a defense against underlying depressive anxieties. However, the strength of the pairing might alert me to the possibility that the group had not adequately mourned the client who had left and created the vacancy for Miss A, and in this connection the loss of parental/conductor attention. I would wonder aloud about loss and sadness, depending on my own affect and my sense of the affect of the group.

More specifically, I would be reluctant to say much about Miss A's confession that she is attracted to another woman in the group, and about her thoughts and feelings about her homosexuality. I would be more concerned with protecting the space for dialogue about these issues within the group. How does the other woman feel about being selected as the object of Miss A's attention and attraction? What do the other women of the group think and feel about this? Are their views diverse? Are their views syntonic with those in the wider culture? In fact, a number of clinical bells would be ringing, but the loudest would be telling me to keep an open mind about the manifest content of these communications and to be alert to the many possible unconscious meanings of them.

I would be cautious because I would not wish to support Miss A's intellectual defenses and various forms of her compliance which, I suspect, are part of a characterological defensive system against profound anxieties about loneliness and failed dependency, which underpin her concerns about homosexuality. However, I am confident that eventually the group and I would explore with Miss A her views about such questions as: Did her parents want at least one son, even if they were not inclined to value boys more than girls? As the youngest, did she signal that her parents would never have a son and that her sisters would never have a brother? Was this especially important to her mother? To her father? Were they aware of this? Might Miss A have been rejected by her mother? Might she have turned to her father prematurely and precipitously? Was she rejected by her father? Might she have been blocked by one of her sisters from making a close relationship with a particular parent? Perhaps Miss A wanted to be her father's son in order to help her compete with her sisters for her mother's love and support.

In what ways might this family history be repeated within the group? Homosexuality might be dystonic for Miss A and her family, but this issue might be carried by Miss A for her family. I would want to explore the personification and scapegoating processes within her family that might be repeated within the group. I would be especially sensitive to the possibility that the disapproval Miss A imagines her family would feel about her homosexuality is based on her sense that the cohesion of her family would be disrupted by it, partly because this is defensive against anxieties associated with the lack of warmth and intimacy among the members of the family. However, this would be balanced by my sense that within a family of three daughters, sexuality is bound to have a homosexual coloration. After all, it is hard for daughters to find a man as desirable and special as their neurologist father is likely to have seemed to be.

Eventually the group would explore the various possible etiologies of various kinds of homosexuality and gender identities. These topics are ubiquitous in my groups. The more we learn about these complex topics, the more we should be ashamed of having perpetrated our clinical ideologies about homosexuality on so many of our patients over so many years. However, political correctness has brought its own problems and scotoma. Be aware of the differences between fantasies and behavior, and realize that in a deep sense, even a relationship between a man and a woman can be "homosexual." Moreover, homosexual love and attraction are often complex defenses against disavowed, eroticized hatred, which has originated in identifications and choices based on extremely painful early life experiences. Nonetheless, Miss A's communication would not panic the group and me to rush into a discussion of these matters. Our goal would be to facilitate Miss A's liberation and maturation based on her increasing knowledge of herself in relationship to others.

REVIEW

You have now had the opportunity to read seventeen different analyses of the same case written by senior clinicians as perceived through their psychological and therapeutic orientations. What is your opinion? Do you feel that all of these paradigms equally help this client? They obviously approach her difficulty in a number of different and provocative ways. Which analysis appeals most to you and why do you think that is?

Chapter 12

The Training Site, Seeking the Truth, and the Problematic Client

SCENARIO

You have just arrived at your new practicum, predoctoral internship, psychiatric residency, or postlicensure training site. Your supervisor, generally an overworked, underpaid individual, briefly welcomes you and tells you that she will be speaking with you later in the day. She also informs you that you will be running a group in about an hour either by yourself or with another student or with one of the staff therapists. Do not panic! Take a deep breath and remember that a fairly large majority of students, interns, residents, and licensed professionals make it through this experience and survive.

Perhaps a short, true story will help alleviate some of your anxiety and show that you are not alone in your feelings. When I was working toward my doctorate and arrived at my practicum site, my new supervisor related to me the exact scenario I just presented. Needless to say, I was sure there was some mistake and that this was a *Twilight Zone* experience, which needed to be immediately rectified, but my supervisor was already gone from view. At first, I wondered if I had heard her incorrectly and misinterpreted the conversation because I was somewhat nervous about beginning a new practicum.

But lo and behold, Nurse Diesel from Mel Brooks's *High Anxiety* movie came around the corner and zeroed in on me. She was everything I had ever feared and fantasized about in an institutional employee. She was quite big, very strong, and light on respect for new practicum students. After she looked me over with a sinister smile (or at least I felt it was sinister), she said, "Follow me." I appropriately chose to introduce myself, but she made no attempt at responding in kind. She walked me down the hall and said, "Stay here." We were at the room in which I was going to run group therapy by myself in about thirty minutes.

I braved asking her how many people would be in the group and, with a sneering smile, she said, "Twenty." What I have not told you was that this site was a state psychiatric hospital that primarily housed chronic schizophrenics and psychotics, who I was later to learn were referred to lovingly by the staff as "snow nuts." Apparently, these individuals would come to Florida in the winter and be hospitalized and then return to hospitalization up north in the summer.

Then I turned to look at the room in which I would be running group therapy by myself with twenty very disturbed individuals. Immediate panic seized me and the impulse to flee was strong. I was aware of the perspiration traveling down my body like white-water rapids. The room itself seemed no bigger than a large walk-in closet without windows. Having personal issues with claustrophobia and beginning something that I felt completely unprepared for gave me an overall feeling of being helpless and psychologically a mess.

I tried to do deep-breathing exercises, which ultimately left me hyperventilating. I probably was breathing too quickly, and I thought I would throw up. The orderlies then began to arrive with their patients. From the way in which they escorted these individuals down the hall, it appeared that they were eagerly looking forward to getting rid of their charges for an hour.

The patients were brought into this closet of a room while I stood outside the door trying to put on my most authentic positive-regard face while I thought my heart would burst from palpitations. The last orderly, a rather nice fellow, briefly said that he would be locking me in with the patients and when the session was over he would return to unlock the door and the patients would be taken back to their respective rooms. I heard myself say, "Lock me in?" He smiled as though this was a very normal procedure and I was just new to the rules and regulations of the hospital. Unbeknownst to him, I kept thinking obsessively, "Oh, shit! I am going to be locked in a room with twenty 'snow nuts.'"

I walked into the room and found that all the chairs had been taken except the one with three legs. I knew then that I was being punished for every wrong deed I had ever done in my life. I was so sorry that I had stolen that candy bar from Mr. Schultz's store when I was eight years old.

Unless schizophrenics and psychotics are completely medicated and half asleep, they are often very verbal. This particular group of individuals was very verbal. It appeared that med time would be after the group. I would like very much to relate that I was brilliant, dazzling, and created an environment for tremendous growth for the patients under my care on that day. I was not! I precariously balanced myself on the three-legged chair in an almost catatonic state. I did not say one word in an hour's time and just watched these individuals have some of the craziest conversations I had ever heard. Fortunately, many of them were in such a different reality than most people that they pretty much thought I was another patient at the hospital.

The hour slipped by in what felt like four days. I made the announcement that the session was over in such a timid voice that no one heard, not even myself, and got up to open the door. The door was still locked. Being an appropriate professional, I began to knock on the door with one hand to alert the orderly who was supposed to be standing outside at the appointed hour to let us all out. I did not hear a key turning the lock. I started to knock louder and still no one arrived. By this time, I was completely crazed and began to bang with both fists in the hope that someone would hear my cry for help, but, alas, no one came.

Just when I was about to run at the door using my shoulder to break it down, one of the patients walked over to me and put his hand on my shoulder. This was a patient who spoke in the group about the fact that he really did not exist. He then said to me, "Hey, little soon-to-be-a-doctor, calm down! We will get you out of here." He then walked me to the far side of the room, which was about eight feet away, and sat me down. He told the other patients to come help him bang on the door. This brought tremendous joy to their lives. They not only banged on the door but on the walls and floor as well.

Finally someone arrived and opened the door. Everyone appeared to leave feeling a lot better—not from anything I did, but rather from expending all that energy banging on anything in the room that was stationary. As the last patient walked out of the room (he was the one who had sat me down), he turned around and said, "This was a great group and I can't wait until tomorrow to come back to group again."

I sat there completely immobile for about forty minutes as every neuron in my body had fired repeatedly during the hour in this, my first psychiatric hospital setting. When I was able to compose myself

I got up, although somewhat disoriented, and thought about that man's statement that this was a great group and he could not wait to come back tomorrow. At that moment, I knew I was not coming back tomorrow.

But as fate would have it, I did come back. In fact, I came back for a year, completing my requirements for the practicum. Did I help anyone? Probably not. Did I hurt anyone? Definitely not. In fact, I was the only person on staff who was not physically attacked by a patient in the entire time I was there. I would like to believe it was because of my great skill and tremendous sensitivity, but now I assume that the patients continued to believe that I, too, was a patient in the hospital and they were not about to hurt their own.

IDEAL SCENARIO

You arrive at your training site and are warmly greeted by your new supervisor who invites you into her office for a cup of coffee and a long talk about your goals and interests in this field. She clearly explains the philosophy of the site plus the rules and regulations that students, predoctoral interns, psychiatric residents, and already-licensed professionals need to follow while completing their requirements at this facility. Then she gives you a manual that basically repeats what she just told you, which you can read at your leisure. Your supervisor says that sometime during your training, she would like you to colead a therapy group with a senior staff therapist, but only when you feel ready.

Her final remarks to you are, "If you have any questions, do not hesitate to contact me at any time, as I am here to make your stay a very profound learning experience and one that will be very pleasant." She offers you some Oreo cookies and milk and sends you off to meet the other staff members who welcome you aboard by throwing rose petals along the hallway you are walking.

Sorry, but this probably will not be the case. Your arrival at your new training site will probably be somewhere between the first and second scenarios. The rose petals will definitely not be included in either. However, if it leans more toward the ideal, there are certain things you can do to help make your transition to leading group in this new facility more effective and reduce your anxiety.

For example, find out if you are going to run the group with another person. Is this person a colleague from your university, another university, a staff member, someone from a different department, i.e., psychiatry, or an already-licensed professional seeking further credentialing? Speak to this person. Inquire whether he or she is at the end of the required training and you are going to take over the group or are you both going to begin a new group together? If the person has been leading the group for awhile, ask what type of group it is, how long it has been active, the number of clients in the group, gender of individuals, ages, what issues are being worked on at this time, whether the clients are voluntary or involuntary, etc. Get to know your coleader. If he or she has been in charge of the group for a while, do not begin to compete with this individual to show how smart you are, as you will be showing your insecurity and will be a general "pain in the butt." Most people are willing to teach and help. If you have the need to take over because of your own control issues, this will set a negative tone for working with this person. When two coleaders are personally at odds, it can become a very uncomfortable problem. Allow your coleader to do just that: lead. Please remember this suggestion when you are coleading. Do not sit next to your coleader. This is not an "us-against-them" situation no matter how insecure you may be feeling, even though sitting near your coleader may reduce your anxiety. Sit across from the coleader as you will be able to observe each other. This helps both of you focus on where the group is going and at the same time enables both of you to give each other nonverbal messages.

If you find that you are going to begin a new group by yourself, there are some things you can do to make it a bit easier but not free from anxiety. If you have the time, find out who is to be in your group. Read the charts to get a feel for the members and then go to meet each person individually and spend some time talking with him or her. Go to the room in which the group will meet and familiarize yourself with it. Allow yourself to feel somewhat secure in the setting. Rearrange the chairs to help make you feel more comfortable while considering the comfort of your group members as well.

When all the clients arrive and are seated, introduce yourself and tell them a little about your history. Do not give them your entire life story, as you are not the client here, but give them enough information so that they feel more comfortable with you, for instance, "I am a practicum student (or intern, or psychiatric resident, etc.) and my goals and interests in this field are . . ." This will help to reduce some of your anxiety and give the group members a model of self-disclosure, especially if it is a beginning group and the members are strangers to one another. It is in your interest to have the group members introduce themselves and encourage them to give more personal information than you have. This will not only help begin to solidify the group, but it will be helpful for you in understanding your clients.

For some group members, this will be very difficult, as speaking in front of others about personal experiences can be quite anxiety provoking. You may wish to speak about the feeling of anxiety after everyone discloses some personal information. There is a good chance that everyone in the room will be feeling some degree of anxiety, as this experience will represent the unknown for them. By introducing the concept of anxiety, you will be helping the clients begin to see that they are not alone in what they feel. The feeling that one is no longer alone is one of the most profound benefits of group therapy. You may wish to open up this topic by simply stating that whenever a new group begins, it is not uncommon for group members to feel various degrees of anxiety, especially if the people in the room are all strangers. If it is an inpatient facility, chances are that many of the clients have seen one another and may not feel as anxious. It is not unprofessional for you to say that you were feeling a little anxious about beginning the group. It not only shows you are human but again models self-disclosure.

It is important that you begin to develop a good memory when it comes to group, as you are going to need to weave past and present disclosures together over time. For example, Anne discloses that speaking in front of groups is quite difficult for her. Bob relates that he too has a similar discomfort. This new information will be of great value as a springboard for later dialogue and to engage these two or more members in speaking about other areas that cause them similar anxieties.

I have found from my own experience with supervising novice practitioners that if I give them certain tools or nonthreatening techniques to begin their groups, they feel a bit more comfortable, as it helps give them some structure in an otherwise unstructured environment. When you are more proficient you will not need these kinds of tools, although they can be quite effective. I have found that if you introduce a poem in the beginning of the group, you not only have a neutral kind of stimulus to begin a dialogue, but a tool for projective analysis. For example, read this poem:

What is it that I feel?
Is it new, is it real?
Has it been with me before?
Is it here to teach me more?
What is it, it has a name?
Inside of me, I'm not the same.

Scott Fehr, 1977

After you have discussed the group agreement and have asked people to introduce themselves, you might want to hand out a poem. You have my permission to use this poem if you so desire, or choose a poem with which you feel comfortable. Please remember that the poem must be neutral in the sense that it can have many interpretations. What I suggest you say before giving out the poem is that you wish the clients to read this poem to themselves and then tell the group what they feel the author is feeling. Also say that you would like the clients to give the poem a title. It is very important that you tell the clients that there is no wrong or right interpretation. This will reduce the fears of members who feel they are being tested and there has to be a right answer. It will also help to reduce the competition of members who believe that their perceptions are the only correct ones. The use of a poem will initially help the clients begin to see that individual personality differences are not to be feared and in fact are welcomed and accepted in your group. Also, it can be quite interesting to hear what other individuals have to say.

Another simple but effective technique I devised a number of years ago which you might consider using in the beginning of the group is to ask the group members, "Who owes you an apology?" It is very interesting to listen to the clients relate the number of people in their lives who have hurt them. I suggest that you do not do an inquiry into the disclosure but rather be supportive and keep this information in the back of your mind for a later date when the clients become more comfortable disclosing intimate information. After they all have disclosed who owes them an apology, ask them, "To whom do you owe an apology?" I have found this to be of considerable interest as generally most people are very sensitive to what has been done to them but often quite insensitive as to what they have done to others. So this little technique not only allows me to glean information for later inquiry and investigation but also permits me to observe the clients' introspective abilities and their level of sensitivity to others in their environment. I have found that by incorporating these two simple techniques in the beginning of a group, bonding begins to develop. Group members will move toward observing similarities in hurt and pain whereas often in the beginning they come into the group looking for differences between themselves and the others, specifically when it comes to their personal experiences. The observation of similarities will help the development of getting the "cohesion ball" rolling. Appendix A will also give you some structured exercises that you may wish to consider if you find that your group is having difficulty coming together.

I think you will be quite surprised at how much information you will be able to glean from these simple exercises, one being a projective tool while the other is a measure of introspection and sensitivity. Please remember to retain the disclosed information in the back of your mind as to what your clients disclose, as you will need to bring these disclosures back at a later date as the group matures. If you find that memory is not one of your stronger areas, give the clients pens to write what they feel about the poem on a sheet of paper. You can place these in their files to be reviewed after the day's group has ended. With the apology exercise, you will need to remember without note taking. There are certain factors that I suggest you keep special note of in your mind. For example, if a man is interpreting the poem, note whether he refers to the author as a man or woman. Look closely and listen carefully to how each group member interprets the poem. Each person is speaking about himself or herself. In poetry therapy, only one person truly knows what the poem means and that is the author. All other interpretations bring forth the interpreter's personal projections. In relation to the apology exercise, at a later date you can ask for greater clarification thus learning more information as to some of the factors that were instrumental in the development of your clients' personalities. As you are aware, previous pain and hurt can be salient factors in how one's personality develops and how one currently interacts with others.

SEEKING THE TRUTH

The truth will set you free. (Sigmund Freud)

The truth will set you free but first piss you off. (Gloria Steinem)

A discussion of the importance of the truth in group psychotherapy and its relationship to anger and projection may appear to be unrelated to the forthcoming section on the problematic client, but without truth in psychotherapy there is no therapy as we know it. Truth, anger, and projection, as demonstrated by the quotes at the beginning of this section, are very much inextricably correlated. This planet and the people who inhabit it would be very different if everyone always told the truth, but unfortunately this is not the case. In fact, the truth seems to be perceived as a negative stimulus to many who present it and many who receive it, but psychotherapy and behavioral change have their foundation in its emergence.

In many interpersonal interactions, as you are aware, there are often conscious and unconscious distortions of the truth in the disclosures between people. These distortions hide what a person is truly thinking or feeling. What is presented in the verbalizations between two or more people frequently masks the truth of what lies behind their words. The same is initially true of our clients as they are having an interpersonal interaction not only with us, as group leaders, but also with the other members in their group.

It is not uncommon to find the expression of truth in a client's anger. Neither is it uncommon to find anger along with a client's expression of the truth disclosed in group psychotherapy. The truth and anger that may be below or behind their disclosures and interpretations of the personalities of their group brothers and sisters is generally unbeknownst to them, especially if it is painful. It can, however, be perceived by us, the group leaders, in the form of their projections onto the other group members. This is why truth, anger, and projection are very often inextricably related. Perhaps a poignant example of an interpretation revealing truth and anger as seen in the projection of the projector may be of help for clarification.

In one of my groups, I have two guys, John and Jim, who are generally quiet in comparison to the other group members. One of the other group members once asked John, "Why are you always so quiet?" John gave a number of rationalizations as to why he did not speak as spontaneously as the majority of the other group members. Jim, the other quiet member, disclosed his interpretation of John's lack of spontaneity. He said that he felt John was quiet because it allowed him to punish people and at the same time indirectly get out his anger. So there we have it: we still do not know why John is reluctant to speak, but we certainly know the truth as to why Jim has been holding himself back and the secondary gain, the anger, he is obtaining from this behavior.

The individual truths of our group members are all in the projections being carried on the back of their interpretations of the other group members. Every interpretation in group, whether accurate or inaccurate, of other group members tells us a lot about the interpreter. Group members are similar to Rorschach cards. The stimulus, rather than the card, is the disclosure of one of the other group members. The interpretation of that disclosure by the other group members is a projection on their parts of who they are. The projection may in fact be accurate, but it tells us something about the person doing the projection. These interpretations, in the form of projections, may be through identification of which they are aware, or unconscious identification of which they are not aware. In either case, we must help them become cognizant of how their interpretation relates to him or her, and, in this case, a truth in a feature of the projector's personality.

My analyst used to say, "I can see myself only in relation to other people." This Sullivanian axiom specifically means that self-analysis in a vacuum is often not very accurate as it does not permit comparisons, identifications, and observations. We must be in the presence of, or at least have interacted with, others to finally develop some understanding of our own personalities. This is why group psychotherapy is a remarkable therapeutic tool with its multiple client format. It permits multiple interpretations carried on the back of individual personal projections of each of the group members. Through this multiple client format, the group members work in tandem to try to learn the truth about who they are as human beings.

Having and accepting this knowledge reinforces the triumvirate concept of truth, anger, and projection being inextricably correlated. It is the encouragement of this trinity that will perhaps help us to understand the hidden reality of what lies behind the words of clients. This provides us access to previously undiscovered parts of their selves, which when acknowledged will ultimately have a major effect on altering their personalities and "setting them free." In a simpler form, we must encourage the disclosure of the truth in our clients no matter how painful that truth may be. How a group therapist will do this depends on the skill of the individual and the environment he or she has created in the group room.

The many forms of this important triad—truth, anger, projection—and how it manifests itself in interpretation in group psychotherapy can be perceived differently by whomever is doing the perceiving. The concept of the truth is philosophical and has a different interpretation for each individual upon its quest. Truth may have different layers. Each truth leads to another truth beyond. Clients new to group therapy analyze their disclosures and interpretations of other group members' personalities on a more superficial level as they have not yet acquired the psychological sophistication and tools that will develop the longer they remain in therapy. For them there is truth in their interpretation at that time. Similar to the psychoanalytic concept of dream interpretation, clients have manifest and latent features in their personalities. It is their manifest personalities that we are initially introduced to when our clients first present themselves to us. This personality is their truth and the one with which they have lived and with which we are working, at that moment in time, as it is an expression of the client's history and life experiences. It is a truth and it is their truth upon which we begin our investigation. What is behind it, features of their latent personality, or to use another term, aspects of their real personality, is solely revealed through the many layers of truth we hope to elicit. These will emerge through projection and interpretation and may be quite different from that which is initially presented.

As stated, a client's manifest personality is a truth. It is a truth that has assisted the client to function within his or her environment up to the point before making the decision to seek psychotherapy. Usually the decision to seek psychotherapy occurs, if the client has not been mandated or forced, when the individual has come to feel that something is not working well any longer and needs to be addressed. This is generally an indication that there is a conflict within the latent or real personality which is making itself felt. The specific conflict or its resolution is unknown to the client. For example, to use a very simple and not uncommon disclosure of a new client, this individual relates that something is just not "right" which he or she cannot figure out.

As therapists we need to be prepared to find the latent truth or that which lies below and probably needs to be expressed but is, for some reason or reasons, being inhibited. Sadly, the direct verbal expression of the latent truth appears to be a great difficulty for many human beings. We see this frequently in the people who come to us for our services. Whether clients are aware of the latent truth but have difficulty disclosing it because of personal reasons known only to them, or are unaware of the truth and its relation to their present difficulties, it has predominantly the same effect. This effect is that unexpressed truth inhibits growth and has a debilitating effect over time for the individual. Helping clients to find this elusive entity, the latent truth or truths, is ultimately the foundation of our work—specifically if we are working from a dynamic paradigm. When working from any paradigm, seeking the truth of a client's behavior is still the foundation of our work. Through this foundation we try to help clients find, sort out, and then make their decisions based in the reality of their real personalities. These more realistic decisions will help them to feel better, give them greater self-awareness, and free them from many of their emotional burdens, as both Sigmund Freud and Gloria Steinem have suggested.

If clients eagerly and openly always told us the truth, our jobs and their recovery would be a lot easier and definitely more expedient. But alas, that is rarely the case, and we spend a great deal of time sorting through information and seeking the truth. When we, as group leaders, offer an interpretation to the material clients present to us, we are simply relating back to them *our* perception of what the truth may be in what we hear them disclosing. We do this in the hope of giving them some insight into their difficulties and to reinforce the courage, which is often needed, when one is on the quest of conflict resolution and self-discovery. The truth in interpretation that we give is not necessarily the ultimate truth but rather another alternative perception which it is hoped the clients may contemplate, as this may loosen the perceptual set and circulatory loop in their thinking. In other words, we are opening up another door for them to go through.

Dr. Steven Van Wagoner, a noted Washington, DC psychologist, has stated the following concerning the truth in a therapist's interpretation with clients:

> If we assume that our patients' verbalizations are the truth for them, and that our interpretations are the truth as we see it (and

hope that our patients will see it), then the extent to which an interpretation is accepted depends upon how divergent these truths (ours and theirs) are.

I have thought interpretations have the capacity to be jarring and unempathic when the chasm between the truths as seen by us and our patients is too wide. I believe that there is a moment in the exchange when an interpretation is more likely to be considered, and felt as empathic, and that moment depends upon how closely we match our interpretation to their experience (i.e., the interpretation might be on the tip of their awareness and we nudge them toward it—the truth); how accurate the interpretation is (i.e., the extent to which we really understand the patients' dynamics and can make an accurate interpretation); and the affective capacity of the patients to receive the interpretation. For example, I typically do not make interpretations when the patient is in an emotional storm—it will likely fail. I have seen many a therapist (experienced and inexperienced) do this, which I think often stems [more] from a countertransference need to get out of the storm, than an empathic understanding of the patient's issues and feelings.

Interpretations should move the patient to a more complete understanding of the truth, if you must use that word. It is why I favor exploration over explanation. I believe that if we can explore an experience with a patient thoroughly, which would include examining all of the resistances to the truth, or the verbalization of it, then we help [the patient] to relinquish the resistances to the extent that [he or she] can receive the interpretation with less confusion and injury.

Of course we can complicate it further with an analysis of the developmental level of the patient. A fairly put together neurotic is more apt to appreciate an interpretation that is more experience distant if it is accurate than a narcissistic patient, but that is another topic. (Personal communication via e-mail, March 2002)

When helping clients seek their truth in group psychotherapy, we are confronted with some clients proactively avoiding knowing its existence. Although this is often the case, Freud astutely declared that, "human beings are not meant to keep secrets" as the truth will eventually work its way out into the open in some form. It is these myriad forms that we as therapists must become acutely aware of in helping our clients, e.g., the meaning behind symptomatology, slips of the tongue, their interpretations of the behaviors of other group members, our sense that clients are withholding information, escalation of their anger when issues are presented, etc.

In the examples of the problematic client in the following section, there appear to be two distinct features that link many clients intimately together. These features or commonalities are the behavioral manifestations of their personalities, which is their truth, although possibly unknown to them at that time, and the direct and indirect expression of anger. A lot of the symptomatology we see in clients, in its many florid forms, is nothing more than the individualized expression of repressed and suppressed anger. If we rule out genetic or physiological damage and deficits and focus our attention to the basically functioning client, we often will see how powerful anger is in affecting his or her life. The manifest difficulties we come to observe in group therapy, in relation to the truth and anger, is seen in the fact that many clients have great difficulty disclosing the truth, which we can observe, and great difficulty appropriately expressing and receiving anger, which we can also observe, without feeling devastated by both.

We consistently hear clients relate that they could never tell another person the truth about how they feel because they would not want to hurt the other person's feelings. So they silently suffer with their feelings unexpressed, which ultimately causes them continuous and ongoing emotional problems. This difficulty in disclosure for them may have arisen through the socialization process in their histories. For example, if they had caretakers who did not allow them to verbally express themselves, and if they did express themselves and these expressions were deemed inappropriate, they were usually physically punished or verbally punished with guilt for having done something wrong. This punishment then becomes internalized and remains in operation inhibiting a client's spontaneous disclosure of what he or she feels and thinks. As an analogy, it is similar to your computer in which programs run behind the screen of which you are unaware, but they have a major effect on control and manipulation of the information which is being manifested on the screen and with which you are interacting.

Because of this, it is not uncommon to hear a client say that he or she was taught "if you cannot say something nice to another person, do not say anything at all." The residual lesson remains in consciousness: "do not say anything at all." The actual emotional pain from that lesson remains behind the scenes or out of consciousness but profoundly influences the client's interpersonal interactions. Whenever repression and/or suppression occurs, I believe anger is predominantly the concomitant feeling being released. Although it may not make itself known directly, it influences the interactions an individual has with most of the people in his or her life.

So with this in mind, we must look behind the disclosures of clients as they relate to others in the group. Basically, when the disclosure or interpretation is related to another group member we seek to find the projection that is in operation. That is why the group therapist must be aware of the concept of projection and its intimacy with interpretation. In these projections we will come to know the truth of the individual whether or not he or she is aware of it. I have found that projection is an easier venue for clients as it often remains unconscious. Whereas the direct disclosure of the truth or anger is perceived as negative, due once again to projection, but in this case the client erroneously empathizes with the supposed feelings of others and at the same time reinforces his or her belief that he or she is a sensitive human being and would not want to create discomfort in another. What this simply means is that clients project onto others their fears and anxieties of being hurt or devastated by hearing the truth or anger from another toward them. Because of this, the client avoids both of these two salient human expressions expressing truth and anger, and sacrifices authenticity, autonomy, and his or her reality.

We now focus our attention toward anger, the final component in our trinity of truth, anger, and projection. Anger is an interesting emotion. It appears to be a part of the emotional repertoire of all humans and most animals. When expressed, it can have the effect of being perceived negatively by both the person expressing it and the person receiving it. Ultimately, its manifestation is usually interpreted to mean that the person expressing it is no longer a nice individual. This is especially true for many new clients initially entering into group therapy. We clearly see this when clients use the ego defense mechanism of undoing. They will disclose that they are feeling angry toward someone and then back pedal with some statement such as, "Well, maybe it really is not anger, it is more annoyance, or I feel a little hatred toward you." Feeling a little hatred is like being a little pregnant. Anger, like truth and all other emotions, when unexpressed directly will make itself known in some way, shape, or form as will be seen in the examples of the problematic client in the next section.

In its obvious, direct form, anger is easily seen. The emotionality is heightened, the voice is raised, and the person expressing it is usually "in your face." Once it has been expressed, the anger generally diminishes because an essence of catharsis has occurred. In the direct form, we know what the individual is feeling and thinking at that moment. We also know, if the anger is directed toward us at that moment, what the individual is feeling or thinking about us. How we then choose to respond to this anger will of course be dependent upon our individual personalities.

In its indirect form, which is the most debilitating over time for both the person feeling it and the person to whom it is being displaced, anger remains hidden but ongoing. In the indirect form we may see a certain degree of passivity in the clients in our groups. There may be a preponderance of the ego defense mechanism called reaction formation. The group therapist should listen to the information disclosed as a projection during interpretation by a group member toward another group member. The therapist should also focus specifically on the tone of voice of that information being disclosed as this will help in having a clearer understanding of what is actually being related when it is not being directly expressed. For example, in a client experiencing reaction formation this individual may speak about another with loving, positive verbalizations or a loving, positive interpretation but feel that what is being disclosed is truly not accurate or sincere. There is something just not right about the tone of voice. It does not comfortably correlate with the words. I think one of my favorite expressions is, "I could just love him to death." Personally, I could do without being loved in that way.

Usually in the reaction formation defense in group, the client is masking anger or hostility. Rarely do we find a client using it to hide true love. Because anger is often perceived as a negative emotion that can affect the positive perception of others toward an individual, it can take many forms. To borrow from science fiction, it is a "shape-shifter." Its direct, heightened emotionality is easy to recognize but one must have appreciation of its indirect and hidden expressions. These expressions are usually more predominant in new groups when clients' egos are not that strong and they are seeking the approval of others. Relating back to a group member that he or she is manifesting these indirect forms of anger and hostility can be an especially interesting experience for the group leader. The client probably will give you an astonished, often hurt look, when you relate that he or she is being hostile. It is the kind of a look that a person would give you if you disclosed that you lived on Saturn. This occurs because the client is often not in touch with his or her feelings. Anger is ego dystonic and the client may not be cognizant of many manifestations. You may find that when you disclose your feeling that the client is being hostile, and after the client tells you how wrong you are, his or her anger begins to overtly emerge—usually directed toward you, the group leader.

Some examples of anger's indirect manifestations can be seen in the following behaviorial characteristics:

- *Judgmental*—Very few people grew up in a Garden of Eden or are perfect individuals who have not done things in their past that they wish they had not done. Whenever a person is being judgmental of another, he or she is being hostile. The person's judgments generally are negative and serve the purpose of elevating the judgmental person over the other by lessening the other's existence. It too can serve the purpose of dragging the other individual down to one's level of development. Judgmental people are very difficult to be around for any prolonged period of time and have a way of debilitating the self-esteem and ego strength of those they are involved with intimately.

- *Indirect insensitivity*—In this behavior, the anger is not direct but rather hidden. The person manifesting this behavior usually is unaware of the negative effect it is having on those in his or her life. If the person was aware and continued this behavior, we would indicate that he or she is being sadistic. Very often, insensitive people are angry and their insensitivity is an expression and displacement of that anger. Rudeness is a form of insensitivity but it is more overt. You know the person is being rude. Indirect insensitivity is not initially that easy to see. For example, if you tell a person to stop doing something because it is becoming annoying and the person continues to do it, he or she is being insensitive to your feelings. Not only is this person being insensitive but this person is also being hostile. If the person does not stop, you will probably be the one to act out the anger that the other person has kept hidden by eventually responding with direct anger at the individual.

- *Competition in an interpersonal relationship*—Competition is fine in business and in sports, but when it comes to interpersonal relationships it is a form of anger and hostility. As you are aware, in competition there is generally a winner and a loser. One does not expect or desire this in interpersonal relationships if one is psychologically healthy. We also see this in people who always need to be right. No matter what, they have to be right; this means no matter what, you have to be wrong. This is hostility on the part of the competitor. You are consistently perceived as an obstacle to be defeated. In an ongoing relationship with this individual you will eventually lose your self-esteem and ego strength because you are constantly placed in the position of defending yourself or being a consistent loser.
- *Emotional ungiving*—We see this a lot. Clients will relate that a significant other in their lives refuses to tell them how he or she feels. With this individual, one never knows exactly where one stands. For them, disclosing their feelings is almost as bad as losing. It too can have a sadistic component, as this individual knows that his or her behavior is upsetting you. However, that is less important than the individual's noncommittal expression of his or her feelings.
- *Setups*—This occurs when an individual sets up two or more people as an indirect form of getting out his or her anger and hostility. For example, when a husband tells his wife that she does not take care of him as well as his mother or his past girlfriends did, he is being hostile. This may elicit anger on the part of the wife toward those other people, when in fact it should be directed back to the husband, who has just gotten out his anger on her and is trying to indirectly manipulate her behavior because she is not fulfilling his needs.
- *Manipulations*—Whenever one person tries to manipulate another for his or her own personal gains, he or she is being hostile. The individual is basically saying, "You are dumb and I can manipulate you for my own hidden needs."
- *Intimidation*—When one person tries to intimidate another by using power, strength, and threats as a form of intimidation for manipulation, he or she is being hostile.

- *Gossip*—Rarely is gossip ever positive. It is frequently derogatory and is a self-stimulating experience for the gossiper at the expense and reputation of another. It is insensitive and hostile and often indicates the unsatisfactory life of the person doing it. It usually has the essence and goal of diminishing another person in the eyes of those who would care to listen.

These are only a few examples of the indirect forms of anger and hostility. Without question, they will manifest themselves in group therapy. Many more exist. It is in the reader's interest to search his or her experiences with others to determine what some other examples may be and to explore the times when he or she may have displaced his or her anger and hostility indirectly.

In conclusion, the reader should feel a little more comfortable with the understanding of the relationships between truth, anger, and projection in their many forms and manifestations. Hiding the truth and repressing or suppressing anger are not psychologically healthy. Learning how to express both appropriately is. No matter what a person's feelings are, they cannot be compartmentalized and maintained over a long period of time without the development of symptomatology in some form. This means that you cannot close the door on one feeling and expect the rest to be fine. Each time a human being does this, he or she further numbs himself or herself to interpersonal experiences with others and foremost with the self. We should work diligently to help clients not only become aware of the truth and what they are feeling but also to be able to express both. Specifically, both truth and anger need to be addressed and expressed in order for us to help our clients in the quest for their self search.

THE PROBLEMATIC CLIENT

The difficulty which arises in the therapeutic relationship is not in the client's behavior but rather in the therapist's behavior. (Altshul, 1977; Ellis, 1985; Kottler, 1992; Lazarus and Fay, 1982)

The concept of the ideal client in group or individual psychotherapy is just that—an ideal. Most of us look forward to working in psychotherapy with individuals who are verbal, bright, motivated to change problematic behaviors, committed to the task at hand, attractive, arrive on time, pay our bill without any fuss, and do not call us ten times a week with complaints. However, this is not always the case. Often we are confronted with a very different kind of client in psychotherapy, whether group or individual. A group member may have some of those characteristics but most assuredly not all of them. It would give one a moment's pause if the individual did manifest all of these characteristics. If this is the case, you are very fortunate, but it is quite possible the person may be acting out a need for your approval, thus manifesting a behavioral style that has caused this client conflicts in the past and present. In relation to the very real human manifestation of needs, it is my belief that all behavior, whether positive or negative, is self-serving. This self-serving expression often has at its core the hope, whether conscious or unconscious, of satisfying or gratifying unmet need(s) from the past. As this relates to the problematic client, it is in the interest of the group therapist to discover what those needs may be and help the client become aware of how those needs are affecting the client's interactions with others.

Admittedly, discovering one's needs can be a Herculean task due to the fact they often have their roots in the past and are out of consciousness. Of specific interest is the fact that this need or needs may be ego dystonic, which makes it that much more difficult for the client to allow into awareness.

For example, a client who strongly and proudly prides himself or herself on his or her great sense of independence is often not going to be receptive to the interpretation that a component of this independence is a flight from a strong unconscious need to be dependent on others. This realization would understandably shake the foundation of the client's integrated personality and create doubt in the individual's personal ego belief system.

So the multirole of the group therapist is not only to help the client become aware of the client's manifest behavior and how it affects others but also the latent need(s) motivating that manifest behavior. A signal to the therapist that he or she is touching upon something that may be of therapeutic value is anger. It will begin to escalate in the group member and at times in the group as a whole. This anger will be directed either toward the group leader or to the group members themselves as the ego of either is beginning to experience anxiety and danger.

The group therapist should search within himself or herself for personal feelings at that moment and ask, "What is it that this client or the group is pulling on in me?" "What do they want from me or the group?" "What need or needs do I or the group seem not to be answering for them at this time?" Generally, the clients we see in therapy are there because personality characteristics have caused distress in both themselves and others in their lives. You may be a therapist, but you are a person first and so are the people who come to see you. In other words, they will be projecting onto you those personality traits that they manifest with others. Although at times distressing and perhaps uncomfortable for you, it is just those personality characteristics of the client and his or her style in seeking need gratification that we hope will appear in the consultation room so that we may do our job. You should realize that these behaviors occur, in many cases, primarily because the client is replaying a behavioral style toward your authority position, a possible defensiveness in your personality, or because he or she is being affected by the multiple transferences occurring in the group.

Altshul (1977), Ellis (1985), Kottler (1992), and Lazarus and Fay (1982) suggest that the difficulty which arises in the therapeutic relationship is not in the client's behavior but rather in the therapist's behavior. Due to some personality conflict of the therapist, the client is perceived as causing the disruption in the therapy rather than the therapist acknowledging his or her own projection and responsibility in causing the difficulty.

A wealth of literature exists on the problematic or difficult client. Bernard and MacKenzie (1994b), Martin (1975), Carroll, Bates, and Johnson (1997), Davis (1984), West (1975), Carroll and Wiggins (1977), Medeiros and Prochaska (1988), Jacobs, Masson, and Harvill (1988), and Greenberg (1984) have provided very interesting and helpful descriptions of this particular population of clients. To help the new clinician, I have done something different in describing these individuals. I have used descriptions that are colorful rather than psychological in the hope that they will help the novice group leader more easily recognize the behavioral characteristic being manifested in the group. Although it is important that you become familiar with these styles of relating, you should also evaluate yourself and determine if you are in some way the catalyst for either creating them or reinforcing them, thus creating iatrogenic disturbances. Perceiving these styles of relating may be difficult and you may find it helpful to refer to this book when you have some experience leading groups. When reading the next section, remember the concepts of the manifest personality, the latent personality, seeking the truth, and the manifestation of anger.

The following list of problematic clients has been gleaned from the input of a number of colleagues. These professionals have had many years of experience with group therapy. They have been on "both sides of the desk" as clients in group and then later as very effective group therapists.

The Idolizer

This particular individual is often a joy to the novice clinician. You are looked upon as brilliant, wise, beautiful, all knowing, always right, someone to model, able to walk on water, etc. This client looks at you with what appears to be love. For the beginning clinician, this is great. Your ego is fed and your chosen profession is validated.

Unfortunately, lurking behind this adoration is a great deal of hostility just waiting to make itself known. In the event that you make a mistake, whether real or imagined, this type of client will seize the opportunity of exposing your "feet of clay." You will be confronted with how much you have disappointed the client. Disclosures such as, "I don't know if I can ever trust you again. You meant so much to me before and now you are just like everyone else in my life," can be completely devastating to the new clinician who does not really understand what has happened.

This change of feeling is very much like Neil Diamond's song, "Love on the Rocks." Try not to be too discouraged, as that is the unconscious goal of this group member right from the beginning. You were doomed to fail in this person's eyes. Obviously, the client is replaying some earlier childhood conflict and you are just standing in, a surrogate for the person to whom these feelings were initially directed. From a dynamic perspective what you are experiencing is the change from a positive transference to a negative transference.

It is advantageous to explore with this individual the concept of expectations of others both past and present and how they relate to each other. A student of mine once said, "Expectation is the foundation for resentment"; this is the case with the idolizer who expects everyone to eventually fail his or her needs and wants.

The Ungiver (Come to Me)

This particular individual should not be confused with the "silent group member," although they may appear to be similar. In the case of the ungiver, we see a group member who rarely volunteers anything without first being "come to" by either another member or the therapist. A group member may say, "John, how do you feel about what I just said, or how do you feel about what the group is discussing?" John actually has a number of thoughts and feelings about what has occurred but patiently waits until someone draws him into the discussion. Novice clinicians often interpret John's behavior as somewhat shy or perhaps fearful. This may be the case, but we also find with this individual a strong need to be in control. By having someone come to him, John is very much in control of the situation. He can either answer or not.

Over time, this individual generally creates frustration in group members. It appears that many group members know individuals similar to John in their personal lives who refuse to disclose what they are feeling or thinking unless prodded, poked, or verbally pushed. Obviously, the transferential component becomes evident and John can become the displacement object of pent-up frustrations from these other group members.

We recommend, with this particular client, introducing the concept of the need for control and what benefits that need is fulfilling. Be advised that rarely does a group member immediately acknowledge the issue you are speaking about. You will need to bring forth this issue and others repeatedly over time. This is probably due to the underlying motivation of the behavior being out of the awareness of the individual and quite possibly the resistance in changing a behavior that is ego syntonic.

The Colleague (The Therapist Helper)

The colleague in group therapy is the client who has taken the role of helping the leader. This group member agrees with your statements, perhaps adding somewhat more or completing your interpretations by saying, "Indeed." Of course, it is wonderful knowing you have an ally in group, but this behavior is a way of distancing this group member's own interpersonal conflicts. By being unofficial co-therapists, clients never have to look at themselves. You will also find that this role, initially, gives the client some power in the group by association with the therapist. Over time, some group members will begin to mention this fact and feel anger not only toward this member but toward the therapist for allowing this behavior to continue.

Some clients who resent this member's behavior interpret the colleague as the therapist's favorite, thus activating unresolved sibling conflicts. Actually, this can be quite therapeutic. It is an opening for multiple discussions. It also activates a new feeling for the client who is an only child and never had to share his or her parents' attention with anyone else.

In the colleague we find a frightened individual. The association with the therapist gives a degree of security and comfort. Such clients never have to look at themselves as they are too busy helping others with their problems. You need to be sensitive to this issue, as it is quite easy to create a narcissistic injury to the client manifesting this behavioral style.

The client may interpret your intervention of changing the role from colleague to client as an act of rejection. Speaking about the need to be special in group and in other areas of one's life is very helpful, not only for the group member but for the group as a whole.

The Transmitter

The transmitter is the client in group who is always on transmit. He or she is extremely verbal without any observable listening skills. Very often group therapists refer to this client as the "monopolizer." Generally this person is the first person to both open and close the group therapy session and proceeds to commandeer as much "air time" as possible within the group therapy session. At first, this client can be helpful to the group leader if there is a preponderance of silent members in the group, but this individual can also sabotage the group by not allowing others to "find their voices." If the group leader is watchful, he or she will begin to see a number of personality features emerge from this particular individual. Perhaps the most salient being competition with an interplay of narcissism and anxiety. It is fortuitous for the group and the transmitter that the group leader address the issues of the transmitter and not permit this individual to consistently take control of the group therapy sessions with her or his personal issues at the expense of other group members not being heard.

The nature and length of time of the group, for example a time-limited or an ongoing group, will also determine the input necessary of the group leader. Usually, time-limited groups require more input on the part of the group leader whereas ongoing groups very often take care of this particular situation on their own. It is not uncommon when the transmitter is confronted by either the group members or the group leader about his or her manifest behavior and commandeering that this client may "cop an attitude." The attitude may be sullenness, disinterest in the group, hurt, total silence as a form of punishing the group leader and group members, or intense anger with a lot of blaming of others for being put in that position because they do not talk.

When all of this comes to light, we have a great deal of information to help this client go beyond his or her self-concentration and move toward establishing more interrelatedness with other individuals. Remember that the group leader and the group members must first work toward helping this person learn how to listen.

The Seducer (It Is Nice to Be Nice)

The term *seducer* is not specifically used to connote sexuality, although there is a possibility of sexuality being part of an unconscious motivation. The seducer is the client who is complimentary to everyone in group. The client operates under the tenet, "if you cannot say anything nice, do not say anything at all." Initially, this client is liked by most, if not by all members of the group.

Who does not like someone who always tells you nice things about yourself? Unfortunately, this group member uses this behavior to render others passive so that nothing negative is said to the individual in question. In fact, when it eventually comes to light that the group feels that the client may be "too good to be true," the seducer is completely bewildered. This client wonders, "How could anyone feel negatively about me when all I have ever been is nice?"

This individual holds a lot of resentment behind the niceties. It is very difficult to be a saint all of the time without feeling some degree of negativity toward other human beings. We find that these people come from homes in which any kind of emotional expression that was less than positive was met with strong parental disapproval, although, in this case, the parents may not have behaved in the manner they required of their child.

It is actually a joy to watch these clients make the decision to finally be real and disclose what they are feeling. We have observed that opening a discussion on the real and artificial personality that one presents to the world is very effective. They often carry a lot of judgment toward others and themselves, which needs to be addressed. It is not uncommon for the seducer to leave therapy when the group begins confronting him or her about lack of sincerity.

The Iron Butterfly
(Don't Hurt Me, I Am Fragile and Sensitive)

The iron butterfly is a most intriguing individual, as this person shows great sensitivity to all living creatures in the universe. Disclosures or dialogues with others tend to have an ethereal tone with an almost egoistic type of connection with the cosmos. This is not to suggest that understanding the connectedness of all life is a negative quality, because it is not. Yet the iron butterfly often escapes pain by saying, "Isn't life beautiful!"

In time, we begin to see a little slippage in this person's armor. This is especially prevalent when other group members whose lives are not so beautiful begin to get fed up with relating to an otherworldly individual.

When confronted, the fragile iron butterfly can turn into a very nasty and hostile person who is actually very strong. In fact, to maintain the denial that the individual's world is always like a garden requires great strength.

We have found that slowly introducing certain realities of this individual's past and bringing forth different interpretations than the ones the individual chooses to see can be very helpful. Although this reality can be painful, it also can be healing. You must proceed slowly with the iron butterfly so that this individual does not fly away.

Convince Me

The "convince me" client can be quite annoying over time for both the therapist and the group members. No matter what is said, the convince-me individual seems to disbelieve your statements or those of the other group members. These statements may not be about the convince-me group member, but there is always that particular look of disbelief or a response that says, "this cannot be so, you must prove it to me." Obviously, this individual has a strong competitive personality component with an even stronger need to be in control.

An open mind is not one of this group member's strong attributes. This person has the need to be right. We have found that in the family of origin of this type of personality, the individual's disclosures were met with uncaring, disbelief, or someone trying to change what this individual said. Nothing tended to stand on its own. Rather, it was changed by another person to help make this other person feel more comfortable or to confer a sense of power.

Unfortunately, this group member has modeled the behaviors of the people who created this problem. We find that this person has a lot of unexpressed rage, which frequently creates frustration in others and eventually causes escalating hostility. When another member expresses this anger, it gives the convince-me individual an open door to release the pent-up anger that is quite close to the surface. In fact, it is easy to see that this behavioral style has been unconsciously designed for the sole purpose of releasing anger. If the individual rationalizes and projects that the other group member is in attack mode, then raging back will appear to be an appropriate self-defense.

We have found with this personality that bringing two salient components into consciousness is extremely effective. Those two components are the repressed rage and the use of frustration as a weapon to lure others into battle. When aware, the convince-me person no longer needs to be convinced.

In Your Face

The "in-your-face" client can be very difficult for the novice clinician who usually operates under the global theme of wanting to help others. Just because you want to help others does not necessarily mean that all others want to be helped.

This individual is usually in your face from day one. Your sensitivities, weaknesses, insecurities, and needs are a focus of this person's interest. This person is not necessarily, at first, interested in personal change, but rather interested in remaining the same. You are the enemy and your vulnerabilities become a focus of this client's goal in therapy.

The other group members are of secondary importance, as you are the individual to defeat. If you can be defeated, this client's personality can remain intact. This can also be a very interesting group member if you can withstand the diatribe that will be forthcoming. It is interesting to note that this client is sometimes admired by other group members. These members would like to be in your face but are fearful that you might reject them or retaliate in some fashion.

As a group member, the in-your-face individual is a catalyst for eliciting emotionality for both the members and you, the leader. A creative web is often woven in which to trap you and to use your own words against you. If you manage to get through the difficulty of being tested and demonstrate that you can take what is dished out, you will find that this person can become a very fine group member.

We find that continuously responding with such statements as, "You seem to be angry with me or you seem to have a need to challenge everything I say," can be effective over time. It shows this client that you are aware of what is occurring and you are not angry, nor are you going to be rejecting.

The Setter Upper

This client can create anger and doubt in both the novice clinician and the senior therapist if neither is aware of what is going on. The underlying goal of this client is to divide and conquer. This goal can be attained in some of the sincerest presentations in group, thus creating division among members and between the therapist and members or between the therapist and another therapist.

The setup occurs when the individual has the need to let out some anger but does it indirectly. For example, the client may say in the nicest of tones that when he or she spoke to Dr. Smith, another therapist he or she is seeing for individual psychotherapy, Dr. Smith completely disagreed with what you said to this client in group. Because both of this client's therapists appear to be saying different things, the setter upper innocently says that he or she is very confused. Or the client may disclose that his wife/husband feels that you are incompetent and a real jerk.

Generally for senior clinicians, this type of setup is expected, but for the beginning therapist it touches on a lot of personal issues and promotes doubt in an already unsure psychotherapist. The setup may stimulate your anger. Since we are human and our immediate response to a narcissistic injury is to give one back, it is in the interest of the therapeutic situation that you do not. Very few beginning therapists are at the point where they can analyze all situations without personalizing some.

You will also see that this client tends to use this technique of setting others up in a number of relationships. You may have a woman in group who discloses that her husband says that she does not make love to him as well as his ex-girlfriend or she does not take care of him the way his mother did. It is not uncommon to hear adolescents relate that their mothers or fathers will say, "Why can't you be like your brother who is a straight-A student?"

Unfortunately, this often works against what the person is trying to accomplish, which is to have some control over the other's behavior. The individual to whom the setup is directed generally feels angry or hurt and rebels against what is being presented.

Making the person aware of this behavior with a clear, detailed explanation is necessary to help this client to change.

The Threatener

The threatener is different from the in-your-face client in the sense that this individual is not in your face. This particular person exudes the feeling that some act of aggression is close to the surface and may be acted out depending upon the type of disclosure presented in the group by either the leader or a member.

A number of students who have been trained in domestic violence groups often have this experience. It is as if the client is lying in wait to let loose a rage that is barely held in check.

This client can be a nightmare for the student clinician because it becomes difficult to concentrate on helping others when there is a feeling that some act of violence may occur. This group member especially intimidates young female clinicians. This is exactly the goal of this client's behavior. Frightening the therapist into passivity gives the threatener a sense of power, plus the individual never has to work on the underlying behaviors that brought him or her into psychotherapy.

We have found that another group member usually brings focus to this issue by disclosing feelings similar to the clinician's concerning the threatening situation. If this does not occur, you will need to address the issue. Work closely with your supervisor and decide when it would be appropriate to introduce this issue into your group. You may find that you will need to do this rather early in the group's history. It may be advantageous to generalize the concept by asking how each member feels when threatened or what each individual does to be threatening and what the goal of that behavior might be.

The Blamer

This particular individual, at first, elicits interest and compassion from the other group members when he or she initially discloses the reasons that brought this person into therapy. Generally, the individual's life story is clear and often exact with many defined details as if it has been worked on over and over again. It is not at all unusual for adolescents to blame their parents, and we expect this as it is often age-specific behavior. It is not unusual to hear adults do the same, but usually an adult will eventually move beyond blaming one's parents and others and take responsibility for his or her lot in life.

This is not to be the case in relation to the blamer. The transition toward refocusing the responsibility of one's life from others back upon oneself is not easily forthcoming with this individual. This client rigidly adheres to the belief that all of his or her woes in life are due to the influence of others. By the way, you as the group leader will eventually become one of those others.

This is not to suggest that many of the life stories this individual discloses did not happen but rather that this person has a heightened sensitivity to most interpersonal interactions. These interactions are often perceived to be negatively affecting him or her unless the other person is consistently attentive and compassionate to the burdens, whether real or imagined, in the blamer's life.

Eventually, we must all move beyond that which previously has burdened us if we wish to have satisfaction and contentment in life. I once had a client in group therapy whose presenting reason for seeking psychotherapy was that she seemed to have a difficult time keeping friends even though initially people seemed interested in her. After three groups, she contacted me and informed me that she was terminating therapy with me but she wanted me to know the list of reasons why. After a rather long diatribe on my incompetence, her last remark, before slamming the phone down on me was, "And I did not lose an ounce of weight in the three weeks I was in group."

Apparently, I was perceived by this client as being remiss in my professional duties because I did not complete a total makeover, i.e., psyche, emotional, physical, and make her relationships last longer in the previously undisclosed three weeks that I was given. It was now my fault, as it had been everyone else's fault in this client's historical relationships. Obviously, there was a transferential component in this client's relationship with me, but the unrealistic demands are more of an interest in this case.

The blamer is an angry person who continually sets up situations and then interprets them in a way that fits this individual's belief system. The belief system is, "it is because of you nothing is right in my life." In relation to group therapy, if the client stays long enough for the process to work, it is in the interest of the group therapist to be aware if a client continually discloses historical and current interpersonal relationships which all have the theme of the client being hurt, burdened, or disappointed. Often, after a few weeks group members will become annoyed and begin to introduce, to this client, concepts and questions, such as, "What was your part in all of this? What do you plan to do about this in the future? We never feel you are interested in us but only that we should be interested in you." This is perfect for the blamer. Once again no one understands the hurt he or she has felt and it may be the springboard for this individual to leave group.

If the individual chooses to hang in and allow himself or herself to take in what the group has related, we have a good chance of providing help and eliciting permanent personality changes. This client will move forward and backward between growth and regression. During those times of regression, when the blaming and "poor me" emerge, it is important not to allow this individual to become a scapegoat because of the group's frustrations with him or her. Actually, the blamer is a wonderful group member as this individual glaringly shows other group members what they must look like when they fall into the blaming trap.

The Good Client

The good client does everything right. This individual is always on time and cooperative, works on issues, pays your bill, does not call you eight times a week, etc. This person appears to deal with anger effectively, whether that anger is toward another member or the anger from another member is toward the good client.

The way this client works in group is almost compulsive. In fact, upon further analysis we often find the need for perfection dovetailed with the need for strong approval to be the underlying motivation. Unfortunately, the underlying issues in this person's life may be lost on the new clinician as this client appears to be doing well and causes little stress or worry to the therapist.

This is not to suggest that a client who works hard in group therapy is always masking a need for approval and seeking perfection. There are certainly cases in which the individual has very strong motivations because of realizations that his or her life is not satisfactory and needs to be changed. But in the case of the good client, it would be wise for the therapist to explore issues of approval and perfection. While exploring these issues, the leader needs to reinforce the client's effort so that this individual does not experience a narcissistic injury, as this will close the client up.

You must remember that a large part of this client's motivation is seeking approval. If you present the behavior as negative, this individual can feel confused and rejected. We often see that certain clients are completely identified with all of their behavioral characteristics. This means that if they fail at a task, they interpret that failure as a total failure in themselves rather than simply not being proficient in one area.

We suggest posing questions such as, "John, you seem to work so hard at always doing things right. This is very commendable, but what happens to you when you have done something and it does not turn out as well as you had expected or planned?" You may find that John will then begin to disclose to you his internal world and the concomitant feelings and thoughts regarding making a mistake. Upon John's disclosure, you may find that many other people in your group have similar issues but perhaps not to the extent John does.

In reducing John's conflict you will need to help him learn how to make mistakes without being intropunitive. Being human and real can be a challenge for this individual, and reinforcement from you, the leader, and the members that it is all right not to be perfect can make a tremendous difference in this person's experience of life.

Am I Getting My Share?

This is an interesting client in the sense that this person operates from a "more or less" perception of events in the group and in life. In the past this client has often had to share attention unequally with other siblings. For whatever reason, more attention was probably given to other siblings.

This inequality created a lifetime pattern of watching to see if someone else was getting more reinforcement than the client was receiving. Group, by its very nature, creates a difficult environment for this person because rarely is everyone given equal time in a session. To compensate for this, the client will identify with what another group member discloses, which at first is helpful in that the other member does not feel so alone in the issue. However, ordinarily it does not stop there. The client always wants the same amount or more of the group's or therapist's attention then uses this identification as a springboard to focus on himself or herself. When the focus is back on the "am I getting my share?" client, this individual can easily go on and on about loosely associated experiences that tangentially touch upon the initial identification.

In time, both you and the group will probably become annoyed with this behavior because it takes attention away from whatever the other client discloses, and, like a magnet, brings it back to the client who has difficulty sharing. Note that this client can get very angry with the therapist if it is perceived that the leader is giving more attention to another member. It is not uncommon for this client to make repeated phone calls during the week after the group session with statements such as, "I really didn't understand what you or another member said during the group." This ploy, which may be based in reality, can also reflect this person's need to get extra time to diminish the concern that others are getting more.

It is very important that you bring up the issue of sharing and how group does not always give each individual equal time at every session. It is also important to help this member understand that group therapy is not individual therapy. You may wish to explore further what it is like for this client to feel that someone is getting more.

The Nontalker (The Silent Member)

At times, this client creates a feeling of failure or success in the beginning clinician. We believe that a chain is as strong as its weakest link and a nonspeaking member can have a very powerful effect on group cohesiveness and dynamics. If the therapist as well as some members of the group are sensitive, the lack of overt responses by the silent member will be felt.

There may be many reasons that this individual does not participate including previous experiences in group situations that were aversive and unsatisfying, or the client's self-esteem is quite low and he or she is fearful that any disclosure may not be as effective as those of other group members. In any case, the lack of disclosure needs to be addressed. It could demonstrate the need to draw attention back to the client, or a total lack of interest on the client's part in what is occurring in the lives of others in the group.

Some therapists feel that a silent member can get as much out of a group as the active members. I do not agree. For one thing, the group suffers in many respects. It is also unfair for the other group members to disclose intimate details of their lives while this member continuously looks on.

We generally address the issue of a silent member in the third or fourth session if another group member has not already done so. We ask the nontalker if this silence is something the individual wishes to maintain. Is he or she struggling with some other issue that may be inhibiting group participation? Although bringing the focus back to them will increase the anxiety of some silent members, this should not inhibit the group leader unless that anxiety is beyond optimal and into the maximal range. Generally, the nontalker begins to disclose some of the discomforts of being in a group situation. If you do not help the silent member find his or her voice, your other group members will begin to manifest escalating anger, and scapegoating may occur.

The Competitor (You Are Wrong)

This type of member becomes an ongoing challenge for the group leader. No matter what you say, this client continuously tries to show you and the group the correct interpretation. This behavior may reflect an underlying need for your approval, but the manifest behavior is to prove you are wrong. Unlike the in-your-face client, this person may compete in the nicest ways. For example, the competitor may say, "If you don't mind me disagreeing with you"—which is another way to discredit you—"I feel that what you might be overlooking is . . ." Or perhaps, phrased in a pleasant voice, "Maybe if you presented it this way to Sabrina she wouldn't look as hurt."

Usually the basic underlying issue of this individual is the need to be in control, and every authority figure becomes a threat to that need. It is not uncommon for this client to spend a lot of energy and time analyzing you and your behavior. This individual may remind you of something you said months ago in group, which the client has been holding patiently to use against you.

Often in the history of this client there was and still may be an inflexible authoritarian significant figure who was always very much in control. Whatever this figure said was the way it had to be and anyone who did not agree was wrong. What you will observe in this particular client through the transference is (1) the repressed anger that needs to come out and (2) the need for the authority figure to finally say, "You are right and I am wrong."

When working with this client you need to be real and to help this individual become aware of the anger and introjection of the personality that initially caused this person's distress. After you get beyond the storm and stress, this client can be wonderful to work with in group therapy.

The Whiner (Why Does Everything Happen to Me?)

This individual becomes an annoyance over time for both the group and the leader. When this member enters group, the majority of the other members are solicitous and understanding of the experiences of this unfortunate individual. As time goes by, it becomes apparent that this person is definitely interested in focusing on, "Why does everything awful always happen to me?"

When the group tries to help, this individual often responds by saying, "yes, but." The level of self-concentration of the whiner is quite elevated—the world revolves around this person. Identification with other group members is limited unless the whiner can use this identification as a competitive springboard to return to issues in his or her life, which are always more intense than those of any other living human being.

No one, according to this person, truly understands the calamities and difficulties this brave soul has withstood. At times, the whining manifests itself in a childlike presentation with an annoying tone that drives many group members to respond with anger. The whining is often a secondary gain, a gratification obtained from an indirect behavior, and probably has been used for a number of years to manipulate others in this individual's environment.

If you watch certain parents whose child continuously whines, you may see the parents give up in frustration and gratify the child's needs to end the whining. In group, it is very important that this client becomes aware of the effect the whining is having on those in his or her environment. In fact, often this person reports that people seem to distance themselves. It is also important to help this client understand that not everyone on earth is here to answer all of this person's needs and wants.

The Paint Dryer (Stimulation Absent)

It is unrealistic to assume that every client that comes to you for professional help will be colorful and interesting. Some clients, upon entering the consultation room, create an environment that is as exciting as watching paint dry. Therapists have been known to fall asleep and group members have been known to completely disregard or scapegoat this member as a means of getting some sort of emotional response.

This individual does not usually have conscious or unconscious motives to put others to sleep. Ruling out depression, there are just some clients whose affect is so flat that speaking with them for any length of time is like being in an environment totally lacking any form of stimulation. In effect, to use a behavioral term, it is like being with a human "time-out room" where all stimulation is removed as a form of punishment.

These clients can be well educated, highly intelligent, and so on, but their presentation and delivery of themselves or information is just plain boring. This individual tends to be emotionally restricted. Perhaps, in this person's history, emotionality was not reinforced or it could have been looked upon by significant others as being childish. It is not uncommon to find that a person with this lack of affect comes from a family with tremendous affect and the child felt over time that his or her voice could not be heard in the family.

In any case, exploring this lack of affect is most important. You will probably find that the individual is somewhat or totally aware that this is occurring but has not been able to find a way out of it. If the therapist is not sensitive to the needs of this client, this member can get lost in a group therapy situation. You may choose to explore the concept of fear, doubt, and anxiety with this person and how it relates to interpersonal situations.

REVIEW

Part A

The truth is philosophically an elusive entity. Often, it is difficult to find, and at times more difficult to accept, and it is often perceived differently by the individual perceiver. How would you go about creating an environment in which your group members would feel comfortable disclosing their truth, the indispensable factor necessary for psychotherapy to be effective?

Part B

You have completed reading a number of different behavioral characteristics of problematic clients in group therapy. Although many of these characteristics overlap, they do in fact manifest different behavioral styles in seeking to get their needs gratified. How do you think these individuals would respond if the presenting issue in group is "I never get my needs met"?

Chapter 13

Group Psychotherapy
As a Negative Experience

Group psychotherapy is an experience, and similar to all experiences in life it can be positive, negative, or a combination of both depending upon the personality of the individual group member. When it is experienced as consistently negative by the client, a number of factors need to be addressed. In cases in which the client has been mandated for group therapy, we are frequently at the outset dealing with a negative situation and often a negative individual. When the client has come on his or her own volition and finds the group therapy process to be a dreadful experience, we need to pursue what is occurring for this particular person.

A negative group therapeutic experience for a group therapy client is considered to be anything that worsens the client's well-being and/or precipitates an early termination from therapy. The negative therapeutic experience can happen at any time within the course of treatment but is predominantly seen at opposite poles in the group psychotherapy experience—the beginning and the end. Between these two extremes, we generally observe a client's positive and negative feelings in relation to their experience in group. This is not to suggest that clients do not terminate along the continuum of the life cycle of the group. Our knowledge of why this occurs is very important for our understanding of both human behavior and the effectiveness of our skills as therapists.

Two possible salient reasons for the negative therapeutic reaction in the beginning of group are (1) improper client selection by the therapist and (2) lack of consistent and clear boundaries within the group. Possible reasons for the negative therapeutic reaction at the end of group seem to be related to (1) the therapist's issues with termination, (2) the client not having accomplished his or her conflict resolution of the problem(s) that motivated this individual to seek psychotherapy and the experience was unsatisfactory or a disappointment, and (3) the group's reactions to issues of separation and loss.

Why these negative experiences occur in group or why these negative therapeutic reactions arise throughout the group experience is the focus of investigation of three possible and different but equally powerful factors. Those factors include the three points on a triangle which symbolize the actual composition of the group itself—the therapist, the client, and the group as a whole.

THE TRIANGLE

The Therapist

The group therapist plays a significant part in the possibility of creating a negative therapeutic reaction in the client. Because of the nature of the work that we do, it is easier to delineate the factors contributed by the group leader, compared to that of the client and group as a whole. This is because we practice within a paradigm or a specific structure. Although not infallible, it does provide certain basic guidelines which, when corrupted, open the door to the possibility that the client will experience his or her therapeutic experience as anything other than therapeutic. Obviously, this places on the group leader a great sense of responsibility. However, it must never be forgotten that the therapist is human and only his or her personal life is subject to the trials and tribulations of life's capriciousness and vicissitudes. If not carefully monitored they can negatively affect his or her work. This is why it is highly suggested that a therapist has his or her own experience as a client in therapy to work through those personal issues which, when resolved, will create a more effective clinician. In this particular case, group therapy would be the more effective route to follow, as it is a relationship-oriented modality.

Korda and Pancrazio (1989) suggest that there are several therapist factors related to negative outcome in group psychotherapy. These factors include incompetency and inadequate preparation of the therapist, inadequate screening and preparation of group members, inadequate provisions for group safety including the lack of a clear statement about ground rules, inappropriate management of conflict, and inadequate handling of early client terminations from the group.

Weiner (1994) states that a negative therapeutic reaction can occur if the therapist has not made the right diagnosis, prescribed the right treatment, and if the therapist lacks the technical skill needed to run a group.

The negative therapeutic experience in group can be a result of the group therapist's unresolved countertransference. Moore and Fine (1990) define countertransference as a situation in which the therapist's feelings and attitudes toward a client are derived from earlier situations in the therapist's life and these feelings then become displaced onto the client. Also, countertransference can be a specific reaction to the client's transference to the therapist and can be seen with how the group leader effectively works with anger and authority issues (Van Wagoner, 2000).

When the group therapist is uncomfortable with the expression and/or acknowledgement of anger in either himself or herself and others, he or she may consciously or unconsciously move the group and its individuals away from this anger. This can become a negative situation for the clients who have been harboring anger inside for much of their lives. When this happens the client may see the situation as being unsafe and will either withdraw further into himself or herself or leave the group—both of which are negative outcomes. Many therapists feel that clients need to behave themselves and that anger is not an acceptable expression of emotion. What the clients need to say can be said in ways other than in the expression of this emotion. I do not necessarily agree with this premise unless it is an anger management group.

When the group therapist has his or her own issues or countertransference issues regarding authority concerns, it will be manifested in how the therapist takes on the leadership role and how he or she manages the boundaries of the group. For example, if the group leader consistently has the need to be liked and accepted and has difficulty wearing the mantle of authority, he or she will tend to ignore boundary issues regarding group attendance and the group's temporal boundaries. Klein (1992) suggests that the leader's role involves boundary identification and regulation. Very often, the setting of limits by the group therapist elicits anger toward him or her. This creates discomfort in the therapist, who would rather avoid the escalation of emotion.

The Client

In relation to the client, the analyses are wide open to interpretation as to why he or she can experience group psychotherapy as being negative. This is because human personality is not easily seen as an either/or entity but rather a combination of multiple and often as-yet-undiscovered factors. Although psychology and psychiatry have come a very long way since Pinel, we are still very much in the dark when it comes to completely understanding another human being. A general consensus is that the following factors contribute to a negative experience and early termination: (1) the client's own personality or psychopathology, (2) the therapist's countertransference and/or technical errors, and (3) the processes occurring within the group as a whole, which the client perceives to be aversive. Since the first factor of this particular triangle is the client, we address and examine possible factors in a client's personality that cause him or her to have a diathesis of a negative group experience. Remember that the client brings into group his or her own personal, unique, and historical experiences that will affect the client's perceptions.

Budman, Demby, and Randall (1980) report that clients who have a negative therapeutic reaction very often have a history of having few intimate friendships, are primarily involved with their family of origin, see themselves as distant and insensitive to others, and have unresolved trust issues which become manifested in the group experience. According to Fielding (1983), who looked at the negative experiences of the silent group member, these individuals often do not permit themselves the process of the group therapy experience and relate that their changes are minimal. These clients have reported that what little change they experienced was both negative and regressive. They have also perceived the group and the group leader as less than satisfactory. The more verbally involved clients related that their experiences were positive and elicited definitive changes in their interactions with others.

According to Rice (1992), the potential for a group member to experience group negatively is historical in origin. This is due to the individual's history, which will be manifested in the phenomenon of transference. Rice explains that transference is an interpersonal, object-related phenomenon in which the members project onto the therapist and one another early, internalized relationships along with their associated feelings, drives, and defenses, and then behave as though they were relating to those early objects. Every client brings into therapy a particular way of relating to certain others. It is this style of relating that creates many of their difficulties in life, which makes group psychotherapy an invaluable vehicle for personality change. Alas, a number of these clients choose not to allow themselves the full reexperiencing of their histories and terminate when their emotional discomfort begins to increase. Embedded within the idea of transference is the client's perception of others, how they see themselves in relation to others, and the feeling that links the two.

Rice (1992) suggests that in group therapy there are multiple transferences between and among the members. A common transferential reaction to the group as a whole includes paranoid-type reactions in which the client perceives the group as an engulfing experience that will swallow him or her up and diminish individuality. Unless serious pathology exists, the fear of diminished individuality often occurs with a client who wants to believe that he or she is unique or "special" and demands to be related to as such. As you are aware, group is a paradigm of equality and the client who demands to be treated as special, different, and unique will find group to be an aversive experience until he or she can adapt and become a group member of parity, if possible, before any therapeutic intervention can begin to occur.

There are also those clients who tend to have poor boundaries thus making it difficult for them to make distinctions between their issues and the issues of others. In the group, these clients will overidentify with the other members' issues and take them on as their own, thus flooding themselves emotionally. They will often comment to the therapist that listening to the problems of others makes them feel worse. If left unexamined, this issue will lead to a negative therapeutic reaction to the group as a whole and the client will likely terminate his or her group therapy experience and relate that he or she is leaving because they feel that they are getting "sicker" while being in therapy.

A common transferential reaction to the group therapist occurs when the client sees the therapist as an all-providing, unlimited source of nurturance and knowledge. When the client's unrealistic, idealized illusion of the therapist becomes more realistic and he or she becomes aware that the therapist is not always available, not an endless well of succor, and does not know everything, the client will tend to perceive the whole therapeutic process as negative and a disappointment. Underneath every idealization is the potential for devaluation (Fehr, 1999). Depending also upon the neediness of the client, he or she will be hypervigilant and supersensitive to the therapist's attention to the other group members. This particular client will become envious and elicit strong negative feelings toward the therapist as he or she perceives the therapist's help toward other clients as being a form of rejection and neglect of the individual whose neediness is unlimited.

Another negative therapeutic reaction occurs when two clients develop an attachment to each other that extends outside of group. Similar to Bion's (1961) basic assumption of pairing in the group itself, these clients believe that their cure lies in their "special relationship" rather than in the whole group process. One of the many possible dangers for these clients is when there is some conflict between the client and the one with whom they are pairing. When conflict occurs in this scenario, it often leads to one or both of the members leaving group with a feeling of disillusionment. The hope that they once carried turns into despair and dejection and the group is projected on and blamed for their failure and disappointment rather than the client taking responsibility for his or her actions. Because this can occur in groups, always write into the group contract that outside socialization should be kept to a minimum. However, we cannot and will not follow our clients around when they leave the group environment. We hope they will honor the contract they have entered into.

Freud (1924) suggests that the negative therapeutic reaction is a result of a patient's unconscious need for punishment. This punishment is related to unconscious, forbidden, instinctual impulses that the client cannot accept in himself or herself. Group therapy, by its nature of creating intimacy, acts as a stimulus for these impulses to once again arise, thus creating a reenactment of the historical punishment the client manifested in the past to ward off the anxiety of the impulses coming into consciousness.

A client's need for punishment can manifest itself in many forms. Because of this, we should be aware of such simple manifest behaviors as group contract breaches, provoking aggressive behavior toward other group members, subgrouping, etc. Although these too can be perceived as testing the limits and boundaries of not only the client, the therapist, and group members, it also can be an unconscious act on the part of the client to be punished for impulses and feelings he or she has not yet disclosed or is not yet aware of. Freud aptly stated, "human beings were not meant to keep secrets and these secrets will eventually make themselves known in some way shape or form." Because some clients manifest a degree of masochism in their personalities, the therapist should search his or her own feelings in relation to the acting out of this type of client. If you feel that this client is pulling on you to reprimand him or her, you may wish to explore that issue. You and the group may be being used in some way as a vehicle to provide a form of punishment for some yet-undiscovered thought or feeling the client may be having toward either you or other members in the group.

Abraham (1919) believed that negative reactions to therapy center on shame and envy. Some clients begrudge the therapist any progress in treatment. Because group therapy can be a powerful facilitator of improvement, it can also stir up feelings of shame and envy in the client. The client with "narcissistic" issues has the potential to feel ashamed at the help the group offers. He or she believes that the acceptance of help from others is an indication of his or her basic unworthiness. Accepting help destroys the illusion of self-sufficiency as it indicates a need. This offering of help from others and the concomitant feelings of shame frequently lead to the wish to destroy that which brings help and comfort. These particular clients are also consistently competitive with both the therapist and the group members. It is a curious conundrum as clients with narcissistic issues seek others to become their narcissistic suppliers. They have developed, over time, exquisite behaviors to elicit adoration. However, when others see negative features in their behaviors and offer help to change those negative features, narcissists become very uncomfortable and often terminate therapy.

Envy can be seen when a group member begins criticizing and devaluing the therapist, the group members, and the group as a whole. Although this can also be interpreted, depending upon the issues presented, that the client is being judgmental but with envy the client is either unaware or aware and withholding that he or she wishes to covet something that another member or members of the group possess. Acknowledging envy would shake the foundation of this client as it would be indicating that he or she is placing a group member in a higher status than himself or herself, which ultimately burdens an already weakly structured ego.

Masterson (1976) believes that the negative therapeutic reaction can be a result of the fear of separation. Group therapy in its essence fosters the development of relationships, which can be frightening to some clients. They believe that getting closer to others will inevitably lead to rejection and loss. These clients then erect emotional walls to prevent themselves from developing feelings of intimacy. These walls ultimately create for them a sense of isolation.

This sense of isolation and the resulting behavioral aversion to close relationships unfortunately inhibits the client from garnering the benefits that group therapy has to offer. In fact, the fear of intimacy and the possibility of loss through rejection is intensely profound and has the power to worsen the client's symptoms and ultimately drive him or her from group before a fear of rejection and abandonment can occur in reality and be worked through in the therapeutic process.

Smith, Murphy, and Coats (1999) suggest that attachment to groups has two underlying dimensions: attachment anxiety and attachment avoidance. They propose that an individual who is high in group-attachment anxiety has a sense of being unworthy as a group member and feelings of worry and concern regarding their acceptance by the group and, as a result, tends to try to please the group by conforming in an unusually rapid time period.

However, this sense of unworthiness and trying to fit in by conforming can boomerang for this type of group member. If this sense of unworthiness is not resolved in the group arena, it can lead to a negative therapeutic perception and experience. This is because the client is aware that he or she has changed to fit in and is not being the person he or she really is, because this real personality probably would not be accepted by the group. Of course, this is not always true but rather a fantasy concerning what the group will consider acceptable in a group member. Group is a wonderful tool for disproving maladaptive beliefs such as unworthiness. However, if these feelings are not addressed by the client openly in the group, the client will continue to assume that his or her beliefs are accurate and there will be a decline in this individual's self-esteem and functioning.

Smith, Murphy, and Coats (1999) further submit that someone who is high in avoidance will tend to view closeness to groups as unnecessary or undesirable and may act aloof and independent, tending to avoid closeness to or dependence on the group. This attitude can also precipitate, if resolution is not forthcoming, not only a negative therapeutic reaction for the group member, but also for some other group members. The group member who has a fear of closeness will not participate emotionally in the group, which will diminish the intrinsic healing power of the group therapy paradigm. Remember Sullivan's statement, "it takes people to make people sick and it takes people to make people well again" (1940, p. 26). This type of client will also tend to elicit negative transferences from other group members who have had unsatisfactory relationships in the past with people who are similar in behavior. Negativity toward the client who fears closeness is almost a self-fulfilling prophecy. Other group members who are transferentially involved with this individual will begin to respond negatively to that group member, which in turn becomes translated by the client who fears closeness as a validation of his or her own beliefs: people are not to be trusted and intimacy leads only to hurt and pain.

Moxnes (1999) suggests that psychoanalytic group analyses often demonstrate that particular individuals emerge in symbolic positions of influence within the group. A number of different forms of symbolic positions have been identified, each representing different emotional themes in the group. Each position in its own way can experience a negative therapeutic reaction.

Moxnes (1999) also suggests that the group selects or drafts its most likely candidate and then forces the person into its needed role. The group members project their disowned emotions and attributes to a single member who unconsciously colludes to absorb and contain some portion of those emotions and attributes.

Fehr (1999) writes about several types of common group member roles. They include the idolizer, the ungiver, the colleague or therapist helper, the seducer, and the iron butterfly, among others. For example, when the person who takes on the iron butterfly role gets confronted in the group he or she will either relinquish the role or play it out to its fullest. If he or she should choose to play it out, the most likely response is to flee group and the feelings of being misused and persecuted.

Klapp (1972) suggests that the central figures in groups are heroes, villains, and fools. These central figures exist in relation to one another and cannot exist separately. There will be those in group who will gravitate to one of these roles and play it out, ultimately risking a negative therapeutic experience.

The person in the hero role will have his or her narcissism fed by the other group members and will thus emotionally close himself or herself off except for when he or she is the recipient of praise. The person in the villain role will be scapegoated and will leave the group feeling angry, misunderstood, and persecuted. The person in the fool role will feel that he or she does not elicit respect from the group and a sense of humiliation will emerge, which eventually motivates this group member to flee the group, feeling foolish.

The Group

It has been my experience that people coming into group therapy arrive with multiple fantasies of what the experience is going to be for them, plus multiple fantasies about the people they have not yet met. This is not to be perceived as an indication of pathology but rather as a very human characteristic for someone entering the unknown, which generates different degrees of anxiety depending upon the individuals' previous histories with groups. When the fantasies correlate in some degree positively with the actual experience, the group member continues in his or her therapy. When the correlation of the fantasies and the actual experience are at intense odds, the client often terminates unless the group therapist can work the two, the fantasies and the actuality, together. This is why many group therapists begin their groups, if it is a time-limited group and all members begin at the same time, with a discussion about the anxiety of being in group and the fantasies the group members may have had. Not only does this give the clients some personal information about one another and encourage them to practice personal self-disclosure, it also gives the group leader some idea as to what has been going on in the minds of the group members. The therapist can monitor the correlation of the clients' actual experiences with their initial fantasies and then determine if a therapeutic intervention may be necessary at a particular time during the group experience.

As you remember from Chapter 6, cohesion is a very important component for an ongoing group. Perhaps the most effective factor in this concept is that the group members have to like one another, as this will elicit in them feelings of wanting to return. If they do not like one another and the therapist does not have the luxury of the format of an ongoing group to work through their individual differences, clients are apt to terminate. Obviously, we cannot always choose group members who we think will get along and have wonderful experiences, but it is certainly a consideration to be well aware of when choosing the people for your groups. Clinicians who do not have the control to choose group members, e.g., in a hospital setting where clients come for two weeks or less, clinics where the clients can afford only group, etc., are in a very difficult and precarious position in creating effective group therapy experiences.

Always remember that each client brings his or her personality and previous history into the group room, which means each client will experience the group as a whole differently unless each group member is identical, and that would be unrealistic.

Yalom (1985) poignantly states that the outcome of a group and a group member's experience is sealed before the first group begins due to the selection of its members. Group members fit together like pieces of a puzzle. This analogy may help the group leader to always take into consideration how well the pieces will fit. Will they hold together during the stresses and strains that are going to be forthcoming, or are the pieces tenuous and is the initial picture missing some very important elements?

According to Rutan and Stone (1993), issues within the group itself can contribute to the negative therapeutic reaction for a client. Powerful regressive forces are activated in group formation, and the interplay between these forces and the individual is generally what prompts a person to drop out. Rutan and Stone add that pressures for intimacy and closeness may be frightening forces that prematurely propel some individuals out of groups. Other group processes that contribute to early departure are scapegoating, avoidance of in-group conflict, and insistence on immediate and intense expression of feelings.

Bion (1961) identified three types of groups that can contribute to the negative therapeutic reaction. These basic assumption groups are called dependency, fight or flight, and pairing.

When a group is acting on the basis of dependency, it tends to see itself and act as if it is inadequate and immature while the therapist is seen as omnipotent and omniscient. In this type of group a negative therapeutic reaction happens because a client's innate strivings for maturity and emotional adequacy are squashed.

When a group is acting on the basis of fight or flight, they behave as if there is an enemy against whom they must defend themselves or from whom they need to escape. A negative therapeutic reaction happens because this type of group promotes an emotional condition of paranoia, which is antithetical to the development of intimacy.

When a group is acting on the basis of pairing, the group will act as if it is meeting in order to reproduce a savior. Two people are picked to carry out this mission. A negative therapeutic reaction occurs for the group when the two people are unable to reproduce a savior that will change their lives. True change occurs when a person works on his or her issues, not when two people create a savior.

The process of scapegoating is a common group process that can lead to a negative therapeutic response. Rutan and Stone (1993) define scapegoating in group therapy as the focusing of hostile, sadistic, and hurtful attention on one particular individual. They add that scapegoating, if left unanalyzed, can be hurtful to the individual and the group. Earley (2000) suggests that scapegoating occurs when a group member is reviled and ostracized by the other group members. There are several reasons why a person would become a scapegoat. They include being especially hostile and blaming toward others, being quite different from the others, and having an underlying need to be excluded.

Yalom (1985) writes that if the group is unable to confront the therapist directly, it may create a scapegoat, which is a highly unsatisfactory solution for both the victim and the group. He adds that scapegoating is a method by which the group can discharge anger arising from any source and is a common phenomenon in any therapy group. Klein (1992) suggests that one of the ways that scapegoating is expressed is in the projecting of desired but threatening impulses onto one client because the group as a whole needs to repress such feelings. The scapegoat often does not go along with this projection and suffers emotionally from this process.

Rutan and Stone (1993) report that central to the understanding of scapegoating is the concept of projective identification. Projective identification is a defensive maneuver in which individuals project onto others those traits or aspects of self-representations and their associated affects that are unacceptable as one's own. When a group member is the recipient of projective identification he or she will tend to react as if he or she is being manipulated which, in truth, is the case. When the whole group uses this defense against a client, he or she is likely to feel demoralized, misunderstood, and unsafe, and chances are that the client will terminate prematurely.

REVIEW

Presented in this chapter are only some of the many possible factors that can create a negative group psychotherapy experience. There are many more, and these can be found in the plethora of books available in the field of psychology. Before you seek these books, what other factors might create a negative group psychotherapy experience for a client that could motivate his or her early termination?

Chapter 14

Issues and Perspectives

The issues discussed in this chapter have been gleaned from the American Psychological Association Group Psychotherapy Forum, an online discussion group. This particular forum was established in 1995 by Haim Weinberg for professionals working in this field who were interested in group therapy. According to Weinberg (2001), the main objective was and continues to be the facilitation of the exchange of ideas among group therapists all over the world. As of September 2002, there were over 500 members from thirty-three different countries. Members on this forum consult colleagues, seek academic references, discuss and suggest new group techniques, dialogue about research, describe their professional experiences, and inform others about important conferences and workshops worldwide (Weinberg, 2001). Any clinician or student seriously interested in group therapy and issues in psychology may wish to join this very worthwhile, erudite, and informative forum on the Internet. To subscribe, send an e-mail to:

listserv@listp.apa.org

In the body of the message write:

subscribe group-psychotherapy YourFirstName YourLastName

If you experience difficulties, send an e-mail to:

group-psychotherapy-request@listp.apa.org

Between the writing of this book and its publication, the e-mail address of the Psychology Forum may change. If this is the case, go to your search engine and type in "group therapy." The APA group therapy forum will be listed. Just click on it and the necessary information will appear.

The identities of the forum members have been deleted for confidentiality. The issues discussed were the initial postings to the group and the responses are from colleagues all over the globe.

ISSUE: HUMOR AND ITS RELATION
TO PSYCHOTHERAPY

Dear colleagues,

Rarely if ever have I seen the concept of humor and its relation to psychotherapy discussed on the forum. I know we are a serious lot in a very serious business but if I don't have a laugh every so often during session, I can feel quite burdened by the end of the day.

I thought I would relate a story to you concerning a client, a fifteen-year-old adolescent boy, who had seen me four times before he was able to disclose what was so terribly burdensome to him. With eyes focused on the floor and in an almost inaudible voice he said, "I broke my penis!" Inquiry into this disclosure brought forth his belief that when a man lies flat on his back with an erection, his penis is supposed to stand straight up like a flagpole, and his lean[ed] toward his chest. Somewhat out of character for me, I said, "I think I must have broken mine also." We both started to laugh in such a way that [it] lifted the oppression from the room and created a most open and wonderful dialogue. Interestingly, my standard adolescent anatomy lesson would not have nearly been as effective as [my] statement for this case.

Are any of you laughing these days?

Responses

1. It is my professional belief that you did a great disservice to the young man by bringing your personal self into his discussion about his personal issue. Clients do not come to us to hear about our lives and in this case our bodies.
2. It never ceases to amaze me how hung up people can be around sexuality and the body. With the young man you mentioned, you probably connected in such a meaningful and human way. Would I do that every day, or have that become a part of a pattern

of interaction? Of course not. Was it unprofessional? Probably. But the spontaneity of that moment with him, and your willingness to drop your professional facade for a moment, and relate to him with such gentle jest and tenderness is arguably a gift. As for the person who believes that you damaged him for life, well . . . maybe his is broken or hers is missing.

3. I find the issue of humor in psychotherapy an interesting one and will try my hand at presenting some of my thoughts about it. Although I find humor most effective in resolving, or at least aerating, resistances in group, I couldn't say that I use it per se. It strikes me that humor is an essentially unconscious process which arises when the therapist has come to understand and accept the resistances of the patient, group, or subgroup, and has resolved those particular resistances in his or her own personality. . . . I find that when I am humorous in a way that signifies a successful hookup between my unconscious and the patient's unconscious, it frequently comes out in the form of a tease. As most of us have probably experienced, being teased by a loving friend or relative is experienced as a great compliment—they are demonstrating that they know and accept our foibles, have affection for us, and are taking a risk on behalf of the relationship—a satisfying communication of intimacy. On the other hand, ego-dystonic teasing is usually experienced as aggressive, confrontive, and embarrassing or exposing. How do you get to the point where you can trust yourself to be spontaneously humorous with group members? The best approach, I think, is to spend lots of time in individual and group treatment with a silly therapist.

4. Yeah, I am laughing. My groups and individuals laugh a lot, as I do. I feel worried about those who can find no humor in their lives, because they don't have the protection humor provides.

5. I couldn't agree more with you—without humor we die! Particularly the spontaneous nature of your experience—you seized the moment, and look at the wonderful results. I've had the same experiences, and find humor to be a great door opener. You're right about it changing the energy also; it can bring trust into the therapy relationship faster and more deeply. Kind of helps us therapists to join the client in his or her world more naturally, and allows them into ours as well.

6. I use humor and laughter a great deal in working with families and children. It has helped the family to enjoy each other during a time of crisis when they are yelling and hurting each other outside of the session. Sometimes I use exaggeration to help the members see each other's side of the issue. Usually it helps the family to see the lighter side, for a moment of light in a very dark situation, and allows them to enjoy one another. It is a very effective tool as someone can't strike out at another when he is laughing.

7. I agree with . . . your use of humor was inappropriate with the young man. I'm glad my son is not going to you.

ISSUE: THERAPIST SELF-DISCLOSURE

Dear colleagues,

The issue of therapist self-disclosure [TSD] has always been a sticky one. When I was a student we were told never to disclose anything about ourselves, as it interferes with the therapeutic process. I have found of late that when I do disclose some minor aspect of my life, it seems to have a positive effect on the client.

What do you think?

Responses

1. I read the inquiry regarding TSD the other day and this topic always intrigues me, as it has for years. I do not believe that you can make across-the-board judgments regarding this use of the therapist self. There are too many variations in terms of the depth of the work (i.e., transference-based or not), the diagnosis of the patient(s), the stage of treatment, age and developmental age of the patient(s) and, of course, the modality. I think it's a tougher call in groups where one must be cognizant of numerous people's reactions and the impact of the disclosure. And by therapist self-disclosure, do we mean of one's feelings and reactions or information that is usually private and unavailable in the therapeutic relationship? . . . I agree with others' comments that one must guard against using disclosure for one's own needs; back to the discussion re: importance of the therapist's own therapy. We could also question genuineness and what that

means. . . . I would love to hear others' reactions, comments, and experiences.

2. It depends on what is meant by disclosure. Telling a patient about one's life outside the office, if done, must be carefully monitored—whose need is it serving, why now, etc. Disclosing one's experience with the patient as dealing with the inter-subjective nature of therapy is an essential part of therapy if done as part of the psychotherapeutic transaction and is analyzed as one would all other material. Some therapists use the euphemism "self-disclosure" as a means for narcissistic self-indulgence. Appropriate self-disclosure—see Sid Jourard's *Transparent Self* or Stolorow's *Intersubjectivity*—can be valuable for treatment. And even here it would depend on the particular patient and for what purpose.

3. I find myself in complete agreement. For me the fundamental question is in whose service is the disclosure being made, and typically self-disclosure by the therapist about his or her own life experience in a certain arena is confusing for the patient, and potentially meets some narcissistic need of the therapist.

4. I think the statement for "whose benefit is the disclosure" encapsulates the essence of all disclosures on the part of a psychotherapist—whether this disclosure is personal or professional. But in our world, knowledge known to civilization so very much remains a mystery. Is it truly in the patient's interest for us to continue to be another point of this mystification or is it in the patient's interest that he is in the presence of some reality? Although reality itself is quite subjective. The concept of de-mystifying the therapist often brings forth intense feelings in psychological quarters. The orthodox Freudians tend to squirm and appear to become quite uncomfortable with this issue. Often theirs is a flat out, no! Except Freud was far from being an orthodox Freudian. Certainly patients did not come to us to hear about us but rather to unburden themselves from the trials and tribulations of living. Often I have found that many patients feel very much alone in their sufferings. That is why group psycho-therapy is so invaluable. They have the opportunity to hear others relate similar conflicts. I have found though that I generally know when a patient's therapy is coming to an end when he/she begins to see me more for who and what I am rather than who or

what they want me to be. In any case, self-disclosure remains a hard call.

5. It is better not to disclose anything. Then you don't have a conflict if it is right or wrong.

ISSUE: SHOULD A GROUP THERAPIST HAVE THE EXPERIENCE OF BEING A GROUP MEMBER?

Dear forum members,

When I was a graduate student, my professor of group therapy used to say, "If you really want to become a fine group leader, go into group therapy as a group member." But then I had other professors say, "You don't have to have a heart attack to be a heart surgeon."

What do you feel about this?

Responses

1. Your colleagues are right, "you don't have to have a heart attack to be a heart surgeon," but then again surgeons, especially cardiologists, are just mechanics. I can safely say this because my wife is a physician. Our profession is different. We deal with the human soul . . . psyche. And that ain't no mechanic.

2. Just a couple of thoughts about the desirability of group experience before practicing. Spending time in a group may or may not help one be a better facilitator, but how does one know how to proceed without at least watching someone lead a group? The more styles one observes, the more possibilities one has for finding a style most useful for him or her to use in leading a group. I would wonder how I could expect a client to come and share his or her life in a setting such as a group if I have been unwilling to do so myself. Also, when people are in a group setting the issues are universal. If the group leader hasn't experienced this type of activity there may be issues of the therapist's that are touched and then the therapist may feel moved to share that material. This seems mostly to be inappropriate. We should have worked that out before, in a group experience of our own, so that now we can be wholly (or as much as possible) present for our clients.

3. I had to throw in my two cents' worth as a group therapist: Maybe I'm rigid, but if I were running a graduate program in counseling or psychology from which students intended to graduate and practice psychotherapy, I would make it a requirement for graduation that they attend a psychotherapy group led by a professional psychotherapist outside of their department for not less than one year of their program. First of all, this eliminates the problems of dual roles on the part of the faculty teaching group psychotherapy, and the resulting ambivalence among students with regard to how safe they feel disclosing intimate personal data to those who are evaluating them. . . . I believe that a therapist has no business doing psychotherapy who has not experienced his/her own psychotherapy process, and likewise a group therapist should have experienced group therapy, not merely for the experience, but to have what may be called the self-search. I would seriously question the choice of occupation of students who meet the expectation that they be introspective with hostility!!!

4. If some members of the forum are unaware of therapist-induced hurtful, harmful, or simply useless experiences in group or individual therapy, [after] years of doing and supervising group therapy, I have a somewhat jaundiced view of how constructive it is to simply say to trainees: "It would be useful for you to experience being in group therapy." I don't think any one of us would argue [with the idea] that therapy is beneficial—but to add it as a requirement does not make a great deal of sense. If we had some outcome studies, we would have better ground for argument. . . . I would suggest that we should avoid giving general answers to oversimplified questions ("Therapy for the therapist: yes or no?").

5. I notice that there is a general assumption that being in a group is such a uniform experience that we can discuss whether group therapy as a generic experience is a desirable or undesirable educational experience for a therapist. . . . My personal experience as a member in group therapy is decidedly mixed. I have been a member of two different regular outpatient therapy groups, one didactic therapy group, and two Tavistock conferences. I would judge two of those experiences as having been good for both my psychological state and my learning about groups. One of the

others was close to traumatic with a balancing amount of learning from a bad experience, and one of the therapy groups which lasted for almost a year was largely a waste of time although I kept hoping that I would get something out of it beyond the regular billings.

6. Personal individual and group therapy for practitioners—I agree 100 percent. I believe [this] in spite of the fact that there may be no empirical evidence to support the contention that personal therapy should be strongly recommended for all practitioners. Not only will it help the practitioners empathize with their patients, it is a great way to gain an appreciation of the practice of psychotherapy from both sides of the couch. In addition, personal psychotherapy (group and individual) certainly would help deal with countertransference issues, increase self-understanding, etc. And last, even if there is no evidence that it helps produce better outcomes, it couldn't hurt, and it's a good rite of passage.

ISSUE: MONOPOLIZERS

Dear members of the forum,

Occasionally I have a monopolizer in group therapy and I am not sure what is the most effective route to go with this particular individual. Can anyone help?

Responses

1. I am just about to go get some supervision about this very topic—monopolizers. In my situation, the client and I have made a mutual decision that she will leave the group. It is, of course, a very painful decision for all, after months of struggling. However, we have all learned a lot from this, particularly about identifying projections and expressing anger productively. There will be much material for her individual therapy and for the remaining group members to ponder for months/years to come. It is interesting to me that others have suggested that some people are not ready for group and need more individual. This is exactly my conclusion in this situation and I can say we tried, we learned a lot, and now we know what is needed!

2. I work with monopolizing as a resistance or a group resistance and find it to be one of the more difficult, delicate, and common dynamics to occur in groups—the task of intervening while being noninjurious is always the challenge for me. One story about possible underlying dynamics: A long-standing group member who is in the midst of resolving this resistance has been asking other members what they have felt about her tendency to be a group hog (her self-attacking words) and when asked about the gain for her, she said spontaneously that if she ever decided to leave the group, this would make it easier; she could tell herself she doesn't deserve to be in group or convince herself she's a misfit and leave. Having verbalized this repetition will probably prevent any such termination. Much more to be explored here related to the group resistance.

3. My preference in dealing with monopolizers is to allow things to unfold until group members begin to comment. Of course, sometimes that approach—especially with several shy group members—could be some time coming. You also raise an interesting point in regard to receiving criticism for some of the more indirect methods you use. This may make for some interesting discussion here. I think many therapists would tend to say that if you are having a reaction to a certain group member, let your feedback be directly to the member; this is more honest, and models effective feedback for others in the group.

4. Monopolizing can often be a failure of self-control, i.e., the inability to stop oneself. Where a group contains more than one somewhat narcissistic individual, I find that they control one another's speaking episodes. The protocol becomes one of interruption by what I often refer to as "walking on the other guy's last sentence." The interrupted person often appears relieved as the new person assumes the burden of occupying group time, perhaps. . . . At other times, it appears more effective to characterize the pressure speech directly as expression of anxiety. Sometimes, after I have had the opportunity to make an empathic response to the content of the monopolizer, I will add a comment such as this: "As [name] was talking, I began to have a very strong image of him running around and around the room. It was as if each word were a panicked footstep." (Looking directly at him), "It seems to me that your distress makes it hard

for you to sit down and actually reflect about your troubles with others. . . ."

5. I've noticed myself being hesitant to put my two cents in this monopolizer discussion, since colleagues have sometimes considered my standard methods of dealing with monopolizers to be slightly controversial in that it doesn't directly change levels to explore the dynamics or motivations of the monopolizing but instead brings the experience of that moment of the group into focus through an indirect form of nonconfrontive experiential elucidating. And, I'm not saying that approaching on one level is better than another, just that I go about it a little differently. However, I do have a pretty consistent method of dealing with certain types of monopolizers in my groups. First I will just let it unfold a while and see if the group will handle it themselves and somehow share the time. If this does not occur and the monopolizer continues, I may simply turn to another member of the group, one of the listeners to the monopolizer, and ask a question. My question might be one of two forms. First form, asking group member A (to whom I am addressing the question) how group member B (another listener who might be showing some body language response to the monopolizer) is responding to group member C, the monopolizer. This has the potential of pulling responses out of two other members. The second option I might resort to is to simply turn to another group member, one of the listeners who had mentioned some important or pending event or situation in the previous group and will ask a question about that event, totally changing the topic. Both of these techniques seem to also function as a release valve for the group's frustration about the monopolizer and often gets a slightly aggressive response from the monopolizer or from other group members in terms of my impolite technique. . . .

6. I find telling the group member to please be quiet for a while to be very helpful. Certainly, it doesn't bring out the best of feelings but it does help to create a group-as-a-whole dialogue at what had transpired.

7. The groups I conduct mostly have people contracting for "airtime" so monopolization is less likely to occur. I like to give group members the opportunity to give feedback before I offer it myself and will only do so myself if they don't, or if I have

something to offer they haven't thought of themselves. However, if I see signs of restlessness when someone is rambling or going on too long in an untimed group, I might invoke the self-care agreement all group members make with each other by looking at the restless person(s) and asking them, are you being passive? This requires that they either deal with the restlessness by addressing the monopolizer directly or hold themselves accountable for it in some other form sooner or later. They need to deal with my question to them. . . .

ISSUE: SUBPOENA GROUP MEMBERS

Dear colleagues,

I thought you might find this most interesting. I had been seeing a client in group therapy for about three months. He had been and continues to be going through a very nasty divorce. He called to say that he had to drop out of group therapy due to his lawyer's recommendation. His rather bitter wife and her attorneys feel that my client, her husband, may have disclosed pertinent information in group that she could use in her divorce settlement. Because of this, her lawyers were determining whether to subpoena my other group members to disclose any and all information that her husband may have related in group. Upon conferring with my attorney as to the legality of this possibility, he related that he felt it highly unlikely a judge would require me to disclose confidential information, i.e., the names of the other group members. If this ever did evolve into a disclosure being legally enforced with its concomitant breaking of confidentiality, the end of the history and practice of group therapy would most surely arrive.

Responses

1. Reading your post, I immediately felt anxious and then outraged for you, for your group members, and for the profession. . . .
2. What a frightening situation. It certainly is a threat to the integrity of group work.
3. I agree that if a judge allowed this, I would probably seek another profession. Having worked with court-ordered populations, I might offer some cautious solace. I have been subpoe-

naed a number of times in cases of divorce or child custody, and
as you might guess, these were nasty proceedings. In each case,
however, I would be required to appear before the judge with the
record in hand, only to have the judge in every case, rule that
[she/he] would not set the dangerous precedent of toying with
privileged communication. . . . Also keep in mind (and this has
been my experience with some attorneys, not all) that an attorney can subpoena whomever [she/he] wants, and often threatens
to do so as an intimidation strategy.
4. You might want to let your client know that he should not disclose material from his therapy sessions as part of his divorce
   strategy, because then he implies waiver of consent. . . .
5. It is my understanding that the privilege of confidentiality can
   be waived explicitly or implicitly in certain circumstances. These
   include: (1) all child custody matters, (2) whenever a third person is present when the information was divulged, (3) whenever
   the litigant raises his or her mental status as an issue, e.g., asks
   for additional damages due to pain and suffering. . . . I always
   include as part of my introduction to the idea of joining a therapy group, that law in this state does not protect confidentiality
   in group therapy. I always continue that I hope that individuals
   will realize the importance of honesty in psychotherapy and that
   whatever they have on another member, other members have on
   them.

ISSUE: WHEN A CLIENT IS SEEING YOU
IN GROUP THERAPY AND ANOTHER THERAPIST
IN INDIVIDUAL PSYCHOTHERAPY

Dear colleagues,
   I have been seeing a client in group psychotherapy and this individual is seeing another therapist for individual psychotherapy. Occasionally, this creates problems in the therapy. Do any of you ever have
problems with this issue?

Responses

1. My own experience is that it is generally easier for me to do both
   the individual and the group work, but it can't always be. I have

a patient who has more or less blocked my attempts at communication with the individual therapist—yet I must say now that I no longer believe he is game playing around that issue (which was my first thought). He is frank that he sees the individual work as cognitive and pharmacologic and the group as the laboratory in which he tries out the ideas, skills, and the attitudes he is trying to learn with the other therapist. He is indifferent to the differences in our orientation, which sometimes are pronounced. It is working out well for him—I think.

2. Your question opens an area of great controversy. To begin with, there are more than two camps who feel strongly from oppositional positions. There is the one camp that feels it is quite all right that a patient be seen by two different therapists, one for group and one [for] individual. Then there is the other camp who feels this is not a good procedure as it creates not only problems for the patient but problems for the therapist(s). Unfortunately, not all therapists can work effectively together nor are all therapists trained in the same modality, thus creating even further problems. I have tried over the years using both of these procedures and have found that seeing the patient in individual and in the group works more effectively for me. Not only does it create less confusion for the patient but it also lessens the patient's need to "set the two therapists up" with each other with statements such as, "Dr. J. said this and now you are saying just the opposite." In some ways, we are regressing the patient with the two therapists' modalities as he/she begins to recreate what he/she did in relation to his/her parents. This is not necessarily a negative thing as it helps us to see the patient in action but this can just as easily be seen in the group situation.

3. I inform patients in the pregroup appointment that I require free communication between therapists. When I and the individual therapist are in good communication it certainly facilitates the patient's progress. This good communication does not always occur (how shocking!!!). In the last week I discovered that one patient's individual therapist did not know that this member was in a group.

4. An added dimension to this topic that I deal with has to do with coleading a group with a therapist who sees a majority of the members individually as well. This presents an interesting and

challenging dynamic for us as leaders. Often the group will refer to insights they have gained in their individual sessions, as well as comment on how wonderful and insightful my coleader is as a therapist. Sometimes I feel like the mean parent (my stuff?). My coleader and I plan to process this group.

5. I tend to make it a practice first of all to determine from all patients who come specifically for group therapy to inquire as to whether they are in current individual treatment. If so, I always have a release signed and contact the individual therapist. I make it a practice to tell the patient as well as the individual therapist that the individual therapist is the quarterback for the patient's treatment. I tend to subordinate group treatment to individual treatment in those instances. I then periodically check in with the individual therapist, perhaps every three months. I also encourage the individual therapist to check in with me. It is interesting to me how few take the initiative to do so.

6. That is one of the reasons why I try to stay away from a patient/client seeing me and another therapist. Although there appear to be other clinicians who have had more positive interactions with colleagues concerning this particular issue, I haven't had the good fortune to have had that experience. Generally, I sense from the other clinicians a concern of losing the patient/client as if the patient/client was a possession and I now become a threat to that loss. At this point, having to comfort a colleague for fear of loss and helping a patient/client effectively make the transition is just not worth it as I feel the individual is not getting the best service possible with these other agendas in operation. Perhaps, I am causing the problem. As I read your posting about the individual therapist being the quarterback and group secondary, I have very different feelings. I don't feel group is secondary to any modality in psychotherapy nor do I feel is my work. I believe there is a parity of both.

ISSUE: THERAPIST ABUSE

Dear members,

One of my staff members called today because she was distraught over three phone calls she received from a patient. This particular patient called and was verbally abusive to the staff member. My question is, where does a therapist draw the line on therapist abuse? Although part of our job is to create an environment where a patient can disclose all of what the individual feels, when does "all of what" become too much and enough?

Responses

1. I think that it is not a therapist's job to put up with abuse, and I doubt if there is any therapeutic value in allowing it. There is a difference between "strong feelings" and abuse. . . .

2. I think that it is important to acknowledge the client's feelings, how they were communicated, and, in some cases, how they were received. I think it is equally important to educate the client about the different ways that his/her feelings can be communicated, what kind of reactions they are likely to encounter, and appropriate versus nonappropriate ways of communicating (i.e., violent, etc.). . . .

3. A patient can disclose all that they think and feel during the session. After the session is over, one should have all their thoughts and feelings but *act* with discretion. One cannot defecate wherever and whenever one pleases. A therapist has the right to say in a calm voice "I'm hanging up now, abuse is not allowed." Having an accepting attitude is quite different from masochism and therapists do not have to tolerate aggressive acts. . . .

4. Having endured my fair share of abuse over the years, I have tried to devise somewhat flexible boundaries around this kind of acting out. I seem to have less tolerance when counselors under my supervision are abused. Part of the group norms each client agrees to asks that they treat others with respect as a condition of treatment. . . . The most frequent problems seem to occur with personality-disordered clients suffering narcissistic insult or devaluing the therapist. Exploring this can be valuable for both client and therapist. . . .

5. One of my most revered mentors once told me of a patient who spent the session telling him he was just like her horrible father, and viciously reviling him. He finally said to her, "I am not your father, and you may not abuse me." To which she replied, "What's the matter, can't you take it?" He answered, "Yes, but I don't have to."

6. I find it difficult to believe that anyone can go twenty years without feeling/being abused by a patient. I read a book a few years back by John Beebe about integrity in psychotherapy. He was so open about his own need to maintain his integrity (of the self) in his early years, that went on for many years. He shared that his patients always seemed to appreciate him, his warmth, his capacity for empathy (read sympathy and compassion). But he also noticed that they reached a plateau in treatment past which many did not progress. In his own self-examination he came to discover the subtle, but no less powerful, ways he thwarted his patients' expression of rage. This struck such a chord in me, resonated with such familiarity, that I have never forgotten this notion.

7. I find this thread interesting. Makes me ponder, what do we mean by "therapist abuse"? Given that we are working with troubled individuals, their behavior, however difficult and challenging, is their attempt to do what they do as best they can. What makes it abuse rather than "acting out" or "hostility" or "anger" or "aggression" or projection, transference, etc.? . . .

8. No one enjoys being the object of intense rage. It is frightening, anger provoking (a defensive reaction), at times rendering us feeling like we are on the edge of some kind of decompensation. It gets even more threatening when it stimulates our own primitive or early memories. I think that the manner through which this unfolds and the feelings and fantasies that are produced are unique to each individual, but I believe (gee I hope so!) and yet difficult to access and accept.

ISSUE: SUICIDE

Dear colleagues,

It is with trepidation that I pushed the send button on this posting. I had begun seeing a patient last week for the first time and was informed late last night that he had committed suicide. I can't, at this moment, think of anything as emotionally devastating to a therapist as to be informed that a patient has taken his own life. The many unanswered questions and the turmoil of the obsessive thinking, "What more could I have done to prevent this tragedy?" adds to the burden. I would very much appreciate it if any of you who has had a similar experience would relate how you felt. It would be a help. If you do not wish to put it on the forum, I can understand.

Responses

1. I can only imagine just how difficult a time it must be for you right now. I had a fairly new client die many years ago when I was a therapist at a rape treatment center and he had been raped fairly recently. Because of what he said, when I discovered he was dead, I was sure it was suicide and was devastated with all the predictable questions: "What had I missed?" "Why hadn't I recognized it sooner?" "Was I competent to be a therapist, etc.?" It was a tremendously frightening time for me on a really deep level. . . . Grieve both his death and the loss of innocence [for] any therapist who has a client suicide—but be gentle too.
2. I am sorry to hear of your loss. When I was twenty-one, a total novice, I evaluated a young man in the state hospital. The next morning I learned he had committed suicide in seclusion during the night. I will never forget him, the situation, and my grief—as well as feeling inadequate.
3. It is a sad event and perhaps an "occupational hazard" for those of us who work with depressed and despairing patients. But before you assume too much responsibility, I have a question. If someone had called to notify you that one of your patients had committed suicide, would you have immediately known which one it was? It would take a psychic, in many cases, to have divined their plans.
4. Your patient came to you for permission to die.
5. I was only a year or two into this profession when I met a client who said he had felt for a very long time that he was a misfit with other humans and wanted to end his life. He was not responding to a life event, rather he had a pervasive attitude toward life. I was set to go on vacation and asked him to agree not to do anything while I was away. He agreed. I had been taught that clients have a high compliance with these contracts. I returned on a Sunday afternoon. The phone rang and no one answered when I said hello. I thought nothing of it. The next day I learned that my client had committed suicide Sunday evening.

I suspect it was he, conforming to the letter of our contract, but not its spirit. I felt tricked. I felt guilty. I was angry. And I wanted to learn all I could about suicide, and I brought many professionals together to help me learn. And even though I have not had a client suicide since, I have no belief that I am wise enough or powerful enough to guarantee myself. All I have is my belief.

6. It is with equal trepidation that I respond publicly. This happened to me last week. I have been in private practice twenty-five years and it is only the second time (although I have heard from the grapevine of a few more who killed themselves some time after I had seen them). Anyway, it's devastating and I have no great insight about it yet. One thought is that I talked to my patient's mother and she said, "It is a grief beyond grief "—and I realized that it is not so for me. I would want to talk with her more, much more, but feel that I could not avoid being the therapist in such conversations, and that such a stance would be lacking in decent humility. Then of course, unseemly as it is with the poor man not yet cold in his grave, I cannot help but wonder about the future malpractice action. Are my notes adequate to demonstrate that I took reasonable precautions—blah, blah, blah. It is a nightmare, isn't it?

7. A patient's suicide is something we never get over—we only get through.

REVIEW

You have now read some of the many issues posted each day from a group psychotherapy forum on the Internet. What is the most predominant feeling you have after reading this chapter?

Chapter 15

Group Psychotherapy As a Specialty

The performance of every job is a self-portrait of the person who did it. (A sign taped to the inside window of West's Diner in Little Falls, New Jersey, 1952)

Nick Cummings, a prominent and substantial psychologist for many years, researched the concept of hypochondria in the early 1960s as it was related to the many repeat office visits medical doctors were seeing in their practices. Through Dr. Cummings' extensive research, he found that approximately 60 percent of these visits were a somatization or a displacement of symptoms from unresolved stress being manifested in the soma of the patients studied (Simon, 2001). It was hypothesized and realized that psychotherapy could and would save the insurance companies medical dollars far beyond the cost of providing the actual psychotherapy. This wonderful study was the impetus for Kaiser Permanente to become the first insurance company in 1963 to include psychotherapy as a regular benefit in its insurance coverage (Simon, 2001).

Dr. Cummings, in a recent interview, predicted that the future of psychotherapy will be in the area of group. These time-limited groups will be "psychoeducational." They will help to lessen medical costs by helping patients become more self-sufficient and cognizant of their medical conditions. They will also be "population-based," by focusing on issues that are not medically oriented but have caused difficulty for the clients' ongoing functioning (Simon, 2001). He further related that current research indicates that the efficacy of group treatment over individual treatment is astronomical and predicted that in the future only 25 percent of all psychotherapy will be in an individual, one-on-one relationship with a therapist, compared to 75 percent which will be in group (Simon, 2001).

Psychotherapy is a business similar to any other business, but in this case it is the business of helping people with intrapsychic, interpersonal, and medical concerns. It needs to be approached as such and those individuals who can see beyond the selfless altruism of "saving the world" and embrace the reality of our profession are likely to be more successful psychotherapeutically, economically, and emotionally over time. My practice over the past twenty-four years has been predominantly group psychotherapy. It is not uncommon for both students and colleagues to ask, "How does one develop and begin to implement group psychotherapy in their beginning or ongoing practices?" I certainly cannot speak for all practitioners, but rather I speak from my own personal experience and what I have done—in the hope that one or two ideas may help a colleague develop his or her practice in the modality that I consider to be one of the finest psychotherapy paradigms in helping people resolve those aforementioned concerns.

Upon reflection, it may be my sincere belief and proactive encouragement in the process of group therapy that clients and prospective clients experience when speaking with me about this wonderful modality. I feel that I inspire (at least that is what has been related to me) my future group members to feel confident and hopeful when making the step into becoming a group therapy member because I truly believe in this modality and consider it to be far superior to individual psychotherapy for the resolution of many human difficulties. I genuinely speak of its benefits in a most positive and reverential manner because I was a group therapy member for six years and I saw the tremendous positive effect it had and continues to have on me.

It is vitally important that a clinician go into group therapy as a client before beginning to implement group therapy into his or her practice. The general training of group psychotherapists, no matter how effective or efficient the professor(s) may be, is not sufficient to teach group dynamics in an academic setting, nor are practicum, internship sites, or psychiatric residencies sufficient in creating truly effective group therapists. Only experience on "both sides of the desk" and life experience in general, in my personal opinion, create a truly effective group therapist. Personal experience in group therapy and working through one's own interpersonal issues as a member is perhaps the best route to go if you wish to truly learn about yourself and experience the process of group psychotherapy. There is an old psychoanalytic belief, which I have incorporated, that proposes "we can only take a patient as far as we ourselves have gone." In order for you to sell the process—and you must sell the process—you too must wholeheartedly believe in it; one of the best ways to do that is to experience it firsthand as a client.

Granted and accepted by many clinicians is the belief that there exists both positive and negative group experiences for a group member but that does not discount the effectiveness of learning, as one can just as easily learn what not to do as to what to do when running your own groups. This argument should also include the fact that individual psychotherapy—which at this time historically is the prominent psychotherapeutic paradigm—can also include both positive and negative experiences. Individual psychotherapy also distinguishes itself, in comparison to group therapy, as generally the area of malpractice suits against therapists, but that does not seem to be discussed when anti-group therapists give their opinions. Another opinion that really must be done away with is that group therapy is a second-rate modality to individual psychotherapy. Perhaps the most profound reason that group therapy is considered as such arises out of the unawareness of the profession itself and the education of new clinicians. Inadvertently, the American Psychological Association and many universities, which have and seek its approval in their doctoral psychology programs, do not require group psychotherapy training to be a course or courses in their programs. It is amazingly possible for a doctoral candidate in clinical psychology to go through an entire doctoral clinical program without ever having taken a course in group therapy. This absence in academia sets the tone to and for the new clinician that group therapy is not of great value, otherwise it would be a core or required course in their training.

Group psychotherapy provides a very timely increase in affect specifically for those groups designed to change behavior, and it offers the wonderful opportunity of multiple transferences occurring, thus permitting the client to work on a number of interpersonal difficulties at the same time. In individual psychotherapy, the therapist must become the virtual surrogate of all those problematic people from the past in order for the patient to resolve these multiple historical interpersonal conflicts.

Often, because of time or economic constraints and due to perhaps the nature and skill of the individual psychotherapist, these multiple transferences do not occur and the client leaves therapy with an incomplete opportunity to work through as many interpersonal issues as possible within a shorter period of time. Besides being a finer therapeutic advantage, group obviously is economically more feasible. The patient can have a longer therapeutic experience, it is less costly than individual psychotherapy, and offers more to be gained for the client who may or may not have insurance. Obviously, I am prejudiced and opinionated when it comes to my specialty, but professional experience and current research is validating my beliefs. The interested reader is directed toward the April 2001 *International Journal of Group Psychotherapy* for further in-depth validation of the efficacies of group.

As previously discussed, psychology is a business. Those individuals who have a greater acumen in business will do better in generating income into their practices than those who find the concept of helping others and making a living mutually exclusive concepts. Specialization is the direction to follow, and group therapy is a specialization which can have within it many other specializations. For example, one may run groups for learning interpersonal skills, anger management, self-search, eating-disordered clients, obsessive-compulsive clients, male or female batterers, etc. Being a "jack of all trades and master of none" is probably the best route to go in one's developing practice in order to generate income and to make oneself known. To remain as such creates restrictions on the capacity of the business to obtain economic growth and as a result you will be considered to be one of many other similar therapists in the community.

The specialization of group psychotherapy offers a therapist a way to generate more income in a shorter period of time, besides providing an arena for clients' timely growth. For example, if we run a ninety-minute group of eight members and charge, for example, a fee of sixty dollars per client, we have generated $480. Very few therapists make $480 in a ninety-minute session seeing a client in individual psychotherapy. So group therapy is not only a tremendous psychological paradigm and experience for clients but also a wonderful income producer for one's private practice. In addition, clients who belong to psychotherapy groups generally attend on a more consistent basis than do clients in individual psychotherapy, thus providing a greater sense of economic security for the practitioner.

Interestingly, our profession seems to elicit in many new clinicians a terrible conflict between money and care. In other words, if you charge for your services, you have muddied the purity of the psychotherapeutic relationship. If you feel that your service is worth nothing, then it is worth nothing and will be seen by the client as worth nothing. Granted, wanting to help out a struggling individual seeking psychotherapy is a most honorable deed. We occasionally do this, but if you cannot afford to do this and continue to set the tone of your private practice as if it is a clinic, you are probably indicating an issue in your own personality as its correlates to your self-worth. The issue of money and charging for one's services is an amazing and very important issue in this profession. I have never seen this in any other profession. For example, the plumber has no problem charging me when he comes to do work, and neither does the lawn man or the electrician. The guy who gives me a massage has no problem charging sixty dollars for the hour even though he has only had a year of massage school, but new therapists and some seasoned therapists who have spent thousands of dollars and invested years of time for their education seem to have difficulty when it comes to charging for their services.

The reality is we have only two things upon which we can charge and make a living: (1) *our knowledge* and (2) *our time.* The care we give is free as a price cannot be placed on that commodity. We do not give a tangible product, as does a grocery store, and if you feel your knowledge and your time are not worth anything of value then you will have some problems in this profession unless you seek some sort of paid position. It truly does not matter how many lives you have saved that month. The companies that provide service for your office are not interested, and if you cannot pay your bills, e.g., rent, electric, phone, you will not have a roof over your head in which to practice your profession. Also, if you cannot help yourself, how can you truly expect to help others help themselves?

In returning to psychology as a business, your office itself does not generate any income but only debt, e.g., rent, electric, malpractice insurance, phone, etc. All revenues from one's office come from outside of the office in the form of clients, corporations, writing, etc. This indicates that the private practitioner must go outside of his or her office to generate income. What is meant by going outside of one's office is that you need to make yourself known in the community in which you practice. Foremost, you must be cognizant of your community. Is psychotherapy a viable profession in the location of your choice? For example, it would be foolish to place a gourmet market in a lower socioeconomic environment, as it would be foolish to set up a practice in an area where there is a paucity of potential clients.

In my case, I chose to settle in an environment in which the professions, i.e., doctors, lawyers, psychotherapists, are respected and used. I wanted people in my community to think "Dr. Scott Simon Fehr" when looking for a psychotherapist. How does one make himself or herself known? Obviously, this comes about through interaction with the community in which the therapist lives. By interaction, I mean generously volunteering your time to give talks on all kinds of psychological issues to any organization that will listen, offering help on committees, writing columns in the local newspaper, teaching at an academic site, joining community organizations, etc. It really is not any different if you live in Hollywood, Florida, or New York City, as there is a community of individuals out there who will accept your offer to give of yourself for their benefit. No matter how proficient you may be as a clinician, if you are unknown the chances of your practice filling up is really quite unlikely unless you have a wonderful referral source and someone who is consistently looking out for your economic well-being. Simply put, in the beginning of your practice— think pro bono!

Remember that you are selling a product and in this instance that product is defined as group therapy. You are also selling yourself. As uncomfortable as that last sentence may seem, it is a reality. It is important that you give those community activities a positive experience not only of your profession but also of you. When people walk away from their experience of "you" they should be able to say, "I liked that man or woman and I could see coming to him or her to talk, or referring my child, friend, lover, uncle, aunt, etc., who I feel also might feel comfortable talking with that psychotherapist." Sadly, many well-intentioned and often very bright clinicians are just not approachable. They seem to have taken the "distant therapist stance" from the office out into the real world. If you have difficulty giving talks and making yourself known, either work on getting over that or seek employment in a clinic setting in which you will be required only to do therapy and not required to seek out clients. For many people, this is a more comfortable route to go which has its obvious economic limitations. I am by nature a relatively shy man but have encouraged and at times forced myself out into the community with a pep talk. I have refused to allow this shyness feature of my personality to limit my success as a professional and what I wish to establish in my career.

After having established my presence in the community and receiving referrals from these talks, I began to build my individual psychotherapy practice. From my individual psychotherapy practice, I chose those clients that I felt were ready for group therapy. I personally do not place a client in group therapy immediately, although other therapists do with apparent success. The majority of clients in my groups have seen me for at least three months previously in individual therapy. These people have initially come to my office through referrals from other clients, making myself known in the community, and referrals from colleagues who do not run groups in their practices for whatever reason(s) they have chosen.

I believe a relationship must be developed between the client and the therapist before he or she can make a positive transition into group therapy. It is important that the client has an initial positive experience in his or her first group session. Group can be a highly anxiety-creating stimulus for most people. If the first meeting has been aversive, chances are that the client will not be coming back. In fact, that might definitely be a healthy response on the part of the client, as I would not go back to a group that was initially an aversive experience. For the client, having at least one person, the therapist, with whom he or she feels relatively comfortable and safe makes the adjustment easier and increases the probability of the client continuing in this modality. In addition, you have at your disposal a wealth of previous material because you have had a relationship with the client over the past three months.

In summary, if you do not believe in what you are doing and its validity, you will have a very difficult time doing it and selling your product. Yes, it is unfortunate after all your hard work, time, and finances for your education that doors have not been flung wide open for you professionally, but that is one of the harsh realities of life and of this profession. The old model of scientist/practitioner has now been expanded to practitioner/scientist/businessperson. If you wish to succeed, you must implement all kinds of feasible routes to that goal. If you wish a group therapy practice, you must make it happen and part of that is being approachable as a person, flexible and creative as a clinician, and ethically beyond reproach. Never give up or be stopped and defeated if success does not all happen at once. This profession is definitely a journey—a journey I feel privileged to have been on and of which I continue to be a part.

Appendix A

The Many Forms of Group Therapy

For every human suffering there is probably a group that addresses that particular issue.

ADHD groups—These groups are for children and adolescents. They are designed to teach them different techniques to deal with their problems. One focus can be on teaching problem-solving skills, learning how to slow down, stop, think of the problem, think of possible actions and their possible consequences, act, and then review the consequences of their actions.

Agoraphobia and phobia groups—Individuals manifesting fears, whether real or imagined from previous experience, are greatly helped with these groups. The therapy is generally and systematically in vivo. Group members are helped to confront their fears by experiencing the actual dreaded stimulus. Phobias such as leaving one's home, fear of flying, water, malls, etc., are but a few of the wide range of phobias that can be helped within these often successful groups.

AIDS groups—AIDS groups provide a supportive environment so that members can discuss their medical problems and experiences with the medical system; explore issues related to death and illness and difficulty telling family members, partners, and friends; discuss new treatment methods; and support healthy behaviors.

Alcohol/substance abuse groups—The focus of these groups is on abstinence. Members receive support from other members. They openly discuss their substance abuse and acknowledge that it is a problem. They look at the effect their substance abuse has had on their lives, and what led them to abuse substances. They deal with ways to avoid situations that create temptation, thus building the cycle over again.

Anger management groups—These groups teach members techniques to handle their anger in ways that are less harmful and destructive. Role-playing and modeling are key components.

Anorexia/bulimia groups—These groups address the members' faulty body image and related underlying issues as well as provide support and encourage healthier eating behaviors.

Anxiety disorder groups—Anxiety groups can be cognitive-behavioral, focusing on teaching techniques to decrease anxiety in different situations, or more dynamic, focusing on looking at issues underlying the anxiety.

Art therapy groups—These groups utilize art media, images, the creative art process, and patient-client responses to the created art productions as reflections of an individual's personality, interests, concerns, and conflicts. The use of art, whether as an already-established form or created by the individual group member, is the stimulus for understanding the expression of one's feelings and inner life. The acknowledgment and awareness of these feelings and inner life becomes the focus of analysis.

Assertiveness training groups—The goal of these groups is to teach passive members to be more assertive through role-playing, modeling, and discussing real-life examples.

Bereavement groups—These groups focus on providing a support network for grieving individuals. The groups are designed to help them discuss and realize the effect their loss has had on them. Through education about the grief process, the individuals are taught new skills to help them move on in their lives.

Breast cancer groups—The goal of breast cancer groups is to boost the immune system and to increase compliance with treatment by helping members to discuss their feelings about their illness and treatment in an environment of mutual support.

Conduct disorder groups—These groups are for children and adolescents. Group members are helped to confront their behaviors and the effect they have on others, especially other members. These groups stress taking responsibility for one's actions. Underlying family dynamics are explored, as well as teaching problem-solving skills and how to express anger in a healthier manner.

Current events groups—These groups are often found in psychiatric hospitals and geriatric centers. Group members are exposed to current events and engaged into discussion. Helping to keep group members current is very important for these populations.

Daily living skills groups—These groups teach individuals the rudiments of basic living skills. These skills can range from shopping, to personal hygiene, to washing one's clothing, etc.

Depression groups—Insight-oriented group therapy for depression focusing on the underlying causes of members' depression and how their behaviors and relationships maintain their depression.

Event trauma groups—These groups are specifically designed to help individuals suffering from post-traumatic stress disorder. They are very powerful groups and require great skill on the part of the therapist. Colleagues working in this realm and working with individuals who experienced the horrendous World Trade Center tragedy, as an example, report that they often feel overwhelmed by the emotionality of their clients.

Gay and lesbian groups—These groups help members to accept their sexual orientation and decrease personal homophobia while providing support and assisting members in dealing with conflicts that result with family, friends, co-workers, and society due to their sexual orientation.

Gay parenting groups—These groups specifically address the difficulties of being a gay parent. Issues of concern may include adoption, finding a surrogate mother, artificial insemination, legal difficulties, etc. Integration into mainstream society is often a very important concern, and these groups are not only support groups but also very important for the passing on of information.

Interpersonal relatedness skills groups—These particular groups are designed to help individuals feel more comfortable when relating to others. They learn new skills in how to engage others in dialogue and overcome some of the shyness that has previously inhibited them from developing new relationships.

Marital problem groups—Couples who attend marital groups benefit because their styles of interacting are pointed out to them by the other group members and they may be able to see similarities and differences between their faulty styles of interacting and other couples' styles. Also, each member's issues that affect the marriage are likely to be acted out toward other group members. These issues can then be pointed out to the individual.

Medical support groups—These groups are specifically structured to address the issues, the dissemination of information, and the education of group members in relation to a particular medical diagnosis. These groups tremendously help the members to not feel alone in their medical difficulties and offer the most current information available in relation to a specific medical diagnosis. These groups truly embody the definition of a support group.

Music therapy groups—In these groups, music is used as the stimulus to elicit feelings and awareness. Certified music therapists, working from a number of paradigms, help individuals come into contact with repressed emotionality, thus liberating them to live more satisfactory lives. Similar to art, dance, and poetry therapy, the therapist is often very creative and seeks new and different uses of his or her medium to help group members.

Outdoor venture groups—These groups are usually geared toward children and adolescents. They teach problem-solving skills, trust, and how to work well with others.

Parent training groups—These groups teach parenting skills through the use of role-playing, modeling, observation, and mutual support.

Personal growth groups—These groups help members to become more aware of themselves and how they affect others. These groups are similar to psychotherapy groups in theme but often not in intensity.

Poetry therapy groups—These groups are as different as the different group leaders. Poetry is used, in its many forms, as a springboard to elicit feelings and dialogue. Many certified poetry therapists use different techniques with poetry in their work with group members.

Psychotherapy groups—The focus of these groups is toward restructuring personality. It is predominantly a longer-term group experience and individual members are there of their own accord. They have found their lives to be unsatisfactory and wish to make permanent changes regarding how they relate to both themselves and others.

Sex offender groups—The goal of sex offender groups is to keep individuals from offending again by helping them learn what led to their offense. Breaking the cycle of secrecy, helping them and others to be aware of the beginning grooming phases that lead to offending, and intervening when these occur are important aspects of this type of group. These groups work with the underlying issues that led to offending in the first place—especially tracing the individual's own life history, which usually reveals that the offender was abused as a child.

Sex-change orientation groups—Individuals seeking a change in their gender are required, before surgery, to be a part of these groups in order to understand their motivations and help with the transition to surgery.

Sexual abuse groups—These groups provide a supportive environment so members can talk about their abuse and explore the impact it has had upon them. It takes them through the healing process, allows them to deal with resulting sexual and trust issues, and helps them not to view themselves as victims.

Sexual dysfunction groups—These groups are designed to help individuals experiencing some form of sexual dysfunction. In men it may be erectile difficulties, and with women it may be frustration of not being able to achieve orgasm.

Shyness groups—These groups help shy members to act out situations related to their particular fears. These groups use modeling and mutual support to teach members new ways to deal with the situation and their anxiety. They then try the behaviors outside of the group.

Significant other groups—These groups are designed for the relatives, friends, and caregivers of the individuals in all the aforementioned groups. These groups help caregivers to understand not only what their friends or relatives are experiencing but also help them deal effectively with the emotionality that they themselves feel.

Single-parent groups—The design of these groups is often focused on helping single parents deal with the trials and tribulations of being the primary custodial care individual of their children. It generally is a support-oriented group with the passing on of information plus the venting of feelings as to the difficulties that may arise as a single parent.

Social skills groups—These groups teach individuals with poor social skills or social discomfort how to handle difficult situations by modeling, role-playing, and in-group experiences.

Spiritual awareness groups—Members of these groups seek to find other meaning in their lives that they have sensed either has been lost or not developed in the realm of spirituality.

Stop smoking groups—This support group-oriented paradigm is designed to help individuals overcome their addiction to nicotine.

Stress management groups—This type of group teaches members how to identify when they are stressed, how to learn what is causing the stress, and ways to make situations less stressful and increase relaxation.

Surviving divorce groups—Divorce is often a devastating experience for couples. This can be especially true if children are involved. Individuals seeking these supportive groups are specifically in the presence of others experiencing similar thoughts and feelings. Not feeling alone in one's adjustment difficulty can be extremely helpful.

Test anxiety groups—These groups teach members different techniques to help decrease test anxiety, such as relaxation, study skills, and test-taking skills.

Vietnam veterans' groups—These groups help Vietnam veterans come to terms with their experiences in war and the negative reception they experienced when returning to the United States. Many of the members of these groups are experiencing post-traumatic stress syndrome. Throughout the country, many veterans' centers work in conjunction with the Veterans Administration hospitals in creating outpatient facilities for these individuals.

Weight loss groups—Groups that provide psychoeducation about nutrition and weight loss in a supportive environment while addressing faulty conceptions about health, nutrition, and exercise. They address dynamic issues underlying weight gain and difficulty losing weight.

Appendix B

Structured Exercises for Developing Group Cohesion

There has been some question as to whether some form of group structure might be helpful in facilitating overall cohesion building or whether it may hinder natural group development. Rogers (1967) views the group experience as requiring a great degree of freedom and very little structure, as this seems essential in allowing the member to forego some of his or her traditional defenses and instead develop different means of interacting with others. Rogers sees this lack of structure as integral in allowing the individual to feel free and open, thereby permitting the indiviual the chance to change and adopt new ways of thinking and acting. Without structure, the group may move through periods in which there is little stability or equilibrium, but as the group learns to cope and stabilize itself, it will move to stages of greater trust and cohesiveness.

In terms of the possible positive effects of structure on the group, the leader may be able to provide cues and behavior guidelines that can benefit group development. In addition to the pretherapy training that the members should be exposed to, there are structured exercises which can help to alleviate the anxiety and discomfort associated with the first part of the group-building process. Aiding clients in working through the initial anxiety may prove invaluable in cutting dropout rates and reducing the stress experienced by the members (Bendar, Melnick, and Kaul, 1974). One study by Crews and Melnick (1976) examined the effects of structured exercises on the level of anxiety, group cohesion, and quality of interpersonal interactions experienced by members at three different points in the course of an interpersonal growth group. The results of the study showed that the structure aided members in clarifying the group task and helped in starting behaviors which were more appropriate to the group setting, such as engaging in more self-disclosure (Crews and Melnick, 1976). Although the initial structure was not seen to influence group cohesion, the increase in self-disclosure may have, in some manner, aided more rapid development of the cohesion needed to keep members in the group during those difficult initial sessions.

In the early group period the goal is to help clients express the specific content of their own issues and to allow them to engage more quickly at higher levels of emotional expression and openness. One should not foster a group culture that cannot operate without the structure provided by a group leader, in a sense creating dependency on the leader. Group leaders need to be aware of this fine line between providing structure to the group while helping the members achieve deeper levels of communication faster. The leader must be aware when approaching this structuring that dependency on the leader may mean that the only means of interpersonal interaction is through following the leader's orders (Bendar, Melnick, and Kaul, 1974; Dreiss, 1986; Vinogradov and Yalom, 1989).

Structured exercises may also allow the members to bypass the traditional social behaviors that prevent individuals from getting close to one another, or they may help group members in reaching suppressed emotions by exploring parts of themselves that are foreign to them. Structure may even take less obvious forms, such as dealing with a group that seems tense and blocked by stopping the group and having a quick go around in which each member discusses his or her own experience at that moment (Vinogradov and Yalom, 1989).

In choosing the type of group structure, one needs to choose between verbal and nonverbal exercises. Research has shown that based on measures of commitment to the group and involvement with fellow group members, nonverbal interventions tend to increase members' commitment to and involvement with their fellow group members more than verbal group interventions (Shadish, 1980). One study that compared nonverbal exercises with modeling of intensive group interaction, exchange of autobiographical information, and no exercise, found that nonverbal exercises were the most productive in promoting self-ratings of extroversion (Freidman, Ellenhorn, and Snortum, 1976). Other research that has focused more on the actual mechanism of touch within the group format found that the touching and physical contact component seemed to result in more positive feelings and greater openness within the group (Shadish, 1980). One study in particular by Cooper and Bowles (1973) looked at the level of self-disclosure when there was physical contact as compared to no physical contact. Results showed that subjects who participated in the exercises with physical encounter had significantly higher levels of self-disclosure following those exercises.

NONVERBAL EXERCISES

In a study by Shadish (1980), one of the nonverbal exercises utilized is labeled "nonverbal give and take." The group members are told to stand and form a circle in the room, then one person chooses to be the focus of the group. This person stands in the center of the circle with his or her eyes shut and all the members approach this individual and express their feelings nonverbally in a positive or negative way. Typically, this takes the form of hugging, stroking, massaging, lifting, etc. After this, the focal person may discuss what his or her experience was of being touched, such as what was pleasant, unpleasant, surprising, and so on. This last part is optional as some leaders may feel this somehow lessens the effectiveness of the experience.

Two simple exercises, described by Carroll, Bates, and Johnson (1997), are specifically aimed at initiating discussion and increasing the level of trust and cohesion in the group. One is called the "two-foot square" and involves marking off a square area in the room that is obviously too small for the number of people in the group. The task is to get everyone in the group into the square. It is hypothesized that this exercise will point out the necessity for the group to work together and act as a whole in order to reach the goals all of them have for their time in therapy.

Another exercise, the "blind walk," involves breaking the group in half. One half is blindfolded or just closes their eyes; the others serve as partners who act as guides. The pairs are allowed ten minutes to explore the building inside and outside if permissible. After ten minutes, the pairs switch roles. Following the exercise, the members discuss the feelings that arose during the exercise, especially honesty, trust, independence/dependence, and responsibility.

In the Cooper and Bowles (1973) study of physical encounter, three interpersonal exercises taken from Encounter tapes by the Human Development Institute of Bell and Howell, are used to promote self-disclosure. The first exercise, called "impressions," involves having the members form a circle. One at a time, each member is face to face with everyone in the circle. While face to face, the individual is told to touch the person, look directly at him or her, and give his or her first impression.

The second exercise, called "break in," involves the group members standing in a circle, with one member moving outside the circle. The outside group member is instructed to attempt to break into the circle. The members in the circle are instructed to link arms and prevent the person from breaking in.

In the third exercise, termed "rolling," the group stands in a circle and each individual in turn stands in the center of the circle, relaxes as much as possible, then falls into the arms of the group members and lets himself or herself be passed from member to member.

After each of the exercises, the members are given time to discuss their feelings about what they have just done. The first exercise appears to help with cohesion as it involves physical contact and the practice of giving feedback based upon affective reaction. The members are encouraged to discuss what it feels like to have to give honest feedback to others, whether it raises anxiety, fears of rejection, etc. The second exercise appears to have value in that it provides the stimulus for a feedback session about rejection and isolation, especially the experience during the exercise and at other points in the individuals' lives. The third exercise seems to bring up feelings regarding trust and how this relates to feelings for other group members and for those outside the group.

Some techniques Corey (1982) suggests for accelerating awareness in short-term therapy groups involve attempting to bring the intrapersonal and interpersonal conflicts of the clients into the group arena through immediate and spontaneous conflict-oriented demonstrations. These exercises are active and interactive in nature, which aids in developing trust and a more cohesive group.

One such exercise is called "stand up—sit down," in which the group is broken down into trios. One of the three is told to leave the room, while the other two are told to stand on opposite sides of a chair, with one instructed to get the third individual to stand up and the other instructed to get the third to sit down. The two may use anything short of physical force, such as flattery, ordering, threatening, and begging to get the third to do what they wish. The third is then told that he or she is the type who seeks to please everyone and so must try to please the two individuals. The three are then left to this task until the third resolves the situation through being assertive, giving up, or coping negatively. The way in which the third resolves the task is examined and related to the client's everyday life as a means of coping with stress and significant others.

The next exercise, called "give me a pillow," is aimed at individuals who are always giving to others and never getting their own needs met. These individuals are surrounded by those who always take from them and/or they may drive away their true friends because they are smothering in their attention. In the exercise, the individual sits in a chair with a stack of pillows and the others are told to ask for the pillows. At some point, the seated person is out of pillows and must deal with the others' begging, pleading, etc., for them. The individual is shown how constant selflessness is draining and is not healthy. A similar exercise involves the person lying on the couch and others putting pillows on him or her; the person must say thank you and never refuse any. This demonstrates the way his or her friends experience being around this particular individual.

The third exercise by Corey (1982) is called "push the wall" and is designed to demonstrate how much energy many individuals spend trying to get others to change, which may be a useless task. The group members are told to place both hands on the walls of the room and push as hard as they can. They are told to say the names of the individuals in their lives who they try to change the most, along with phrases such as, "please change." It is believed that the intense emotion this arouses, along with the hopelessness created, will lead to group discussion and self-change for those who have issues in this area.

VERBAL EXERCISES

One exercise cited by Vinogradov and Yalom (1989) that might be useful in the early sessions of a group involves breaking the group down into dyads and having each person describe himself or herself to the other person for a few minutes. The group gets back together and each partner introduces the other partner, making sure to describe personal characteristics, brief life biography, likes and dislikes, aspirations, etc. The next step is to have the members explore what it is like to describe themselves in detail to another person and have that person share the description with the group.

In terms of other low-intensity interpersonal verbal activities that are used early in the growth process, any number of topics can be introduced by the leader to spawn discussion and feelings. Examples are birth order and the problems associated with being in that position in the family, first memories of conflict and any personal problems or behaviors that serve to create conflict, symbolic substitution—meaning what bird, animal, or plant a client would be and why, or the best and worst possible way of life and where clients are on this continuum.

One exercise that aids in identifying and labeling affect is called "color strips." In this exercise, the participants are asked to close their eyes and think about the day's experiences and get in touch with their feelings right at that moment, then describe the colors that represent the feeling, the texture, and whether it is big/small, jagged/smooth, linear/round, etc. The members are asked to describe the shape and color they have chosen and why they selected it (Carroll, Bates, and Johnson, 1997).

To develop feedback skills, within the verbal intervention component of Shadish's (1980) study an exercise called "verbal expressions" was used. The exercise can be manipulated, changed, and used in any number of ways, but the basic premise is that group members are expressing feelings and giving feedback to other members. This can be extremely lengthy, so it may be best to limit the time provided for feedback. The exercise may be done in one of two ways: either someone volunteers to receive feedback or the group goes one by one and gives feedback to all the other members. It is important for the leader to establish some norms for the feedback as follows: (1) try to give both positive and negative feedback; (2) be specific in the feedback—give behavioral measures; and (3) include your own personal feelings about other members and their behaviors.

Some medium-intensity interpersonal exercises recommended by Carroll, Bates, and Johnson (1997) are designed to serve as a catalyst for pulling members into interaction and fostering intermember interaction. The first of these is called "metaphors" and involves each of the members coming up with impressions in their minds of their group mates and associating food, animals, automobiles, weather, color, or anything that summarizes their impression. It is vital that the individual providing the metaphor gives reasons for choosing that particular one and tries to be positive, if at all possible. One example provided is, "You seem like a teddy bear; you're physically powerful looking but very gentle in disposition."

Another similar exercise is to have group members reflect on their lives and choose a specific time, place, or event that proved to have a significant influence on their present situation. The group should not get caught in a storytelling mode focused on the past, but members should associate to their present situation and how they are dealing with those around them.

An exercise of similar intensity that taps into the level of cohesion in the group is termed "as a group member." Typically, this exercise is used at the end of a group, but it also appears to be useful in the early sessions as a gauge for the leader to develop a sense of "we-ness." The members are asked to complete the phrase, "As a group member, I _____." It is hoped that this will help members explore the meaning of the group for themselves, their level of commitment, and their therapy goals (Carroll, Bates, and Johnson, 1997).

Another exercise cited by Vinogradov and Yalom (1989) which can be used to push the members into deeper levels of self-examination and which may allow the group members to get to know one another at a deeper level deals with each members' personal identifying characteristics. Each member gets seven index cards and a pencil and is told to write down seven identifying characteristics. The members are told to arrange the cards with the most superficial characteristic on top and the most profound on the bottom. They then start with the most superficial characteristic and think for several minutes about what it would be like to give that one up. They move down the stack, doing the same for each of the characteristics. The members move back through the cards and reassume the characteristics from most profound to most superficial. The group then discusses the thoughts and feelings evoked by the exercise.

Carroll, Bates, and Johnson (1997) employ an exercise called "lifeline," which is not appropriate in the very first sessions but is useful when some level of trust has developed. This involves having the members draw a line on a piece of paper that represents the course of their lives, with all the highs and lows included and indicated by peaks, valleys, and plateaus. The group members then explain their lines to the others, with the other members encouraged to look and ask questions. Members learn more about one another personally and are able to accelerate the process of universality and shared experiences.

Another exercise that would accelerate self-disclosure, especially in terms of personal values and interest, is the "perfect day." The leader instructs the members to plan a day that is perfect for them, regardless of time, money, or freedom, and write down the central characteristics. The members describe these perfect scenarios to the group, sharing personal aspects of themselves and at the same time recognizing the different values of others.

Appendix C

Group Therapy from A to Z

A number of years ago, Dr. David Cantor, a psychologist and group psychotherapist, contemplated how he could explain group therapy, in a simple written form, for a client considering group therapy for his or her personal developmental growth. He was acutely aware of the anxiety new group members experience when they make the decision to enter into this special form of psychotherapy. It represented not only the unknown, but also the vulnerability of permitting strangers into one's own personal world. He wanted this written explanation to be positive and in a form that would be generally familiar in format. He creatively approached this task using the English alphabet.

I have found that a number of clients, after reading Group Therapy from A to Z, feel excited about their decision to enter into this microcosm of society, improve their interpersonal relationships, and the strong possibility of understanding their familial histories.

A is for Acceptance. It is important in group therapy that you learn to accept yourself and to accept others. To feel accepted is an important ingredient in the success of this type of therapy. However, to accept others is a sign that this type of therapy is working for you. The more that you accept yourself and accept others, the more you will feel a part of the group and less isolated and alone. In addition, during the course of group therapy, you will find yourself confronted with some things about yourself that you may not like. This is good and very important, as it will be the motivation for change. Change only occurs when acceptance is first permitted in oneself.

B is for Beliefs. During the course of group therapy you will be learning to explore your and others' beliefs. These beliefs are about you, others, and the world. Everyone has a whole set of beliefs, part of which we are very much aware and part of which are not fully in our awareness. Crucial beliefs are those we have about how we are supposed to be with others and how they are supposed to be with us. During group therapy you act and react toward others based on your beliefs. It is important to pay attention to these beliefs so that you can change the ones that are not effectively working in your best interest.

C is for Curiosity. First of all, curiosity did not kill the cat; it was a lack of awareness of itself and its environment that killed the cat. Curiosity about yourself and the people with whom you share the experience of group therapy, your group brothers and sisters, is perhaps the most important value/behavior that one can possess. Curiosity is the royal road to improving and enriching your life. It is also a valuable skill to have in group therapy and in life. Curiosity communicates caring and concern and it also enhances the process of acceptance within and between group members. Everyone in group has his or her own special story and is waiting for someone to listen to him or her. This will be true for you as well.

D is for Disclosure. To get the maximum benefit from group therapy, one has to disclose personal information. This information may be embarrassing and, at times, painful depending upon the thoughts and feelings of the experience. Some of the obstacles to disclosure are shame, humiliation, vulnerability, or the risk of being judged by others. We normally turn ourselves away from this as disclosure often elicits anxiety, but by not taking the risk, one perpetuates the feeling(s), which have remained hidden for perhaps a very long time. However, it is this turning away which perpetuates the many underlying feelings that have shaped one's current life and possible interpersonal inhibitions for intimacy. It is important to remember that disclosure includes giving information about yourself to others while at the same time giving information to yourself about you. Disclosure is the opposite of denial.

E is for Empathy. Empathy can be defined as being able to put yourself in the other person's shoes and understand their situation from their point of view. It is similar to two tuning forks. If they are sensitive to each other, when one is set to vibrate the other will respond in kind. It basically means being emotionally sensitive to a situation and having the capacity to feel what the other person is feeling. Empathy is a temporary identification with another person. It is the basis for relatedness. When one feels that the other person is empathizing with them, there is an increase in the amount of curiosity that they will have about their life, and an increase in the amount that they will disclose to themselves and to the group. Empathy is a good group skill to work on and practice because how you respond to people in group is very similar to how you respond to people in your personal life.

F is for Fears. In the course of group therapy, you will begin to notice that you have certain fears in relation to yourself and others. It is important that you become curious about what fears you have especially those you have about your interactions with others. It is these fears, based on our beliefs, that decrease our intimacy and feelings of closeness with others. It is our fears which propel us to seek reassurance from others, and it is our fears which propel us to distance ourselves from others. Of note, is that it is fears which stand most in the way of our empathic skills/behavior. For example, if a person in group is expressing rage toward a parent or a spouse and we have some fears around the issue of assertiveness or passivity, then it will be much harder for us to identify with the person and get into what they are feeling and trying to express. We will distance ourselves from that person and that particular issue. The effect that this has on the other person is that they will feel less accepted, perhaps alone in their issue and will disclose less to themselves and to the group.

G is for Growth. The goal in group therapy is personal growth and maturity. Often when people enter into any kind of therapy, they focus on relieving their symptoms instead of focusing on themselves and how they live their lives. Symptoms and interpersonal behavior are very much connected. If one will worry about their own growth and the obstacles that are in the way of this growth then the symptoms will take care of themselves. Symptoms are warning signs and they are not altogether bad. In fact, though they are painful, they are quite useful. They do point the way to personal growth and maturity. It is also important not to be misled by the symptoms of others in group. Everyone can also use symptoms as a way of avoiding or dealing with more difficult areas in their lives such as their beliefs and their fears.

H is for Here and Now. To be effective, group therapy needs to be centered in the present which is referred to as the here and now. A person's past is very important and past experiences certainly affect a person's current way of relating to others. However, the focus needs to be on how the person is relating to others in the present and any understanding of the past needs to be used to understand the here and now. To focus too extensively on the past is a way of distancing oneself from the present. It does not lead to the birth of more intimate and mature relationships in the here and now. There is no urgency in understanding, for example, how one has been passive to parental figures in the past. It is, however, in your interest to be aware how you are passive in the present as that is something that can be worked on. History cannot be changed but the future can.

I is for Intimacy. Intimacy can only live in the present. It cannot live in the past and it cannot live in the future. It is fully in the "Here and Now." Intimacy depends on acceptance, curiosity, disclosure, and empathy. It also depends on trust. It is our fears which prevent us from feeling truly close to others. Although the group member relationships have several distinct differences from other relationships, it is still possible to achieve a healthy level of intimacy. During the course of group therapy, it is important to monitor this process and to ask yourself "how intimate am I being with others" and "how intimate are they being with me and to the other group members?" Again, signs of intimacy include acceptance, curiosity, disclosure, and empathy.

J is for Judgment. Being judgmental of other people results from our fears and our own unresolved issues. In group therapy, judgment of others is detrimental to acceptance and disclosure and to intimacy. It is hard to accept ourselves, let others know about us, and to establish intimacy with others if we feel that they are going to say that we are bad people. It too works conversely. If others in a group feel we are judgmental, they will be reluctant to disclose intimate aspects of themselves. A way of fighting your own judgments of others is to find within yourself the particular things that you are judgmental against. For example, if you are judgmental about another person's selfishness, then you should examine your own selfishness. People sometimes use their judgments as a way of distancing themselves from others. They avoid intimacy by negatively judging the other person and their beliefs.

K is for Knowledge. The most important thing that a person can gain in group therapy is knowledge of themselves and others. This increases a person's sense of personal control and sense of pride in himself or herself. Curiosity is the foundation for acquiring knowledge. A very important maxim is "Know Thyself." There are many types and levels of knowledge and there are many paths to gaining information. One type of knowledge that you will be seeking and gaining during group therapy is the knowledge of yourself and others. Remember that there are several paths to this knowledge and you may have to unlock several doors before you find the one that reveals to you what you need to know. It is also important to use the knowledge that you gain in group therapy in your personal life. People in group therapy are not and will not be much different than the people that are in your daily life.

L is for Listening. Listening is one of the most important skills that you will learn in group therapy. Unlike individual therapy where you do most of the talking, in group therapy you spend most of the time listening to others. It is important to listen for a person's beliefs and their fears. During the course of group therapy, you will learn to listen to what the person says and to what they do not dare mention. The group as a whole needs to listen to the various levels of what a person is saying. An important level of listening is listening to what the person is saying about their relationship with you even when they are not directly speaking about it. This takes curiosity and empathy. It also takes mastering one's fears of rejection and one's fears of not being in control.

M is for Motivations. People have different motivations for their actions. During the course of group therapy you will learn to pay attention to your own and others' motivations. Motivations can be known or they can exist outside of the person's awareness. Usually the most important and powerful motivations are those which lie outside of our awareness. Many of our motivations are related to our beliefs and our fears. The most important motivations are those that have to do with our relationships with other people.

N is for Nonverbal. People communicate verbally and nonverbally through body posture, tone of voice, facial expression, and through their eyes. Our feelings about others and ourselves are usually sent through nonverbal cues. We often say nonverbally what we cannot say out loud. It is important during group not only to pay attention to what a person is saying verbally but also to listen to what a person is saying with their eyes, their faces, their body, and so on. It is also important to be open to feedback on how you present yourself nonverbally. This kind of feedback can be frightening at first, but is usually extremely helpful to you in your personal growth.

O is for Observation. It is important to observe yourself and the other group members during the course of the group experience. Observing how you and others feel and behave in different situations gives you very good information that can be used to further your and others' personal growth. It is especially important to observe other people's emotional reactions or in other words, how they feel. It is also important to observe yourself when different topics come up or when different people in the group are speaking. For example, are you more interested and involved when one person is speaking and sleepy or bored when another person is speaking? This is important to observe and then to be curious about why.

P is for Projections. All people use projections from time to time. A projection happens when we see another person as having some particular negative quality that we do not see in ourselves. For example, when we are acting controlling with another person but cannot acknowledge that aspect of our personality, we run the risk of seeing that other person as being controlling. People generally use projections in order to protect their self-esteem or to help them feel better about themselves. It is sometimes difficult for us to acknowledge and know our less attractive sides. In group therapy, you will tend to see in others (project) aspects of your own personality. One problem in doing this is that it does not lead to intimacy. It also does not lead to accurately perceiving others or to accurately perceiving oneself. It is also important to remember that other group members will be seeing in you aspects of their own personality. This makes it important that you become very knowledgeable about your own issues.

Q is for Quietness. In order to listen to both yourself and to others there must be a sense of quietness within you. You must be able to shut down all the internal distractions and make yourself quiet so that you can hear others and to hear your feelings about what they are saying. In group therapy, there are many times when it is beneficial to have a sense of quietness. It is the cornerstone of effective listening. It is also the first step in effective communication. Having a sense of internal quietness allows one to be aware of different feelings and then to express them.

R is for Relating. Learning to relate to others is a very important goal in group therapy. Many people live in interpersonal isolation. They do not truly relate to anyone on a deep and meaningful level. In many cases, people have not learned the skills to effectively relate to other people. It is important in group therapy that you pay attention to how you and the rest of the group relate to each other. For example, does your interpersonal style communicate acceptance and concern or does it communicate hostility and/or competitiveness?

S is for Solutions. In group therapy, we are looking for solutions to help ourselves and each other live our lives in more meaningful and adaptive ways. We primarily look for solutions that will help people relate to each other in more fulfilling ways. Remember, most if not every problem has a solution. These may be hard to grasp at first, but they do exist. Sometimes, solutions take longer because we are asking the wrong questions or because we are working on the wrong problems. For example, if a person comes into group and states that their problem is depression, it does not give us a lot of information in order to help them find a solution. However, if we think of their depression as resulting from loneliness and bitterness then we can come up with different solutions that may be helpful. Do not be misled by what people say their problem is. Look beyond the particular symptom such as depression or anxiety to how they are living their lives and to the state of their interpersonal relationships. Of note is that certain feelings are not problems which require a solution. For example, the feeling of sadness is appropriate after losing someone and anger is appropriate if someone has mistreated you.

T is for Transference. Transference is when you develop feelings, perceptions, or actions toward someone that are similar to those that you had toward parents, siblings, or other important childhood figures. Transference happens when you have not resolved or gotten over what happened in previous childhood relationships. Transference is a way of misperceiving others or their roles in your life. For example, if one or both of your parents did not acknowledge your feelings, you would probably expect other people who had personalities similar to your parents to do the same thing. In fact, you may begin to feel that historical hurt from the past in the present. In group therapy there will be people who remind you of your parents or some other significant person from the past. These are useful people for you in that you can learn something about a past relationship through a current relationship. You will also find yourself relating to others in ways that you learned in your family. This too is a transference type relationship.

U is for Unconscious. There are many things we do not know about ourselves. In group therapy, you will be told many things about yourself that you do not know. This can be very frightening to you and may even cause you to be defensive and to say "No, that is not me." It is important that you keep an open mind to the feedback that you get from others. Not all of it will be accurate and useful but much of it will be and it is important to think about all the feedback about yourself. Actually, unconscious is often more easily understood as being out of awareness.

V is for Verbalization. In group therapy or any kind of therapy it is important that you learn to verbalize your feelings rather than to act them out. If you can learn to put into words what you normally put into action then you will increase your ability to get along with other people.

W is for Work. Group therapy is hard work. It takes commitment and dedication in order for it to be of benefit. The degree of benefit for yourself is dependent on how hard you work, not on how hard others work for you. To succeed in group therapy, one must also work on issues while not in group. This means that if an issue is pointed out to you while in the group, you will think and talk about the issue during the week. The issue will be on your mind. It also means that you will allow your mind to be open to the issues of others. Very often we can lean a lot by just seeing how others effectively or ineffectively work with their own distinct personal issues.

X is for X Rays. Like an X ray, group therapy looks below the surface at where the pain really is. You also learn to look deeper into your own and other people's lives than what you normally do. It is important to realize that all of us cannot fully talk about what is troubling us. Many times, what is troubling us lies just underneath or out of awareness. Group therapy teaches you to look beyond what is said. For example, it is important to observe how a person says something such as their tone of voice or what emotion they are expressing. It is also important to pay attention to what a person does not talk about. For example, if a depressed person is in the group and they do not talk about their anger, then you have learned something about how they feel about this emotion.

Y is for Yearnings. In group therapy you will learn about what you yearn for most of all and you will learn about the yearnings of others. Most people yearn to be accepted and to be listened to. Often people hide from themselves and others what they most desire. In group therapy, these yearnings will become apparent to you and to others. In other words, the process of group therapy will activate all your old and new yearnings and desires. You will learn more about what you need or yearn for both from others and from yourself.

Z is for Zestfulness. One purpose of group therapy is to give you zestfulness for life. One key to zestfulness or aliveness is becoming involved with other people and things outside yourself. The opposite of zestfulness is self-concentration or self-involvement. One cannot be zestful and involved in life if they are involved only with themselves. In order to become more zestful in life, it is important to get more in touch with your feelings and to express them. Many people report feeling "bottled up inside." This leads to a lack of zestfulness and vitality, which can best be helped by dealing more with your feelings. Group therapy is very helpful in getting to know your feelings. Because of the number of issues that are presented, it is nearly impossible not to have a feeling about at least one of them. Group therapy will give you a chance to experience these feelings as well as help in expressing them.

Welcome to group therapy and one of the most extraordinary experiences you will have in your life . . .

Glossary

acculturation: A process of attitudinal and behavioral change that occurs as a result of being exposed to a new society or culture.

acting out: Putting into action sexual or aggressive impulses in order to reduce tension or anxiety. A physical or motor action to lessen anxiety.

adjustment: A series of results to compensate for or meet special conditions. The outcome of an individual's energies to effectively deal with gratification of needs and reduction of stress.

affect: The subjective experience of feeling or emotion. It can be attached to an idea or complexes of ideas. May be seen in disguised form in dreams as related to an object other than that to which it would ordinarily belong. Can be an unconscious manifestation for an individual and at the same time be noticeable to others.

albatross: The albatross reference is from the poem "The Rime of the Ancient Mariner," by Samuel Taylor Coleridge written in 1798, where it is used as a symbol of guilt or a burden.

altruism: This is concern and affection for others. This concern is without a selfish underpinning. In group psychotherapy altruism is expressed by group members helping each other through support, reassurance, suggestions, and by sharing similar problems with one another. This is one of Yalom's eleven factors which help groups become effective.

ambivalence: Simultaneous feelings or attitudes within the same person which are contradictory (e.g., love-hate, acceptance-rejection). Ambivalence generally is universal. It does not become significant until the conflicting feeling increases to such a point where action seems unavoidable. At these times, only one of the conflicting feelings is brought to consciousness.

American Psychological Association Group-Psychotherapy Forum: An Internet discussion forum founded in 1995 by Haim Weinberg that brings together professionals interested in working with groups. This forum provides an avenue for group therapists to exchange information, provide support, and dialogue about group work including their professional experiences, ongoing research, and consultation. Often, since the group is made up of over 500 members, many of whom are group therapists, the discussion also focuses on the dynamics of the mailing list. Other past topics have included intimacy in groups, difficult patients in groups, entering a group, working with special populations in groups, and large groups.

anachronistic: Something out of its place in time. Here, it is suggested that a genuine relationship with the therapist is not being developed, but rather that the relationship is transferential, or a representation from a past relationship.

anthropomorphized: Interpreting behaviors of animals in terms of human traits.

anxiety: An uncomfortable subjective emotional state characterized by apprehension and dread. It generally is accompanied by an increase in physiological arousal. Depending upon its level of arousal, it can be either a motivator or debilitating.

atavistic: Here it is used to mean the reverting to an older, simpler, infantile, or more primitive state.

authenticity: The quality of being genuine and real.

autocratic: A system where one individual (here, the therapist) is seen as the authority and also possesses and exerts all the power. It is perceived as an asymmetrical interpersonal relationship.

biological determinism: The philosophy that current behavior is determined by biological or chemical influences.

bridging: The techniques used in group therapy that facilitate meaningful interaction and dialogue between individuals. These methods develop an emotional connectedness between the members and help the group to function as a cohesive unit.

case study: The organization of historical and biographical data on a particular individual.

catastrophize: To exaggerate the consequences of events.

catharsis: Release or discharge of emotional tension or energy. In therapy it is associated with reexperiencing repressed material and verbalizing that material with concomitant emotional affect. It literally means to purge. Observed by Aristotle in relationship to audiences watching a play and experiencing intense emotional identification with the actors and the situation. The release of emotional tension associated with a forgotten or conscious event through recalling and reliving the forgotten experience, or through talking about the conscious event followed by the expression of the emotion. The technique was first used by Josef Breuer (1842-1925) in Vienna.

cathartic method: Introduced by Breuer as a procedure or technique in therapy whereby the patient relives a past trauma with its concomitant emotionality.

cognitive restructuring: Changing the thinking process of a client by replacing maladaptive thoughts with more adaptive ones in order to alter the client's emotions and behavior.

cognitive-behavioral mode: A theoretical perspective in psychotherapy which has as its underpinning that thoughts play an important role in one's behavior and affect. Cognitions that are causing the individual distress are identified and techniques are used to identify new ways of thinking. Examples of behavioral interventions include visualizations, modeling, and practicing.

cohesion: Mutually attractive or hanging together. In group psychotherapy this term is used to describe the overall attraction of a group for each of the participating members. Cohesion gives members a sense of belonging, which facilitates the group process. It is analogous to the rapport established between a client and his or her individual therapist.

compensation: A defense mechanism in which one engages in a substitutive behavior to make up for real or perceived deficiencies in another area of one's personality. Compensation can be conscious or unconscious.

consciousness: The individual's awareness of both the internal and external environment belonging to certain processes or events in a living organism which are unique. Ordinarily employed as a synonym for awareness.

contagion: In social groups this occurs when behavior patterns spread due to suggestion. A term used by Bion which suggests that within groups individuals give up their own personal interests for the interest of the group.

contingency contracts: A technique used in behavior therapy. It is based on cooperative responses in which a patient must comply with certain identified behaviors and in doing so will be reinforced accordingly. The goal is to decrease unwanted behavior by increasing positive reinforcement and minimizing negative reinforcement and punishment.

conversion: An ego defense mechanism in which unconscious emotional conflicts are transformed into physical symptoms. These symptoms can take several forms including motor, sensory, and visceral problems such as blindness, vomiting, tremors, paralysis, difficulties swallowing, and pains that serve the function of protecting the individual from anxiety.

corrective emotional experience: A concept developed by Franz Alexander in which he argued that intellectual insight was not enough to produce change. He believed that the patient must face, under different circumstances, emotional situations that he or she was unable to handle in the past. Under these new circumstances with the therapist, the patient is able to experience the emotions and begin to see the reality that the therapist is not recreating the patient's past experience(s).

countertransference: Feelings and thoughts that a therapist has toward a client. They can be both positive and negative resulting in either a benefit or an obstacle to the therapeutic situation.

decompensation: The loss of self through the deterioration of defense mechanisms, often leading to a pathological state.

defense mechanism: In psychodynamic theory, intrapsychic operations employed by the unconscious to defend the ego from anxiety caused by a threatening event, thought, or emotion by preventing these materials access to conscious awareness. Some examples are: denial, projection, and reaction formation.

democratic: A system in which all individuals have equal say and where minority views are tolerated. In therapy, this is done by reducing the power of the therapist as an absolute authority and increasing the responsibility of the clients as active participants.

denial: A primary ego defense mechanism in which an individual's thoughts and impulses are blocked from consciousness. Denial is a component of many of the higher order, or more sophisticated defenses, such as reaction formation and rationalization.

desensitizing: Reducing anxiety, or the tendency to react less strongly to emotion-arousing stimuli such as violence, through repeated exposure to the stimuli.

diathesis: A predisposition or propensity toward something. For example, a child from two clinically depressed parents may have a diathesis toward depression.

diatribe: Speech or writing which is biting and abusive.

didactic: Instructional.

directive: A psychotherapeutic situation in which the therapist assumes a more active role in the therapeutic process.

displacement: A psychoanalytic defense mechanism in which an affect or emotional attachment is transferred from its intended source to an alternate, less threatening object.

dissociation: An ego defense mechanism in which conflicting thoughts, impulses, or feelings are split off and kept separate from the remainder of the individual's personality.

dovetail: Interlocking or combining to create a unified whole. Fitting well together.

eclectic: In psychology, refers to combining knowledge from several theories or orientations rather than strict adherence to one theory (such as psychodynamic or behavioral).

ego: An individual's experience of the self, or the conception of self. It is that part of the person which is in direct touch with external reality and is conscious and includes the representation of reality as given by the senses. It is responsible for decision making and appropriately seeking objects for self-gratification.

ego ideal (self-ideal): Part of the personality that is concerned with what one "ought" to be. Often developed through identification with significant others from the person's past.

ego strength: An individual's ability to recognize and accept reality, despite it being unpleasant at times, without utilizing primitive defense mechanisms. Primitive defense mechanisms include denial, splitting, and projection.

ego-dystonic: In opposition to the ego and its standards. For example, an individual may be aware of certain personality characteristics that he or she dislikes. These characteristics would be dystonic for the individual. In psychotherapy, change can often occur when an ego-syntonic behavior, which can be inappropriate, is changed to an ego-dystonic behavior and the individual seeks to change this dystonic feature to something that is emotionally comfortable.

ego-syntonic: In harmony with the ego and its standards. For example, an individual manifests certain behavioral characteristics and is comfortable with those characteristics. Those behaviors would be considered ego syntonic to the individual.

emotional insulation: An ego defense mechanism in which an individual responds to disappointment or frustration by becoming detached and indifferent. An extreme example of this defense is seen in a catatonic stupor. More commonly, its function is to shield an individual from disappointment.

empathy: The awareness of another's thoughts and feelings. Often referred to as identification with another. Very necessary component in the personality of an effective therapist.

empirical: Based on results that are obtained by experimental procedures or naturalistic observation.

encounter group: A type of therapy that promotes personal growth and interpersonal communication. The leader hopes to facilitate openness, emotional expression, and sensitivity toward others through interpersonal experiences in a small group setting.

equilibrium: A state of balance in a system.

Erikson's stages of development: Erik Erikson is an American psychoanalyst who furthered Freud's theory of psychosexual development. The emphasis of Erikson's stages of development was based more on the ego and emphasized psychosocial factors. He included stages ranging throughout the life span and emphasized the crises that occur between the individual's needs and needs of society. These crises must be resolved in order for an individual to progress in social development. The stages of development include trust versus mistrust, autonomy versus shame and doubt, initiative versus guilt, industry versus inferiority, identity versus role confusion, intimacy versus isolation, generativity versus stagnation, and integrity versus despair.

erotic transference: The sexually charged feelings developed by a client toward the therapist or other group members when they become a symbolic representation of a significant other from the client's past.

etiology: The factors that contribute to an illness or disorder. It is the investigation of a given phenomenon or series of phenomena as the cause of disease. In psychology, it is the historical investigation of the client's presenting problem(s).

euphemism: Using a pleasant or benign term as a substitute for a more unpleasant term.

existentialism: A philosophical and psychological movement emphasizing human existence and taking responsibility for that existence.

facilitator: Another term used for a group leader; a professional or layperson who aids the group in moving forward.

fixation point: A point at which an individual is stuck in his or her way of doing something that is no longer serving a beneficial function. In psychoanalysis, this term is used to describe a stagnation at an early stage of psychosexual development.

foreground figure and background: Gestalt principles of perceptual organization emphasizing that humans organize stimuli into a foreground superimposed on a background. The foreground figure is always associated with more prominent features than the background.

fragmentation: Used in this context to refer to the group losing its cohesion and integration. Literally, it means the separation into parts or the inability to integrate.

free association: A fundamental technique used in psychoanalysis in which the patient reports, without censure, every thought and feeling that comes to mind, no matter how irrelevant, disturbing, or embarrassing it might be.

genogram: A schematic diagram originally developed by Bowen and utilized in psychodynamic approaches to therapy. It provides a systematic way of gathering information regarding family structure. The information gathered and plotted on the "map" includes marriages, deaths, and closeness of each member of the family to the identified patient and helps to identify recurring patterns across generations.

genuineness: Being true to oneself and real to oneself and others. This quality is at the base of all therapy. In relation to group therapy, it implies that there is no facade or pretense in the therapeutic relationship and there is no front separating the therapist from the client or group.

gestalt: A theoretical orientation developed by Perls in which the group focuses on the "here and now" and through this experiencing of the present moment, members gain insight into their personal behaviors. These discoveries facilitate decisions for which behavior change can occur. Group members in this modality are constantly "in the moment" and are taught to take personal responsibility for their behaviors and feelings. Group therapists using this model try to integrate all aspects of the individual with the goal of achieving an integrated whole.

group contract/group agreement: Often used interchangeably, refers to a set of rules or guidelines agreed upon by all group members to ensure confidentiality, safety, and to promote group cohesiveness. The term contract implies a strict adherence to established rules rather than the cooperation implicit in the term agreement. It is one of the few structural components in a generally unstructured environment, group therapy.

guilt: Aversive feeling(s) arising from actions, desires, or impulses in contradiction to one's ethical principles. Includes growing apprehension and fears of punishment. It is an emotion having its origin in the development and maintenance of civilization.

here and now modality: Focusing on the immediate interpersonal interchanges as they are occurring in the group. The group therapist's role is to maintain the focus on the present, what is transpiring within the group at that moment. This focusing on the present allows each member of the group to experience and examine their own personal feelings, reactions, and responses as well as those of the people around them, giving them an appreciation for how they relate to others in the real world.

heterogeneous: Having different constituents. In group psychotherapy, a heterogeneous group would be characterized by individuals who show dissimilarities such as age, gender, sexual orientation, and ethnic background.

homeostasis: The self-regulating process that helps an organism maintain a constant or steady internal state. For example, the body keeps its temperature constant through homeostasis. In psychology, it refers to the mind seeking a state of equilibrium.

hominid: The family of bipedal mammals that consists of humans and all of their immediate ancestors.

homogeneous: Having similar characteristics. In group psychotherapy, a homogeneous group would be composed of individuals who are alike such as those suffering from panic attacks, or all adolescents, or all substance abusers.

humanistic psychology: A theory of psychology, developed from the work of Abraham Maslow, which focuses on the human process. It is an outgrowth of existentialism and phenomenology and values the individual's subjective experience, uniqueness, freedom of choice, and maximizing one's potential. The emphasis is on developing potential through an experiential process instead of through behavior modification or focusing on unconscious processes.

hypochondriasis: A somatoform disorder in which common bodily sensations are consistently misinterpreted as indications of major illness despite medical evidence to the contrary. It often represents unacknowledged anxiety translated through the soma.

iatrogenic disturbances: A disease or disorder that is unintentionally induced by a physician. This can occur by providing the patient with more information than necessary or giving the individual's complaints more attention than necessary. This is commonly seen in patients who have hypochondriacal or hysterical tendencies.

id: Designated by Freud to indicate the interacting energies or forces constituting the unconscious. In psychoanalytic theory, along with the ego and superego, the id is one of the three components of personality present at birth. The id houses unconscious instincts and is composed of all the energy of the psyche. It acts on the pleasure principle and seeks immediate gratification of its needs. It is that feature of the primitive personality that requires socialization for civilization to develop.

inductive reasoning: Proceeding from the specific to the general. As used by Horowitz, it is a way to account for individual differences in group. The therapist goes from an individual's disclosure to the universal theme of the entire group.

insight: Awareness of one's underlying motives, reactions, and impulses previously not understood by the individual. In psychoanalysis, this is considered an essential component to the therapy process.

intellectualization: A higher order ego defense mechanism. This is seen when a person talks about feelings in a manner which seems emotionless as a way to defend against the confrontation of experiencing feelings. This defense is typically accompanied by the use of rationalization and emotional insulation.

interpretation: A method by which the therapist reveals the meaning behind a client's statement or behavior. The technique, as used by dynamic therapists, can reveal defense mechanisms and demonstrate repressed meaning behind dreams and verbalizations. In group therapy, unlike individual psychotherapy, interpretation is kept at a minimum.

introjection: An ego defense mechanism in which objects (either loved or hated) are internalized. For example, the emotions that one is experiencing are turned back upon the self. This can be seen in a depressed person who turns their aggression back on themselves. It might help to understand this defense by noting that it is the opposite of projection.

intropunitive: Responding to stress and frustration by blaming oneself.

introspection: Awareness of one's unconscious experiences and feelings.

labile: Unstable or shifting. It is usually used to describe emotions and affect.

latent content: The real meaning behind a thought, action, or dream as interpreted by the therapist. The latent content reveals information that was altered or previously hidden because the information may have been threatening to the ego. For example, the latent content of a dream about an evil witch may have to do with hostility a client feels toward a woman in his or her life. *See also* MANIFEST CONTENT.

learning theory: A body of general principles offered to explain the nature of learning.

libido: In psychoanalytic theory, the psychic energy generated by the id or the sexual pleasure-seeking instincts or drives.

lifestyle: The consistency of the behavioral style of an individual. The pattern of assumptions, coping mechanisms, cognitive functioning, and motives. A possible predictability of the individual's behavior.

managed care: A predominating, organized system in the United States whose function is to create a balance between health care users and the cost of benefits. The goal of the managed care system is to provide the best care possible in the most cost-effective way. This is done by monitoring the duration, setting, and provider of services. The most frequently used managed care system is known as HMOs (health maintenance organizations).

manifest content: The uninterpreted or symbolic content of a dream or thought as it is remembered. The manifest content of a dream often hides threatening information by altering the real (or latent) content of the dream. For example, sexual objects could be symbolically represented as neutral objects such as a jet plane taking off.

masochistic: A term used to describe self-defeating behaviors. Psychologically speaking, individuals who manifest masochistic behaviors endure pain and suffering in the hope that some greater good will come out of it. This hope can be either conscious or unconscious.

medical model: An approach to conceptualizing psychological disturbances. This model views these disturbances as analogous to organic diseases and this affects the type of treatment intervention utilized.

mental health: A state of being in which a person is well adjusted, has an enjoyment for life, and is seeking to attain a level of self-realization. This term indicates the absence of any psychological disorder, and refers to a positive state of existence. According to Adler, it is the ability of individuals to engage with others in cooperative, reciprocal relationships and achieve significance intrapersonally as well.

microcosm: In group psychotherapy, the group represents a miniature world of interpersonal relationships that the individual has outside of the therapeutic situation. By working in this miniature reality, the individual learns how to relate more effectively and develop more meaningful relationships outside. This is why group therapy is seen as an ideal place to solve interpersonal problems.

modeling: In behavioral theory, learning behaviors through the observation of others (models). The likelihood of a behavior being performed depends on several factors, including the observed consequences of the modeled behavior.

narcissistic injury: Any action or verbalization interpreted as a personal attack or affront to the self. In psychotherapy, this is when a client feels abused by something a therapist says. The therapist may also experience a similar feeling of abuse when a client responds negatively. The problem with narcissistic injuries is that often when they occur either the client or the therapist may feel the need to retaliate.

nationalism: A sense of loyalty to one's country.

negative transference: The development of hostile attitudes or feelings toward one's therapist. In other words, it is the transferring of negative feelings onto the therapist.

neuron: A nerve cell that sends and receives signals from other nerve cells or other muscles or glands.

neurosis: Emotional disorder characterized by unrealistic anxiety that is nonpsychotic in nature. Many of the disorders previously labeled as neuroses are currently classified as anxiety disorders. Neurosis was perceived as an exaggerated use of avoidance behaviors with defense mechanisms to ward off escalating anxiety.

nondirective: A term used to describe the way in which a therapist works in therapy. The therapist refrains from directing the client's communication and through clarification, nonverbal mannerisms, and restating reflects back what the client has stated. The therapist attempts to facilitate the client's responsibility for himself or herself but does this without making interpretations, correlations, or evaluations.

nonverbal communication: Communicating without the use of writing or speech. Examples of this type of communication are facial expressions, body gestures, and eye contact. These may at times be subtle or obvious. It is important for a therapist to attend to these signs as they relate to the therapist the patient's unstated ideas and feelings.

normal curve: In psychology, a bell-shaped curve indicating the distribution of a measurable trait depicting most people in the center. Remember that it indicates a statistical number and a "majority rule" evaluation and should not be confused with the concept that the trait being measured is an indication of "normal," meaning healthy.

occupational therapy: The use of occupational training as a form of psychotherapy.

orthodox Freudian: Another term used to describe those who maintain and preserve the concepts that Sigmund Freud developed. They tend to use these theories to the exclusion of others in clinical practice today. Often referred to as the "strict" Freudians.

outpatient: A term used to describe any ambulatory individual who receives treatment from a hospital or clinic. In relation to psychotherapy, these individuals leave the site of intervention (e.g., office, hospital, clinic) after the group or individual session. This term is contrasted with inpatient. These individuals receive psychotherapy within the hospital and clinic and remain in these facilities after their psychotherapy session is complete.

overcompensation: The process by which a greater than necessary effort is made to correct a real or imagined deficit. This process can be conscious or unconscious.

panic attacks: A sudden and discrete period of intense fear or discomfort accompanied by somatic or cognitive symptoms such as palpitations, sweating, feelings of choking, chest pain, and fears of dying or losing control. It can be a terrifying experience for an individual who has never experienced this event previously. Often, if not treated, it can lead to agoraphobia in which the individual is afraid to leave home.

paradigm: A design or framework within which theories are proposed and experiments to support these theories are outlined.

parataxic distortion: A term coined by Harry Stack Sullivan that essentially means the same thing as transference and is used to defend against anxiety. It refers to the distortions we make, specifically in our current relationships, due to our need to relate to others in a manner that is consistent with our previous life experiences.

perseveration: Persistent repeating of ideas or words, often observed in schizophrenia or certain neurological disorders.

pleasure principle: A psychoanalytic term in which an instinctual need seeks immediate gratification. This gratification transcends the appropriate boundaries of reality if the need is not processed through the ego and superego.

predisposition: A diathesis toward responding in a certain way, whether genetic or learned. For example, a particular stressor may affect one person in one way and another person in another way.

process group: A type of group whose primary function is to provide a forum in which individuals learn about themselves and how they relate to others.

progeny: Descendants or followers.

projection: An ego defense mechanism in which the individual unconsciously attributes his or her own traits, attitudes, desires, and faults to others. This usually is a defense against feelings of guilt and inadequacy.

protagonist: The leading role in a drama or novel. In psychodrama, this is the individual who is acting out an event in order to gain greater self-understanding.

psyche: The mind.

psychoanalysis: The theory and techniques of dynamic psychology founded by Sigmund Freud that focuses on the unconscious forces (i.e., repressed impulses, conflicts, and memories) and the effect they have on an individual's current adjustment. It seeks to modify the personality so as to eliminate the neurosis that is impacting the individual. This is accomplished through the transferential relationship between the patient and the analyst. This relationship helps the therapist identify and interpret the unconscious material that has contributed to the development of the neurosis.

psychodrama: A group therapy model developed by Moreno in which the client takes on certain roles and "acts out" the incident. By doing this with an "audience" (or other members of the group taking part in the enactment), it is hoped that the actor will reveal what social relations mean to the individual.

psychogenic disorders: Physiological disorders that are due to psychological rather than organic factors.

psychotic break: A state or loss of ego boundaries and reality testing that could result in delusions or hallucinations that often comes about through prolonged stress.

pyromaniac: A term used to describe an individual who has an uncontrollable impulse to set things on fire.

rationalization: An unconscious process of developing justification or plausible reasons to support a decision, practice, or belief when they are challenged either by others or by oneself.

reaction formation: A higher order ego defense mechanism in which an individual expresses feelings, thoughts, and behaviors that are the opposite of the impulses they actually feel. This might be manifested in group when a member states that they appreciate the feedback the group has given them, when in reality they are unappreciative of the advice and see the other group members as teaming up on them.

reality testing: A behavior designed for testing and exploring the nature of the individual's physical and social environment. It is the exploration of the limitations of one's existence and the permissiveness of one's environment.

reductionistic: Theory of reducing a complex phenomenon to simple parts, especially for the purpose of studying the phenomenon. In science it is the modernistic approach as represented by the scientific method. It is the belief that all things can be reduced to a finite unit.

regression: Literally, regression means moving backward. In psychology, this term is used to describe the return to an earlier state (or a return to more primitive behaviors) when gratification was easier. In group psychotherapy, one of the most common forms of regression is seen when a new member enters the group. The group as a whole returns to a less developed stage.

reinforcement: In classical conditioning, it is the procedure of following a conditioned stimulus with an unconditioned stimulus. For example, Pavlov used a bell to elicit salivation in dogs. In operant conditioning, it is rewarding a desired response to increase the likelihood that it will be repeated.

repetition compulsion: An irrational need that causes a person to engage in a behavior over and over again. By repeating this behavior pattern, the individual's anxiety is relieved. Transference is a form of repetition compulsion in that an individual repeats previous maladaptive relationships in the present.

repression: The first defense mechanism identified by Freud. It is a higher order defense mechanism in which the individual forgets or ignores something as to keep it out of consciousness because consciously remembering and experiencing the emotion or event will upset the individual. This defense differs from suppression, as this is not a conscious mechanism. It can be seen in its most basic form, for example, when an individual fails to remember the name of a teacher who generated anxiety within him or her in grade school or a more extreme form when an individual cannot recall traumatic experiences that have occurred in his or her life. Repression also operates in many of the other higher defense mechanisms.

resistance: The conscious or unconscious defense against allowing unconscious thoughts from coming to the surface. It can be viewed as a barrier to keep people, thoughts, and feelings at a distance. Some examples of resistance include coming late to group, the group's unconscious working together to keep the group from advancing, and focusing on external events rather than on the "here and now" group process. It is important to explore and modify the resistance as it impedes the progression of the group.

role theory: Social psychology theory concerned with the impact of roles imparted by society on individual behavior.

role-play: A technique used in psychotherapy in which a patient acts out a role in a contrived situation in order that the interaction be viewed in a more objective manner. This technique can be used for several purposes. It can enable patients to understand how they interpret social roles and how they function within those roles, to gain insight into the roles of others, and to allow the patient to practice more adaptive ways of fulfilling roles or dealing with issues. In group therapy, a group member can practice confronting a member in his or her life by acting it out with other group members in the safety of the group setting. The feedback received can be used to prepare the individual for the actual confrontation outside of group.

scapegoat: An individual or group of individuals toward whom displaced aggression is targeted. In psychotherapy groups, often a member of the group is "chosen" to fulfill the role and receives blame and hostility from other group members.

schizophrenia: A group of psychotic disturbances that affect thinking, motivation, and mood characterized by both positive symptoms (delusions, hallucinations, disorganized speech, inappropriate affect, and disorganized behavior) and negative symptoms (anhedonia, alogia, avolition, and flat affect). The disorder(s) peaks in late adolescence and early adulthood and effects about one percent of the population.

secondary gain: Any external gain that is derived from an illness. For example, a female group member might remain depressed because she receives attention and sympathy from the group.

self-fulfilling prophecy: An expectation an individual has about a given situation which plays a factor in that expectation being met. It is similar to circular causality. For example, a group member may have the expectation that others will reject him or her. To avoid being rejected, the individual does not speak in group. Other group members get frustrated at his or her silence and begin to disregard his or her presence. In turn, the individual perceives the group as rejecting, further supporting his or her belief that people are in fact rejecting.

shame: An emotion that results from feelings of disappointment. Often this emotion is the result of failing to fulfill expectations and is often characterized by feelings of guilt and embarrassment.

social phobia: An anxiety disorder that revolves around the persistent fear of social situations. People who experience social phobia fear that participating in a social situation might expose them to scrutiny and produce anxiety symptoms within them that will be embarrassing. This typically leads to the avoidance of situations that can be one specific social act (e.g., speaking in public) or it can occur in most social situations.

social psychology: An area of psychology that studies social behavior. It is the study of individuals' behavior in a social environment and how this behavior is affected by other individuals.

sociopathic: An older term used to describe an individual with antisocial personality disorder. An individual with these features lacks social responsibility and does not adapt to social standards. This term was used in the DSM-I.

spectator therapy: A phenomenon that Corsini and Rosenberg, as well as Yalom, identify as one of the dynamics of effective group therapy and psychological change. It is believed that members benefit from observing and imitating other individuals with similar issues as they begin to identify and resolve their problems within the group setting. Often this allows for the beginning of experimentation and trying new behaviors for the observing group member. This is also known as vicarious therapy.

splitting: A primitive ego defense mechanism in which a single object (e.g., the therapist) is seen by the client as two separate objects. This allows the patient to deal with the anxiety of ambivalent feelings (e.g., wanting and rejecting) toward the same object. This defense is often seen in individuals with borderline characteristics who have difficulty with ambivalence. To deal with the anxiety of feeling opposite feelings toward an object, these individuals will "split" and will see the therapist as either all good or all bad. This explains why when working with a borderline patient, at one session the therapist can be the greatest person in the world, and at the next session the therapist could be the worst person in the world.

status quo: The existing situation or state of affairs.

subgroup: A smaller unit that develops within a group. This usually develops when two or three people within a group perceive themselves as having similarities with one another and form a bond in which they believe they can gain more from one another than from the rest of the group members. Subgroups can form within groups or outside of group. For example, group members meeting for coffee or speaking on the phone with one another. Subgroups can be destructive to the group process in that members may show loyalty to those in the subgroup, avoid sharing information, and keep secrets from the rest of the group, or change their behavior in order to remain part of the subgroup.

sublimation: An ego defense mechanism in which unacceptable sexual or aggressive urges are rechanneled into more personally and socially acceptable expression.

subpoena: A command typically sent by a litigating party requiring the appearance of the receiving party to show up and testify at a stated time and place. It is important to note, however, that a subpoena in and of itself is not a court order which forces a testimony. Unless signed by a judge, a subpoena merely indicates that the court has issued an order for the receiving party to attend.

subsystem: An organized unit within a larger system. It is similar to a subgroup.

Sullivan's interpersonal theory of psychiatry: A theory developed by Harry Stack Sullivan in which he conceptualizes and understands an individual in relation to others around him or her. Sullivan believes that one's personality is developed through interactions with other significant individuals in one's life and that psychopathology develops when these interactions and relationships are distorted.

superego: In psychoanalytic theory, along with the ego and the id, the superego is one of three components of personality. It forms from the teachings of and internalization of identified parental and cultural standards. The superego is concerned with ethics, morals, and values, and acts as a person's conscience.

suppression: Consciously forcing out of awareness any thoughts, feelings, or impulses.

sympathy: Shared feeling *with* another person. This is felt most often in relation to painful or unpleasant experiences.

taboos: Social prohibitions.

tangential: Irrelevant or off course. This is a term used to describe a type of thought process in which one responds in a manner that is irrelevant to the question being asked.

Tavistock Conference: A conference of psychoanalysts that focuses on the mode of group therapy known as the Tavistock group approach. This mode was developed in part by Bion and used by many therapists during the 1960s and 1970s in the United States and in Britain. The theory was based on the concept that focusing on the whole of the group process (or the mass group process) was the predominant function of the therapist. Therefore, a therapist utilizing this model would make interpretations related to the mass group rather than the individual members.

teleology: Belief that events or behaviors serve a purpose. Also refers to any philosophy that attempts to study a series of events in terms of their purpose or goals.

therapeutic alliance: This is essential to the relationship developed between a patient and therapist. It is the level of cooperation between the patient and therapist that persists even in times of emotional stress that might develop during treatment.

topographical perspective (theory of psychoanalysis): Freud's model of the structure of the mind, which shifted from conscious-preconscious-unconscious to id-ego-superego.

transactional analysis: A theoretical position for group psychotherapy developed by Eric Berne. He conceptualized three internal ego states: the parent, the adult, and the child. The goal within groups is to gain awareness as to which ego state the individual predominantly functions in the group interaction. In addition, this approach involves identifying the games each member uses in their social interactions as well as understanding the unconscious map (by examining the messages received from parents and the early decisions regarding worth and position) in order to find the source of the individual's emotional turmoil. The theory has at its roots that whatever has been decided can be decided again.

transference: The positive or negative feelings developed by a client toward the therapist when the therapist becomes a symbolic representation of a significant other from the client's past. For example, unresolved issues a client may have with a particular parent may be transferred onto the therapist as a virtual surrogate of that parent.

unconditional positive regard: A necessary and sufficient condition of person-centered therapy that brings about change. It is a term coined by Carl Rogers to mean an attitude of concern, warmth, and acceptance toward the client by the therapist. Rogers believed that by accepting the client as a human regardless of the therapist's own personal values and ideals, growth would be facilitated.

unconscious: Originally identified by Freud as one realm of his topographical model of the mind and later became part of his structural model. This part of the mind contains unacceptable wishes, impulses, and memories that have been repressed and are inaccessible and outside of awareness to the individual.

universality: One of Yalom's eleven factors that is consistently experienced by group members. Specifically, this factor helps the individuals to no longer feel alone, which frequently produces a sense of relief that his or her problems are not unique and are shared by others.

vicarious learning: As described by Bandura, refers to learning through the observation of what happens to others when they exhibit a behavior. Bandura expanded the range of vicarious learning to include role-playing, contagion stereotype, and moral values.

working through: A time-consuming, difficult process in which the patient accepts the analyst's interpretation and effectively deals with the repressed material creating the intrapsychic conflict until it is resolved.

References

Abraham, K. (1919). A particular form of neurotic resistance against the psychoanalytic method. In Abraham, K. (Ed.), *Selected Papers of Karl Abraham* (pp. 303-311). New York: Brunner/Mazel.

Alexander, F. (1946). *Psychoanalytic Therapy: Principles and Applications.* New York: Ronald Press.

Altshul, J. A. (1977). The so-called boring patient. *American Journal of Psychotherapy,* 31(4), 533-545.

American Association for Counseling and Development (1989). AGSW ethical guidelines for group counselors. *Journal for Specialists in Group,* 15(2), 119-126.

Amighi, J., Loman, S., Lewis, P., and Sossin, K. (1999). *The Meaning of Movement: Developmental and Clinical Perspectives of the Kestenberg Movement Profile.* Amsterdam: Gordon and Breach Publishers.

Bendar, R. L., Melnick, J., and Kaul, T. J. (1974). Risk, responsibility, and structure: A conceptual framework for initiating group counseling and psychotherapy. *Journal of Counseling Psychology,* 21, 31-37.

Berman, A. and Weinberg, H. (1998). The advanced stage therapy group. *International Journal of Group Psychotherapy,* 48, 499-518.

Bernard, H. S. and MacKenzie, K. R. (1994a). *Basics of Group Psychotherapy.* New York: The Guilford Press.

Bernard, H. S. and MacKenzie, K .R. (1994b). Difficult patients and challenging situations. In H. Bernard and K. Roy MacKenzie (Eds.), *Basics of Group Psychotherapy* (pp. 123-156). New York: The Guilford Press.

Berne, E. (1958). Transactional analysis: A new and effective method of group therapy. *American Journal of Psychotherapy,* 12, 735-743.

Berscheid, E. and Peplau, A. (1983). The emerging science of relationships. In H. H. Kelly, E. Berscheid, A. Christensen, H. H. Harvey, T. L. Huston, G. Levinger, E. McClintock, L. A. Peplau, and D. R. Peterson (Eds.), *Close Relationships* (pp. 1-19). New York: W.H. Freeman.

Bion, W. R. (1961). *Experiences in Groups and Other Papers.* London: Routledge.

Bion, W. R. and Rickman, J. (1943). Intra-group tensions in therapy: Their study as the task of the group. *Lancet,* 245, 678-681.

Blatner, A. (1988). *Acting-In: Practical Applications of Psychodramatic Methods* (Second Edition). New York: Springer.

Boszormenyi-Nagy, I. and Spark, G. M. (1973). *Invisible Loyalties.* Hagerstown, MD: Harper and Row.

Boszormenyi-Nagy, I. and Ulrich, D. N. (1981). Contextual family therapy. In A. S. Gurman, and D. P. Kniskern (Eds.), *Handbook of Family Therapy* (pp. 159-187). New York: Brunner/Mazel, Inc.

Bowen, M. (1978). *Family Therapy in Clinical Practice*. New York: Jason Aronson.

Bowen, M. (1985). *Family Therapy in Clinical Practice* (Second Edition). Northvale, NJ: Jason Aronson, Inc.

Brook, M. (2001). The evolution of modern group process: An overview. In L. B. Furgeri (Ed.), *The Technique of Group Treatment: The Collected Papers of Louis R. Ormont, PhD* (pp. 11-20). Madison, CT: Psychosocial Press.

Buber, M. (1958). *I and Thou*. New York: Charles Scribner's Sons.

Budman, S., Demby, A., and Randall, M. (1980). Short term psychotherapy groups: Who succeeds, who fails. *Group*, 4, 3-16.

Burrows, T. (1928). The basis of group-analysis, or the analysis of the reactions of normal and neurotic individuals. *British Journal of Medical Psychology*, 8, 198-206.

Carroll, M., Bates, M., and Johnson, C. (1997). *Group Leadership* (Third Edition). Denver, CO: Love Publishing Company.

Carroll, M. R. and Wiggins, J. D. (1977). *Elements of Group Counseling* (Second Edition). Denver, CO: Love Publishing Company.

Cohen, A. (1996). Process-Directed Counseling Training Manual. Unpublished. Vancouver, Canada.

Coleman, J. C. (1976). *Abnormal Psychology and Modern Life* (Fifth Edition). Glenview, IL: Scott, Foresman and Co.

Cooper, C. L. and Bowles, D. (1973). Physical encounter and self-disclosure. *Psychological Reports*, 33(2), 451-454.

Corey, G. (1995). *Theory and Practice of Group Counseling* (Fourth Edition). Pacific Grove, CA: Brooks/Cole.

Corey, M. S. and Corey, G. (1992). *Groups: Process and Practice* (Fourth Edition). Pacific Grove, CA: Brooks/Cole.

Corey, M. S. and Corey, G. (1997). *Groups: Process and Practice* (Fifth Edition). New York: Brooks/Cole.

Corey, T. L. (1982). Demonstrations: Techniques for accelerating awareness in short-term group psychotherapy. *Small Group Behavior*, 13, 259-263.

Corsini, R. J. and Rosenberg, B. (1955). Mechanisms of group psychotherapy: Processes and dynamics. *Journal of Abnormal and Social Psychology*, 5, 406-411.

Crews, C. Y. and Melnick, J. (1976). Use of initial delayed structure in facilitating group development. *Journal of Counseling Psychology*, 23, 92-98.

Cribbin, J. J. (1972). *Effective Managerial Leadership*. New York: American Management Association.

Davis, H. (1984). Impossible clients. *Journal of Social Work Practice*, May, 28-48.

Debbane, E. G. and DeCarufel, F. (1993). The context of transference interpretations in analytical group psychotherapy. *American Journal of Psychotherapy*, 47(4), 540-553.

Decker, R. J. (1988). *Effective Psychotherapy: The Silent Dialogue.* New York: Hemisphere.

Donigian, J. and Malnati, R. (1997). *Systemic Group Therapy: A Triadic Model.* New York: Brooks/Cole.

Dreikurs, R. (1951). The unique social climate experienced in group psychotherapy. *Group Psychotherapy,* 3, 292-299.

Dreiss, J. E. (1986). Building cohesiveness in an adolescent therapy group. *Journal of Child and Adolescent Psychotherapy,* 3, 22-28.

Earley, J. (2000). *Interactive Group Therapy: Integrating Interpersonal, Action-Oriented and Psychodynamic Approaches.* Philadelphia: Brunner/Mazel.

Eaton, M. and Peterson, M. (1969). *Psychiatry* (Second Edition). New York: Medical Examination Publishing Co., Inc.

Ellis, A. (1985). *Overcoming Resistance.* New York: Springer.

Epstein, D. and Altman, N. (1994). *The Twelve Stages of Healing: A Network Approach to Wholeness.* San Rafael, CA: Amber-Allen Publishing.

Erikson, E. H. (1956). The problems of ego identity. *Journal of the American Psychoanalytic Association,* 4, 56-121.

Erikson, E. H. (1959). *Identity and the Life: Selected Papers.* Psychological Issue Monograph Series, 1 (no. 1). New York: International Press.

Erikson, E. H. (1968). *Identity, Youth and Crises.* New York: Norton.

Fehr, S. S. (1999). *Introduction to Group Therapy: A Practical Guide.* Binghamton, NY: The Haworth Press.

Fielding, J. (1983). Verbal participation and group therapy outcome. *British Journal of Psychiatry,* 142, 524-528.

Forsyth, D. (1990). *Group Dynamics* (Second Edition). Pacific Grove, CA: Brooks/Cole.

Foulkes, S. H. (1957). Group analytic dynamics with specific reference to psychoanalytic concepts. *International Journal of Group Psychotherapy,* 7, 40-52.

Foulkes, S. H. (1975). *Group Analytic Psychotherapy: Methods and Principles.* London: Gordon and Breech (An Interface Book).

Fraenkel, D. (1983). The relationship of empathy in movement to synchrony, echoing, and empathy in verbal interactions. *American Journal of Dance Therapy,* 6, 31-48.

Fraenkel, D. (2001). *Living Dance: Theory, Method and Experience.* New York: Kinections.

Freud, A. (1946). *The Ego and the Mechanisms of Defense.* New York: International University Press.

Freud, S. (1910). The future prospects of psychoanalytic therapy. In J. Strachey (Ed.), *The Standard Edition of the Complete Psychological Works of Sigmund Freud,* Volume 11 (pp. 141-151). London: Hogarth.

Freud, S. (1912). The dynamics of transference. In J. Strachey (Ed.), *The Standard Edition of the Complete Psychological Works of Sigmund Freud,* Volume 12 (pp. 97-108). London: Hogarth.

Freud, S. (1924). The economic problem in masochism. In P. Rieff (Ed.), *Collected Papers,* Volume 6 (pp. 190-201). New York: Basic Books.

Freud, S. (1960). *Group Psychology and the Analysis of the Ego.* New York: Bantam.

Friedman, S. B., Ellenhorn, L. J., and Snortum, J. R. (1976). A comparison of four warm-up techniques for initiating encounter groups. *Journal of Counseling Psychology,* 23, 514-519.

Friedman, W. H. (1976). Referring patients for group psychotherapy: Some guidelines. *Hospital and Community Psychiatry,* 27, 121-123.

Gill, M. M. (1982). *Analysis of Transference* (Volume 1). New York: International Universities Press.

Glasser, W. (1980). *Reality Therapy.* New York: Harper and Row.

Gray, P. (1993). "The assault on Freud." *Time.* 142, November 29, 46-92.

Greenberg, G. (1984). Reflections on being abrasive: Two unusual cases. *The Psychotherapy Patient,* 1(1), 55-60.

Hansen, J. C., Warner, R. W., and Smith, E. J. (1980). *Group Counseling: Theory and Process* (Second Edition). Boston: Allyn & Bacon.

Hesse, H. (1919). *Demian.* Translated by W. J. Strachan. London: Granda Publishing Limited (1969).

Hopper, E. (1985). The problem of context in group-analytic psychotherapy: A clinical illustration and a brief theoretical discussion. In M. Pines (Ed.), *Bion and Group Psychotherapy* (pp. 330-353). London: Toutledge and Kegan Paul.

Hopper, E. (1991). Encapsulation as a defense against the fear of annihilation. *International Journal of Psycho-Analysis,* 72(4), 607-624.

Hopper, E. (1995). A psychoanalytical theory of drug addiction: Unconscious fantasies of homosexuality, compulsions and masturbation with the context of traumatogenic processes. *International Journal of Psycho-Analysis,* 76(6), 1121-1142.

Hopper, E. (1996). The social unconscious in clinical work. *Group,* 20(1), 7-43.

Hopper, E. (1997). Contribution to the debate on homosexuality. *The British Psycho-Analytical Society Bulletin,* 33(1), 18-21.

Hopper, E. (2001). Difficult patients in group analysis: The personification of (ba) I: A/M. *Group,* 25(3), 139-171.

Hopper, E. (2002). The social unconscious: Selected papers in sociology and group analysis, Volume II. London: Jessica Kingsley Publishers.

Horovitz, E. G. (1999). *A Leap of Faith: The Call to Art.* Springfield, IL: Charles C Thomas.

Horovitz-Darby, E. G. (1994). *Spiritual Art Therapy: An Alternate Path.* Springfield, IL: Charles C Thomas.

Horwitz, L. (1977). A group center approach to group psychotherapy. *International Journal of Group Psychotherapy,* 27, 423-439.

Jacobs, E. E., Masson, R. L., and Harvill, R. L. (1988). *Group Counseling: Strategies and Skills.* Pacific Grove, CA: Brooks/Cole.

Kahn, M. (1991). *Between Therapist and Client.* New York: W. H. Freeman and Company.

Klapp, O. (1972). *Heroes, Villains, and Fools*. San Diego: Aegis.

Klein, E. (1992). Contributions from social systems theory. In E. Klein, H. Bernard, and D. Singer (Eds.), *Handbook of Contemporary Group Psychotherapy* (pp. 108-125). Madison, CT: International Universities Press.

Korda, L. and Pancrazio, J. (1989). Limiting negative outcome in group practice. *Journal for Specialists in Group Work*, 14(2), 112-120.

Kottler, J. A. (1992). *Compassionate Therapy: Working with Difficult Clients*. San Francisco, CA: Jossey-Bass Inc.

Lazarus, A. A. and Fay, A. (1982). Resistance or rationalization? A cognitive-behavioral perspective. In P. L. Wachtel (Ed.), *Resistance: Psychodynamic and Behavioral Approaches* (pp. 86-97). New York: Plenum.

LeBon, G. (1920). *The Crowd: A Study of the Popular Mind*. New York: Fisher.

Lonergan, E. C. (1994). Using theories of group therapy. In H. S. Bernard and K. R. MacKenzie (Eds.), *Basics of Group Psychotherapy* (pp. 189-216). New York: The Guilford Press.

MacKenzie, K. R. (1990). *Introduction to Time-Limited Group Psychotherapy*. Washington, DC: American Psychiatric Press.

MacKenzie, K. R. (1992). *Classics in Group Psychotherapy*. New York: The Guilford Press.

Mahler, C. Q. (1969). *Group Counseling in the Schools*. Boston: Houghton Mifflin.

Malan, D. (1976). Group psychotherapy: A long term follow-up study. *Archives General Psychiatry*, 33(11), 1303-1315.

Martin, P. (1975). The obnoxious patient. In P. L. Giovacchini (Ed.), *Tactics and Techniques in Psychoanalytic Therapy* (pp. 140-163). New York: Jason Aronson.

Masterson, J. (1976). *Psychotherapy of the Borderline Adult: A Developmental Approach*. New York: Brunner/Mazel.

Medeiros, M. E. and Prochaska, J. O. (1988). Coping strategies that psychotherapists use in working with stressful clients. *Professional Psychology*, 19(1), 112-114.

Mindell, A. (1992). *The Leader As Martial Artist: Techniques and Strategies for Resolving Conflict and Creating Community*. New York: HarperCollins.

Mindell, A. (1995). *Metaskills: The Spiritual Art of Therapy*. Tempe, AZ: New Falcon Publications.

Minuchin, S. (1974). *Families and Family Therapy*. Cambridge, MA: Harvard University Press.

Moore, B. and Fine, B. (1990). *Psychoanalytic Terms and Concepts*. New Haven and London: The American Psychoanalytic Association and Yale University Press.

Moreno, J. L. (1940). Mental catharsis and the psychodrama. *Sociometry*, 3, 209-244.

Moreno, J. L. (1966). Psychiatry of the twentieth century: Function of the universalia: Time, space, reality and cosmos. *Group Psychotherapy*, 19, 146-158.

Moxnes, P. (1999). Understanding roles: A psychodynamic model for role differentiation in groups. *Group Dynamics: Theory, Research, and Practice*, 3(2), 99-113.

Ormont, L. R. (1992). *The Group Therapy Experience: From Theory to Practice.* New York: St. Martin's.

Ormont, L. R. (2001). The leader's role in resolving resistances to intimacy in the group setting. In L.B. Furgeri (Ed.), *The Technique of Group Treatment: The Collected Papers of Louis R. Ormont, PhD* (pp. 85-101). Madison, CT: Psychosocial Press.

Porter, K. (1994). Principles of group therapeutic technique. In B. MacKenzie (Ed.), *Basics of Group Psychotherapy* (pp. 100-122). New York: The Guilford Press.

Pratt, J. H. (1907). The class method of treating consumption in the homes of the poor. *Journal of the American Medical Association,* 49, 755-759.

Reik, T. (1972). *Listening with the Third Ear: The Inner Experiences of a Psychoanalyst.* New York: Arena Books.

Rice, C. A. (1992). Contributions from object relations theory. In R. H. Klein, H. S. Bernard, and D. L. Singer (Eds.), *Handbook of Contemporary Group Psychotherapy* (pp. 27-54). Madison, CT: International Universities Press.

Rioch, M. J. (1970). Group relations: Rationale and technique. *International Journal of Group Psychotherapy,* 20(3), 340-355.

Rogers, C. (1965). *Client-Centered Therapy—Its Current Practice, Implications, and Theory.* Boston: Houghton Mifflin Company.

Rogers, C. R. (1967). *The Process of the Basic Encounter Group.* New York: McGraw-Hill.

Rutan, J. S. and Alonso, A. (1979). Group therapy. In A. Lazare (Ed.), *Outpatient Psychiatry: Diagnosis and Treatment* (pp. 612-620). Baltimore: Williams and Wilkins.

Rutan, J. S. and Stone, W. N. (1993). *Psychodynamic Group Psychotherapy* (Second Edition). New York: The Guilford Press.

Schutz, W. (1973). Encounter. In R. Corsini (Ed.), *Current Psychotherapies* (pp. 401-443). Itasca, IL: Peacock.

Shadish, W. R. (1980). Nonverbal interventions in clinical groups. *Journal of Consulting and Clinical Psychology,* 48(2), 164-168.

Simon, R. (2001). Psychotherapy's soothsayer. *Psychotherapy Networker,* 25(4), 34-62.

Slavson, S. R. (1957). Are there "group dynamics" in therapy groups? *International Journal of Group Psychotherapy,* 7, 131-154.

Smith, E., Murphy, J., and Coats, S. (1999). Attachment to groups theory and measurement. *Journal of Personality and Social Psychology,* 77(1), 94-110.

Stein, A. (1981). Indications for concurrent (combined and conjoint) individual group psychotherapy. In L. R. Wolberg and M. L. Aronson (Eds.), *Group and Family Therapy* (pp. 410-416). New York: Brunner/Mazel.

Stock, D. and Thelen, H. (1958). *Emotional Dynamics and Group Culture.* New York: University Press.

Sullivan, H. S. (1940). *Conceptions of Modern Psychiatry.* New York: Norton.

Sullivan, H. S. (1953). *The Collected Works of Harry Stack Sullivan.* New York: Norton.

Toseland, R. W. and Siporin, M. (1986). When to recommend group treatment: A review of the clinical and the research literature. *International Journal Group Psychotherapy,* 32, 171-201.

Trotzer, J. P. (1989). *The Counselor and the Group* (Second Edition). Muncie, IN: Accelerated Development.

Van Wagoner, S. (2000). Anger in group therapy, countertransference and the novice group therapist. In S. Fehr (Ed.), *Group Therapy in Independent Practice* (pp. 63-75). Binghamton, NY: The Haworth Press.

Vinogradov, S. and Yalom, I. D. (1989). *Concise Guide to Group Psychotherapy.* Washington, DC: American Psychiatric Press, Inc.

Von Bertalanffy, L. (1968). *General Systems Theory: Foundations Development, Application.* New York: Braziller.

Wastell, C. (1996). Feminist developmental theory: Implications for counseling. *Journal of Counseling and Development,* 14, 575-581.

Weinberg, H. (2001). Group process and group phenomena on the internet. *International Journal of Group Psychotherapy,* 51, 361-378.

Weiner, M. (1994). Failures in group psychotherapy: The therapist variable. *International Journal of Group Psychotherapy,* 44(1), 21-24.

Wender, L. (1936). The dynamics of group psychotherapy and its application. *Journal of Nervous and Mental Disease,* 84, 54-60.

West, M. (1975). Building a relationship with the unmotivated client. *Psychotherapy,* 12(1), 48-51.

Whitaker, D. S. and Leiberman, M. (1964). *Psychotherapy Through the Group Process.* New York: Atherton.

White, H. (1950). The aggressive forms of the defense mechanisms. In W. H. Mikesell (Ed.), *Modern Abnormal Psychology* (pp. 161-207). New York: Philosophical Library.

Williamson, D. S. (1981). Personal authority via termination of the intergenerational hierarchical boundary: A "new" stage in the family life cycle. *Journal of Marital and Family Therapy,* 7, 441-452.

Yalom, I. D. (1970). *The Theory and Practice of Group Psychotherapy.* New York: Basic Books.

Yalom, I. D. (1975). *The Theory and Practice of Group Psychotherapy.* New York: Basic Books.

Yalom, I. D. (1985). *The Theory and Practice of Group Psychotherapy* (Third Edition). Pacific Grove, CA: Brooks/Cole.

Yalom, I. D. (1990). *Understanding Group Therapy.* Video Pacific Grove, CA: Brooks/Cole.

Yalom, I. D. (1995). *The Theory and Practice of Group Psychotherapy* (Fourth Edition). New York: Basic Books.

Yalom, I. D. and Lieberman, M. A. (1971). A study of encounter group casualties. *Archives of General Psychiatry,* 25(1), 16-30.

Index

THE HAWORTH PRESS
Advances in Psychology and Mental Health
Frank De Piano, PhD
Senior Editor

INTRODUCTION TO GROUP THERAPY: A PRACTICAL GUIDE, SECOND EDITION by Scott Simon Fehr. (2003). "A must read for clinicians and therapists. This excellent book is clearly written, highly informative, and insightful." *Herbert L. Rothman, MD, Medical Director, Mount Sinai Outpatient Partial Hospitalization Program, Miami Beach, Florida (from the first edition)*

RELIGIOUS THEORIES OF PERSONALITY AND PSYCHOTHERAPY: EAST MEETS WEST by R. Paul Olson. (2002). "This is a well-written, unique book. It examines the major world religions, with each represented by a practical clinical psychologist, which provides a common thread so often lacking in such works." *Richard Gorsuch, PhD, Professor of Psychology, Fuller Theological Seminary, Pasadena, California*

THE AGGRESSIVE ADOLESCENT: CLINICAL AND FORENSIC ISSUES by Daniel L. Davis. (2000). "An easily read book that contains numerous insights for all mental health providers, educators, and others who work with this population." *Raymond W. Waggoner Jr., MD, Clinical Associate Professor, Ohio State University Medical School*

THE PAIN BEHIND THE MASK: OVERCOMING MASCULINE DEPRESSION by John Lynch and Christopher Kilmartin. (1999). "This book is men's studies at its best. . . . Lynch and Kilmartin have provided our best articulation to date of male socialization." *Rocco Lawrence Capraro, PhD, Associate Dean of Hobart College, Geneva, NY*

PROFESSIONALLY SPEAKING: PUBLIC SPEAKING FOR HEALTH PROFESSIONALS by Arnold Melnick. (1998). "Touches on virtually everything one needs to think about when preparing to communicate medical issues to an audience. I wish that it was available years ago. It certainly would have helped me be an even better medical speaker." *Bernard J. Fogel, MD, Senior Advisor to the President and Dean Emeritus, University of Miami School of Medicine*

THE VULNERABLE THERAPIST: PRACTICING PSYCHOTHERAPY IN AN AGE OF ANXIETY by Helen W. Coale. (1998). "Professionals involved in the direct treatment of clients and those charged with administrative responsibility of mental health resources and policy will benefit from the author's thought-provoking reformulation of the basis for ethical decision making." *Doody Weekly E-Mail*

CROSS-CULTURAL COUNSELING: THE ARAB-PALESTINIAN CASE by Marwan Dwairy. (1998). "Written by one of the pioneer clinicians among Palestinians in Israel. . . . An illuminating book for all therapists, especially for those who deal with patients coming from diverse cultures." *Dr. Shafiq Masalha, PhD, Clinical Psychologist Supervisor, Counseling Services, Hebrew University of Jerusalem*

**HOW THE BRAIN TALKS TO ITSELF: A CLINICAL PRIMER OF PSYCHO-
THERAPEUTIC NEUROSCIENCE** by Jay E. Harris. (1998). "A conceptual tour de
force that leads the way to an exciting dialogue between the fields of psychotherapy and
neuroscience." *Stanley B. Messer, PhD, Professor and Chairman, Department of Clinical Psychology, Graduate School of Applied and Professional Psychology, Rutgers University, State University of New Jersey*

**BEYOND THE THERAPEUTIC RELATIONSHIP: BEHAVIORAL, BIOLOGI-
CAL, AND COGNITIVE FOUNDATIONS OF PSYCHOTHERAPY** by Frederic J.
Leger. (1998). "A collection of the most erudite issues that any committed scientist or de-
voted practitioner needs to know." *From the Foreword by Arnold A. Lazarus, PhD, Dis-
tinguished Professor, Graduate School of Applied and Professional Psychology, Rutgers
University, State University of New Jersey*